LAW FIRM CYBERSECURITY

LAW FIRM CYBERSECURITY

// DANIEL GARRIE and BILL SPERNOW \\

ABA GPSOLO

Solo, Small Firm and General Practice Division

YOUR SUCCESS, OUR MISSION™

Printed in the United States of America.

20 19 18 17   5 4 3 2 1

ISBN: 978-1-63425-700-8
e-ISBN: 978-1-63425-701-5

Cataloging-in-Publication Data is on file at the Library of Congress

Discounts are available for books ordered in bulk. Special consideration is given to state bars, CLE programs, and other bar-related organizations. Inquire at Book Publishing, ABA Publishing, American Bar Association, 321 N. Clark Street, Chicago, Illinois 60654-7598.

www.shopABA.org

Contents

Chapter 5
Cryptography 57

Chapter 6
ISO Standards 75

Preface

Daniel Garrie

In our society, law firms have long held the position of being problem solvers. They untangle the mess of business, and create rules for society. Since their inception, law firms have devoted significant resources to ensuring the best representation of their clients. But now there are new threats that law firms face beyond the practice of law, namely data breaches and cyberattacks, and they must begin to devote sufficient resources to ensuring the security of their clients' data. If a firm is breached, its client files may inadvertently end up on the darknet, in the hands of investigative journalists, or with other nefarious entities.

Consider the following hypothetical: A small law firm did not have proper access controls for different employees, so any employee could access the highly sensitive data of all the firm's clients. One day, a new associate decides to poke around the firm's files, and finds that the firm has been assisting a local bank in evicting his grandfather from his home. This attorney rashly collects and leaks all of the firm's files, leaving the firm scrambling to figure out what happened, how these documents were leaked, and how to stop and control the subsequent reputational fallout to both the law firm and its clients.

This example is not meant to scare lawyers out of the practice of law, but rather to serve as an explanation of the seriousness of a data breach in the law firm context, and a reminder of why investing in information security is prudent. Law firms, both big and small, need to become cognizant of the risks associated with a data breach, and determine how to protect and secure their clients' confidential data.

Law firms can mitigate the risk of a data breach through a variety of means, including investing in cybersecurity tools, hiring internal and external resources to augment the firm's current information security practices, and—arguably most importantly—changing the firm's culture to be more security conscious. Although no one-size-fits-all solution exists for dealing with cyber threats, with proper focus and resources, a firm can consider its unique factors and develop an information security posture that addresses its most compelling concerns.

While preventing a breach should be a paramount concern for any law firm, it is similarly important to prepare for what could happen in the event that a breach occurs. There are options, such as cyber insurance, to help mitigate the direct costs of a breach, but law firms must also look to other options to resolve these issues expeditiously. As the costs associated with litigating data breach claims continues to climb, it will become increasingly apparent that law firms must begin looking toward other dispute resolution mechanisms, such as arbitration, to mitigate and control costs. This book hopes to give firms information about the tools they need to defend themselves; however, firms must also take steps to create processes to mitigate and control the risk of and fallout from a data breach.

Acknowledgments

I would like to thank Masha Simonova, Benjamin Dynkin, Michael Mann, and Yoav Griver, for their contributing efforts and assistance with pulling everything together.

I would also like to thank Amy Newman, President at ARC, without whose unwavering support and kindness, this book would never have come to fruition.

I also thank my wife, Sarah, and my two amazing children, without whom I could not have done it.

Daniel Garrie, co-author

About the Authors

Daniel Garrie

Daniel B. Garrie, Esq. is a seasoned e-discovery special master, forensic neutral, mediator, and arbitrator with JAMS, retained for complex, high-stakes cases around the country. His deep understanding of both law and technology, enables him to efficiently and cost effectively resolve some of the most challenging disputes.

For over a decade, Mr. Garrie has served as a mediator, arbitrator, electronically stored information (ESI) liaison, discovery referee, special master, neutral, and expert. He has appeared before the Los Angeles County Superior Court, New York Supreme Court, Delaware Supreme Court, and the U.S. Courts of Appeals for the Second, Third, and Seventh Circuits. Mr. Garrie has authored over 200 legal and technical articles and publications. His scholarship has been recognized by several Supreme Court Justices and cited in over 500 articles, publications, and opinions.

Mr. Garrie is the Senior Partner & Co-Founder of Law & Forensics LLC, a technology consulting firm that specializes in e-discovery, software, computer forensics, and cybersecurity. His work with Law & Forensics includes preparing incident response plans for cyber incidents, serving as an expert witness, developing e-discovery playbooks, and conducting digital forensic investigations. Prior to founding Law & Forensics LLC, Mr. Garrie built and sold three separate companies and served as the Worldwide Director of Discovery & Information Governance at Charles River Associates, managing a team of over 200 individuals.

Mr. Garrie is a nationally recognized educator and lecturer on computer software, cybersecurity, e-discovery, forensics, emerging Internet and mobile technologies, and cyber warfare. He has published over 150 articles and is cited in more than 500 articles and opinions. He is the editor in chief of the Journal of Law & Cyber Warfare, a fellow at the Ponemon Information Privacy Institute, and is on the Board of Advisors of several cybersecurity and technology start-ups.

Mr. Garrie also is a Cybersecurity Partner at the law firm Zeichner Ellman & Krause LLP.

Bill Spernow

Bill Spernow is a Director with Law & Forensics in the Atlanta area specializing in forensic analysis, defense-in-depth enterprise level security projects, incident response events, zero-day exploits, and hacking activity.

Mr. Spernow is the former Director of Information Security, Investigations and Incident Response for Experian, the world's largest consumer reporting agency. Prior to Experian, Mr. Spernow was an e-Discovery and forensic litigation expert affiliated with LECG's Digital Evidence Solutions Group. Mr. Spernow is the former Chief Information Security Officer for the Georgia Student Finance Commission and was recruited to revamp the security of this State Agency after it had experienced a significant security breach. His efforts resulted in an agency described by prominent government officials as the most secure in Georgia. Mr. Spernow has an extensive Information Security background at both the strategic and tactical level. His hands-on tactical design and implementation expertise includes firewalls, intrusion detection systems, secure network and Web sites, content monitoring, HIPAA and GLBA privacy and regulation compliance, authentication and authorization methodologies, biometrics, cyber investigations, forensic analysis, incident response strategies, and laptop protection.

Mr. Spernow spearheaded the development and implementation of several projects funded by the US Department of Justice, providing hands-on training to Federal, State and local law enforcement in the area of Cyber Crime investigation. Over a previous five year period with the SEARCH Group he personally trained over 4,000 cyber investigators. As the Assistant Director of the Computer Crime Section with the National White Collar Crime Center, he managed their domestic and international digital evidence training program on forensic acquisition and analysis.

In addition to his training background, Mr. Spernow has extensive experience in Information Security at both the strategic and tactical levels gained from his practice in both the public and private sectors. He is quoted frequently in national and international publications regarding his expertise.

About the Contributors

Dr. Ken Baylor

Dr. Ken Baylor is the President of the Vendor Security Alliance (VSA), an industry led initiative to measure and address third party risk. Dr. Baylor serves as head of Compliance for Uber and in the past had been the CISO of Pivotal, Symantec, and Nuance. He is recognized as a leader in Data Protection, Bank Security, Agile Information Security and Regulatory Compliance. He is a Certified Information Systems Security Professional (CISSP) and a Certified Information Systems Manager (CISM). He served as President of ISACA-Silicon Valley from 2007–2009. In addition to security certifications, he holds a law degree, an MBA, a Ph.D. in Biochemistry.

Richard Borden

Rick Borden is Counsel at Robinson + Cole, and focuses his practice on three core intersecting areas: big data governance and the Internet of Things, cybersecurity risk management, and technology sourcing and transactions.

Before joining the firm, Mr. Borden served as the chief privacy officer and chief information security and privacy counsel of Depository Trust & Clearing Corporation (DTCC). He also acted as the general counsel of Soltra, the DTCC, and FS-ISAC–automated threat-sharing joint venture. During his tenure, Mr. Borden focused much of his outreach on alerting the business community to the risks and vulnerabilities in the cyber network.

Prior to joining DTCC, Mr. Borden was senior vice president and assistant general counsel at Bank of America, where he was responsible for cybersecurity, privacy issues, general technology, commercial contracting, outsourcing, licensing, data, and intellectual property for the bank and broker-dealer.

Before joining Bank of America, Mr. Borden was an assistant general counsel at The Hartford, counsel at Brown Raysman Millstein Felder & Steiner, specializing in venture capital and private-equity-funded companies, and general counsel at Paradigm4, a private-equity-funded wireless data and systems integration company.

Mr. Borden is also an inventor, holding two patents covering insurance-processing systems and methods using mobile devices for medical monitoring application (US9224171B2 and US8510133B2).

Cindy Donaldson

Cindy Donaldson, Chief Operating Officer, Sector Services Division of FS-ISAC, Inc., has 20 years of experience in cybersecurity in both the public and private sectors, supporting organizations ranging from Fortune 500 to small organizations. She has served as a chief security officer for a global $500 million company responsible for both cybersecurity and physical security, and is also an experienced entrepreneur. She was asked to serve as an American Express representative on the Payment Card Industry Security Standards Council (PCI SSC) Technical Working Group, where she co-authored the PCI Data Security Standard. She has led several teams to success and has managed $20 million in professional solutions.

Ms. Donaldson was the founder and inaugural president of the Phoenix Chapter of the Information Systems Security Association (ISSA). She has a Master's of Business Administration degree and a bachelor's degree in Management and Marketing from Indiana University of Pennsylvania.

Ms. Donaldson is leading efforts in assisting communities to establish information-sharing capabilities by providing advisory services, operational support, intelligence-sharing services, and technology capabilities. She provides direction for FS-ISAC's delivery of services that are requested from member-driven ISACs and ISAOs, including the Legal Services ISAO (LS-ISAO), the Retail Cyber Intelligence Sharing Center (R-CISC), the Real Estate ISAC (RE-ISAC), and the Oil and Natural Gas ISAC (ONG-ISAC). Ms. Donaldson takes an active role with the legal services community in defending the industry through her support of the Legal Services ISAO.

Barry Dynkin

Barry Ian Dynkin, Esq., is an attorney in private practice. He is a staff editor on the *Journal of Law and Cyber Warfare*. He completed his J.D. degree at the Maurice A. Deane School of Law at Hofstra University and is an LL.M. candidate at the Benjamin N. Cardozo School of Law at Yeshiva University.

Greg Kelley, EnCE, DFCP

As co-founder of Vestige Digital Investigations and CTO, Greg leads Vestige's digital forensic and e-discovery services.

Greg's responsibilities include helping to determine strategic direction of the company, overseeing the day-to-day operations and internal information systems infrastructure, and personally handling some of Vestige's engagements. He helps in performing as well as managing the digital forensic investigations and leads the data evidence specialists and forensic analysts on the Vestige team.

Greg has 20 years of experience working in the computer industry. His various positions and responsibilities included custom software design and implementation, network management and security, database programming, disaster recovery, and end-user support. For the past 15 years, Greg has helped Vestige become one of the few companies capable of performing comprehensive digital forensic investigations.

He has worked on both criminal and civil matters, covering areas such as intrusion and incident response, intellectual property theft, fraud, and uncovering hidden assets. Greg is experienced and has testified in state court and federal court in both civil and criminal cases.

Greg graduated cum laude with a Bachelor of Science degree in Computer Engineering and a minor in Artificial Intelligence from Case Western Reserve University. He holds the professional designation of Encase Certified Examiner (EnCE) and Digital Forensics Certified Practitioner (DFCP). He is an active participant in the digital forensics industry, having spoken at conferences such as Techno Forensics, ISS World (Intelligent Support Systems), Computer and Enterprise Investigations Conference (CEIC), and Paraben Forensic Innovations Conference (PFIC).

Headquartered near Cleveland, Ohio, Vestige supports litigation work primarily in the Great Lakes region, including Ohio, Pennsylvania, Indiana, Michigan, and Illinois, and routinely supports cases nationally and internationally as well. Prior to Vestige, Greg founded two predecessor computer consulting companies in the Ohio region.

Originally from Chicago, Illinois, Greg and his wife, Stacey, have two children and reside in North Royalton, a suburb of Cleveland.

Matthew Lawrence

Matthew H. Lawrence is a graduate of Brown University (B.A. History, 2012) and attends Fordham University Law School (2018). He works as a legal and IP researcher at Perkins Coie, and has assisted in co-authoring a number of articles on cybersecurity.

David Lawrence

David Lawrence is the founder and chief collaborative officer of Risk Assessment Network + Exchange (RANE). He previously served for approximately 20 years as associate general counsel and managing director at Goldman Sachs. During his tenure, David formed and was the global head of the Business Intelligence Group. His role covered a wide range of legal, regulatory, diligence, and transactional responsibilities for the firm, as well as advising Goldman's clients directly. David served on a number of the firm's global risk-management and investment committees, including its commitments and capital committees.

During his tenure, David worked with his industry counterparts to lead in the development of Wall Street's first design and implementation of controls and technology to safeguard against money laundering, illicit finance, terrorism financing, foreign corrupt practices, and violations of economic sanctions. In 2014, David received the FBI Director's Award for his efforts in combating international terrorism.

While at Goldman Sachs, he helped create and lead the firm's formation of Regulatory Data Corp. (RDC), in which 20 of the leading global banks invested. RDC (www.rdc.com) provides data, technology, and risk management solutions to the private sector in wide-ranging areas such as anti-money laundering, fraud, corruption, and illicit finance, as well as other enterprise risk-relevant fields.

Prior to working at Goldman Sachs, David served for 10 years as an assistant U.S. Attorney, in the Southern District of New York. During this tenure, he served as the deputy chief of the Criminal Division and chief of the Public Corruption and General Crimes Units. David serves as a member of the board of trustees for the John Jay College of Criminal Justice Foundation (City University of New York).

David received a B.A. from Brandeis University in Urban Studies, magna cum laude with highest honors. He attended the University of Texas School of Law and received his J.D. from New York University School of Law.

Timothy P. Murphy

With 30 years of public- and private-sector experience—primarily in the Federal Bureau of Investigation—Timothy P. Murphy is a recognized leader in the global law enforcement, intelligence, and business communities.

A Michigan native, Murphy became a police officer after graduating from college in 1983. In 1988, he joined the FBI as a special agent. He held a number of operational positions in a variety of field offices nationwide, investigating matters as diverse as counterterrorism, intelligence, and cyber and organized crime, and even serving as an FBI pilot. Mr. Murphy served in various management roles, including as a Special Assistant to the FBI Director—a position that gave him a unique, high-altitude view of the global FBI from both operational and administrative perspectives. He steadily climbed the Bureau's management ladder, eventually serving as the Special Agent in Charge of the Cincinnati field office, the Bureau's chief financial officer, and then its chief operating officer. He eventually rose to become the Deputy Director of the FBI, a position he held until retiring in 2011. Prior to joining TRSS, Mr. Murphy was a vice president at MacAndrews and Forbes, Inc.

In his last two FBI positions, Mr. Murphy oversaw the operational and administration aspects of a workforce that was more than 35,000 strong, spread throughout 56 national offices and more than 60 international offices. This included all operational aspects of the counterterrorism, counterintelligence, criminal, cyber, and intelligence programs, as well as human resources, training, strategy management, facilities management, records management, security, financial management, information technology, inspection, internal audit, and leadership development.

Mr. Murphy maintains close ties to the law enforcement and intelligence communities and is frequently consulted for his expertise in global cyber, counterterrorism, intelligence, criminal, and security issues. He is a guest lecturer at colleges and universities on these issues. He is frequently called on to speak on these topics in the media. He is a member of the Police Executive Research Forum, the International Association of Chiefs of Police, the Department of State Overseas Security Advisory Council (OSAC), Deputy Co-Chairman of the FBI/DHS Domestic Security Alliance Council, the FBI Agents Association, and the FBI National Academy Associates. He is also a member of the advisory board of two cybersecurity companies, the chairman of the board of directors for a data analytics company, and on the board of directors for the National Center for Missing and Exploited Children (NCMEC) and the Foundation Board of Directors for Ferris State University.

William B. Nelson

Bill Nelson is the president and CEO of the Financial Services Information Sharing and Analysis Center (FS-ISAC), a nonprofit association dedicated to protecting financial services firms from physical and cyberattacks. FS-ISAC has more than 6,900 members worldwide, including banks, credit unions, payment processors, broker-dealers, third-party service providers, and insurance companies.

The FS-ISAC fulfills its mission through the dissemination of trusted and timely information regarding physical and cybersecurity risks to its membership. In 2013, FS-ISAC received the prestigious RSA Award for Excellence in Information Security. Also in that year, Mr. Nelson was named the fifth most influential person in the field of financial information security by the publication *Bank Info Security*.

Before joining the FS-ISAC, Bill was the executive vice president of NACHA, the Electronic Payments Association, from 1988 to 2006. Prior to joining NACHA, Bill held several treasury management and lending positions within the banking industry.

Jeff Stapleton

Jeff Stapleton has more than 30 years' experience with information technology and cybersecurity in the financial services, payments, healthcare, and government industries. His areas of expertise include authentication, cryptography, public key infrastructure (PKI), key management, biometrics, and trusted time stamps. He also has more than 25 years' experience in standards development, having created more than three dozen ISO, ANSI, and X9 security standards for financial services. Jeff has been an architect, assessor, auditor, author, designer, coder, consultant, and subject matter expert (SME). His book series *Security without Obscurity* from CRC Press includes *A Guide to Confidentiality, Authentication, and Integrity* and *A Guide to PKI Operations*.

Alex Tarnow

Alex Tarnow, Esq., is an Information Technology Law Advisor at RANE Corp. Alex's practice encompasses data privacy law, electronic discovery, cybersecurity, electronic surveillance law, and intellectual property law. Alex received an LL.M.

in Information Technology and Privacy Law from John Marshall Law School. He was the recipient of the National 2014 DISH® Network eDiscovery Legal Research and Writing Competition, for "Conflicts Between American Electronic Discovery Policies and International Privacy Laws—Are the Proposed F.R.C.P. Amendments the Answer?" He also studied Chinese intellectual property law at Peking University in Beijing, China. Mr. Tarnow can be reached at alextarnow@ tarnowlaw.com.

CHAPTER

1

OVERVIEW OF CYBERSECURITY AND THE LAW FIRM

Daniel Garrie

"People have entrusted us with their most personal information. . . . We owe them nothing less than the best protections that we can possibly provide by harnessing the technology at our disposal. We must get this right. History has shown us that sacrificing our right to privacy can have dire consequences."

—Tim Cook,

CEO of Apple, at the 2015 White House Cybersecurity Summit

1.1 Introduction: Law Firm Vulnerability to Cyber Breaches

No one is immune to a cybersecurity incident. Every industry and business sector—including the legal profession—is a target for hackers and cyber criminals. Law firms are especially appealing targets, given that, in the course of their business, they acquire highly sensitive and confidential information from clients. According to a report from cybersecurity firm Mandiant, at least 80% of the leading U.S. law firms already have seen their security compromised via a cyber breach.[1] Even this is likely to be an underestimate, as firms are often unaware they have been breached.[2]

Law firms thus face intense pressure to improve their cybersecurity. Clients are increasingly requesting that their lawyers be allowed to work remotely (often on personal, possibly unsecured devices), while at the same time law firms are being required to verify the integrity and security of their networks and information systems.[3] Large banks are pressing outside law firms to demonstrate that they are using state-of-the-art technology to secure the information the banks are entrusting to the firms.[4] Some financial institutions are asking law firms to fill out lengthy questionnaires detailing their cybersecurity measures, while others are doing on-site inspections.[5] In some cases, banks and companies are threatening to withhold legal work from law firms that hesitate to comply with increased scrutiny, or requesting that firms add insurance coverage for data breaches to their malpractice policies.[6]

---

1 Stuart Poole-Robb, *Law Firms Are a Hacker's "Treasure Trove,"* ITProPortal, http://www.itproportal.com/2015/03/30/law-firms-hackers-treasure-trove/#ixzz3nFgP2mm0.

2 *Id.*

3 Hinshaw & Culbertson LLP, *Cyber Security for Law Firms* (2016), http://www.hinshawlaw.com/services-Cyber-Security-for-Law-Firms.html.

4 Matthew Goldstein, *Law Firms Are Pressed on Security for Data*, DEALBOOK (Mar. 26, 2014), http://dealbook.nytimes.com/2014/03/26/law-firms-scrutinized-as-hacking-increases/?_r=0.

5 *Id.*

6 *Id.*

Moreover, regulators and government agencies are criticizing law firms as a group for the weak protection afforded to the personal data and client information they collect and store.[7] As early as 2009, the FBI cited the legal industry as a group that could easily succumb to cyber incidents.[8] In 2011, the FBI met with major U.S. law firms to discuss their cyber preparedness, and followed up with educational programs intended to help firms implement more secure systems.[9]

Thus, at this point, cyber threats should feature prominently on most law firms' threat radar, yet there is an ominous statistical dichotomy in the legal industry: Most law firms view cybersecurity as a major threat to their organizations, yet many of them say they are unprepared for a significant cyberattack.[10] Marsh's 2014 Global Law Firm Cyber Survey returned the following results regarding law firm cyber security:[11]

- 79% of respondents viewed cyber/privacy security as one of the top 10 threats in their overall risk strategy.
- 72% said that their firms had not assessed and scaled the cost of a data breach based on the information they retain.
- 51% said that their law firms either had not taken measures to insure against cyber threats (41%), or did not know if their firms had taken such measures (10%).
- 62% had not calculated the effective revenue lost or extra expenses incurred following a cyberattack.

As shown by these results, the majority of firms surveyed had not taken into account what kind of financial impact their organization could experience following a cyber incident. More than 60% said their firms had not calculated the effective revenue that could be lost following a cyberattack. Even more (72%) said their firms had not assessed how much a data breach could cost them based on the kind of information the firm retains.

The preceding statistics demonstrate that the legal profession generally lags behind other industries when it comes to preparing for and responding to cyber threats. Although a limited number of law firms have developed satisfactory cybersecurity programs, many law firm programs lack essential elements that are common in cybersecurity programs of companies in other industries.[12] For example, some law firms now have a chief information officer (CIO) and/or chief information security officer (CISO), as is common with companies in other sectors, but it

---

7 Marsh LLC, *More Cyber Preparedness Needed, According to 2014 Law Firm Cyber Survey*, https://www.marsh.com/us/insights/more-cyber-preparedness-needed-2014-law-firm-cyber-survey.html.

8 *Id.*

9 *Id.*

10 Daryn Teague, *ABA Pilot Recommends Law Firms Collaborate on Cybersecurity*, Business of Law Blog (Aug. 24, 2015), http://businessoflawblog.com/2015/08/law-firms-cybersecurity-2/.

11 Marsh LLC, *More Cyber Preparedness Needed, According to 2014 Law Firm Cyber Survey*, https://www.marsh.com/us/insights/more-cyber-preparedness-needed-2014-law-firm-cyber-survey.html.

12 Daniel Solove, *Law Firm Cyber Security and Privacy Risks*, TeachPrivacy Privacy + Security Blog (Apr. 30, 2015), https://www.teachprivacy.com/law-firm-cyber-security-and-privacy-risks/.

is hardly the norm; many law firms still lack any kind of substantial cybersecurity program or dedicated cybersecurity personnel.[13]

Effective cybersecurity programs involve privacy and data security training. The legal industry has been slow to adopt training concerning data protection.[14] One of the difficulties in implementing cybersecurity training at law firms is that lawyer time is so valuable:[15] Time spent training is time not spent on billables.[16] Nevertheless, training is an essential component of good privacy and security protection.[17] According to information technology (IT) executives quoted in a recent *ABA Journal* article, untrained lawyers and office personnel constitute the biggest weakness in a law firm's cyber defense.[18]

1.2 Potential Consequences and Liability for Law Firms from a Data Breach

A cybersecurity incident can cause serious trouble for a law firm, including lawsuits, ethical violations, negative publicity, reputational damage, regulatory fines, and/or disgruntled clients. On top of that, there is the cost of any necessary forensic investigation and breach notification, as well as the potentially tremendous amount of valuable attorney time lost. This section surveys some potential consequences and sources of liability when a law firm is the victim of a data breach.

1.2.1 Ethical Violations May Result from a Cyber Breach

1.2.a Privilege and Confidentiality

Inadequate data security or protection of privacy arguably constitutes a failure to fulfill a law firm's duty of confidentiality. Under Rule 1.6 of the *ABA Model Rules of Professional Conduct*, "a lawyer shall not reveal information relating to the representation of a client unless the client gives informed consent."[19] Lawyers must "make reasonable efforts to prevent the inadvertent or unauthorized disclosure of, or unauthorized access to, information relating to the representation of a client."[20]

---

13 *Id.*
14 *Id.*
15 *Id.*
16 *Id.*
17 *Id.*
18 Rachel M. Zahorsky, *As More Hackers Target Lawyers, Here's How to Protect Client Data*, ABA TECHSHOW (Apr. 4, 2013, 11:15 PM), http://www.abajournal.com/news/article/as_more_hackers_target_lawyers_heres_how_to_protect_client_data/.
19 MODEL RULES OF PROF'L CONDUCT R. 1.6 (AM. BAR ASS'N 2015) (hereafter "Rule").
20 *Id.*, Rule 1.6(c).

Rule 1.6(c), however, does not address whether attorneys have to tell their clients about a data breach. The law governing lawyers suggests that lawyers must self-report a breach in which client data is exposed if the breach results from the lawyers' negligence.[21] Professor Benjamin Cooper, in discussing Rule 1.6, Rule 1.4 (communications with the client), and the fiduciary law governing the lawyer–client relationship, states: "If the lawyer's conduct of the matter gives the client a substantial malpractice claim against the lawyer, the lawyer must disclose that to the client."[22]

Indeed, the ABA Model Rule is written broadly enough that it likely requires disclosure of a breach even if the lawyer did not personally act negligently in exposing the data. Further, various doctrines of secondary liability mean attorneys can be held liable for malpractice due to negligent defects in information security systems caused by subordinate employees.[23] Thus, even if an IT employee at a law firm negligently caused or allowed a security breach through which a client was harmed, the client could have a viable malpractice claim against the lawyers and firm responsible for managing that IT employee, such that the lawyers likely would be required to disclose the breach to the client.[24]

In this regard, Model Rule 5.3, governing law firm responsibilities related to nonlawyers, suggests that attorneys may be liable for ethical violations by their subordinate IT personnel:

> A lawyer shall be responsible for conduct of such a person that would be a violation of the Rules of Professional Conduct if engaged in by a lawyer if:
>
> 1. the lawyer orders or, with the knowledge of the specific conduct, ratifies the conduct involved; or
> 2. the lawyer is a partner or has comparable managerial authority in the law firm in which the person is employed, or has direct supervisory authority over the person, and knows of the conduct at a time when its consequences can be avoided or mitigated but fails to take reasonable remedial action.[25]

Ignorance of IT personnel's negligent actions likely will not be a successful defense against a claim for failing to disclose a law firm data breach, given the requirements of Rule 1.6 discussed earlier,[26] as well as the further requirement of Rule 5.3 that "a lawyer having direct supervisory authority over the non-lawyer

---

21 *See* Restatement (Third) of the Law Governing Lawyers § 20 cmt. c (Am. Law Inst. 2000); Benjamin Cooper, *The Lawyer's Duty to Inform His Client of His Own Malpractice*, http://www.baylor.edu/content/services/document.php/116819.pdf.
22 *See* Cooper, *supra* note 21; Olds v. Donnelly, 696 A.2d 633, 643 (N.J. 1997) (the Rules of Professional Conduct still require an attorney to notify the client that he or she may have a legal malpractice claim even if notification is against the attorney's own interest; citation omitted); In re Tallon, 447 N.Y.S.2d 50, 51 (App. Div. 1982) (an attorney has a professional duty to promptly notify his client of his failure to act and of the possible claim his client may thus have against him). *See also* Section 1.2.2 *infra* on negligence claims against attorneys.
23 *See, e.g.*, State ex rel. Sawicki v. Lucas Cty. Ct. of C.P., 931 N.E.2d 1082, 1088–89 (Ohio 2010) ("The doctrine of respondeat superior operates by imputing to the employer the acts of the tortfeasor, not the tortfeasor's liability").
24 *See generally* Adam J. Sulkowski, *Article: Cyber-Extortion: Duties and Liabilities Related to the Elephant in the Server Room*, 2007 U. Ill. J.L. Tech. & Pol'y 21.
25 Rule 5.3.
26 Lawyers must "make reasonable efforts to prevent the inadvertent or unauthorized disclosure of, or unauthorized access to, information relating to the representation of a client." Rule 1.6.

shall make reasonable efforts to ensure that the person's conduct is compatible with the professional obligations of the lawyer."[27]

Examining these two rules in conjunction, it is clear that lawyers in a managerial position at a law firm must oversee IT personnel action regarding client data, and make sure those actions are compatible with the professional obligations of the lawyer, to avoid possible ethics violations. As Professor Cooper has observed, "firms have a duty under Rules 1.1 and 1.6 to effectively protect their clients' information. If a firm is negligent in carrying out that duty because it has been lax with its security, and that resulted in client files being disclosed, it is potentially a problem."[28] Even if a firm has a very good security system, he states, "the attorney absolutely has a duty to inform clients under 1.4 that their confidential information has been compromised."[29]

Accordingly, a strong[30] security program may help shield a firm from an ethics violation caused by not appropriately protecting client data, and it may help them defend against a negligence charge, but it has no impact on an attorney's ethical requirement to inform clients of security incidents. A good security program does, however, reduce the likelihood that such a painful conversation will have to take place.

1.2.b Competence

Inadequate cybersecurity systems can also raise competence issues. Model Rule 1.1 requires that a "lawyer shall provide competent representation to a client."[31] "Competent representation" means "the legal knowledge, skill, thoroughness and preparation reasonably necessary for the representation."[32] The ABA recently amended Comment 8 to Model Rule 1.1 to emphasize that "a lawyer should keep abreast of changes in the law and its practice, *including the benefits and risks associated with relevant technology*"[33] (added language indicated by italics).

Furthermore, the ABA published Resolution 109 in 2015, calling for firms to "develop, implement, and maintain an appropriate cybersecurity program."[34] The ABA's adopted resolution encourages firms to "create cybersecurity programs that are tailored to the nature and scope of the [firm] and the information to be protected."[35] The resolution also encourages firms to regularly conduct threat assessments, "create controls based upon these assessments, create response plans for possible cyber-attacks, and establish relationships and share information with

---

27 Rule 5.3.
28 Cooper, *supra* note 21.
29 *Id.*
30 Other chapters of this book explore the standards, practices, and technologies that contribute to developing a strong information security program.
31 Rule 1.1.
32 *Id.*
33 *Id.*, Comment 8.
34 http://www.americanbar.org/content/dam/aba/images/abanews/2014am_hodres/109.pdf.
35 *ABA Adopts Cybersecurity Resolution; Says Cyber-Attacks a Top Organizational Risk* (Aug. 18, 2014), http://www.bna.com/aba-adopts-cybersecurity-n17179893912/.

external organizations, where appropriate, as a method of addressing the problem of cyber-attacks."[36]

Based on Comment 8 and Resolution 109, adequate cybersecurity protection now appears to be a material part of the "skill, thoroughness and preparation" expected from competent legal counsel. Thus, in the event of a data breach, law firms may face liability and sanction for breach of the ethical duty of competence, in addition to any other ethical violations or legal claims against the law firm related to the disclosure of confidential information.

1.2.2   Lawsuits Brought by Clients

Law firms that are victims of cyber breaches can be held liable for a number of common law claims brought by clients whose data was exposed. Possible causes of action include malpractice, negligence, breach of fiduciary duty, and fraud. Although case law regarding law firm data breaches is sparse, attorneys now may have a greater duty of care with respect to information security than in the past, in light of the abundance of recent data breaches and the ABA's recent comments and resolutions.[37]

Since the late 19th century, attorneys have been held to what courts have described as an "ordinary" standard of care in representing their clients.[38] In other words, as it is frequently expressed, an attorney must exercise that degree of care, skill, and diligence which is commonly possessed and exercised by attorneys in practice in the jurisdiction.[39] As the recent comments to the ABA Model Rules and Resolution 109 suggest, "ordinary care" for attorneys now seems to include some degree of care with respect to information security. Attorneys should proceed accordingly.[40]

Negligence claims arising from data breaches in other sectors may shed some light on what "ordinary care" means for attorneys with respect to information security in this age of increased cyber threats. Following the highly publicized 2014 Target data breach, customers and financial institutions affected by the breach brought a number of lawsuits against Target, primarily asserting claims of general negligence in Target's implementation and maintenance of its information security systems.[41] The District Court of Minnesota's order identified three distinct duties

---

36 *Id.*

37 To establish a cause of action for legal malpractice, a plaintiff must demonstrate that its attorney was negligent in representation and that such negligence proximately caused actual and ascertainable damages (*see* Bixby v. Somerville, 62 A.D.3d 1137, 880 N.Y.S.2d 205 [3d Dept. 2009]); *see also* Comment 8 to Rule 1.1.

38 For example, in Babbitt v. Bumpus, 41 N.W. 417 (Mich. 1889), the Supreme Court of Michigan held that attorneys must be held to a standard of "ordinary care and diligence"; in Hill v. Mynatt, 59 S.W. 163 (Tenn. 1900), the Court of Chancery Appeals of Tennessee held that an attorney should be liable for injuries caused when the attorney fails to exercise "reasonable diligence" or ordinary care.

39 *See, e.g.,* Spangler v. Sellers, 5 F. 882 (C.C. S.D. Ohio 1881); Davis v. Associated Indem. Corp., 56 F. Supp. 541 (M.D. Pa. 1944), *appeal dismissed,* 150 F.2d 1005 (3d Cir. 1945); Rapuzzi v. Stetson, (1914) 160 A.D. 150, 145 N.Y.S. 455 (1914); Armstrong v. Adams, 102 Cal. App. 677, 283 P. 871 (1929).

40 A court may conclude that a negligence suit is appropriate where a business failed to take reasonable steps—as defined by statutes, regulations, industry practices or even retroactively applied standards determined by a judge—to secure its network, resulting in a data breach involving client data. *See* Sulkowski, *supra* note 24.

41 *In re* Target Corp. Customer Data Security Breach Litig., MDL No. 14-2522 (PAM/JJK), accessed at https://drive.google.com/a/pulseadvisory.com/file/d/0Bzqf52Yc4ogyaURWZ1A0b1lxMTg/view?pref=2&pli=1.

that Target (and now other companies) have in the data breach context: (1) a duty to safeguard its and its business associates' customers' data; (2) a duty not to disable security features that would prevent a data breach; and (3) a duty to heed the warning signs of an attack and respond appropriately.[42] Though nothing is set in stone as of this writing, since the Target case is ongoing, the initial phases of the litigation indicate that the court is willing to consider recognizing what some see as a new species of tort: negligent data security.[43]

To date, data breach victims have been only marginally successful in breach lawsuits, but the field is developing rapidly.[44] Recent filings have sought to broaden plaintiffs' arsenal of weapons by alleging negligent misrepresentation and applying products liability theories. For example, class action plaintiffs suing Ashley Madison[45] claimed that its duty of care stems from the availability of commercially reasonable safeguards against breaches.[46] These plaintiffs claimed that Ashley Madison failed to follow industry standards, citing the Data Security Standards for the payment card industry to demonstrate the kind of steps that plaintiffs assert would have been sufficient to protect data.[47] The theory behind this claim is that, had Ashley Madison adhered to industry standards, the breach could have been avoided. This approach is much closer to a products liability claim, alleging that a defendant's failure to take commercially reasonable and viable steps to protect consumers led to harm, than to a general negligence claim.[48]

Should the "commercially reasonable options" approach prevail, the consequences would be substantial; under this analysis, the burden shifts to the defendant, who must demonstrate that it kept up with, and abided by, industry standards on data security.[49] Such a standard would put significant pressure on many businesses to identify applicable industry standards and raise their information security to that level. However, this rule could also allow defendants in industries with low information security standards to get claims dismissed on the grounds that their security—however poor it is—meets those industry standards.

---

42 *In re* Target Corp. Customer Data Security Breach Litig., MDL No. 14-2522 (PAM/JJK), accessed at https://drive.google.com/a/pulseadvisory.com/file/d/0Bzqf52Yc4ogyaURWZ1A0b1lxMTg/view?pref=2&pli=1.

43 Philip R. Stein, *Legal Precedent May Come from Ashley Madison Breach*, Law360 (Sept. 3, 2015), http://www.law360.com/articles/698349/legal-precedent-may-come-from-ashley-madison-breach; *see also* techielawyer85, *Cybersecurity Liability: Is There a Duty of Care for Customer Information?* (Jan. 22, 2014), https://nicoterablawg.wordpress.com/2014/01/22/cybersecurity-liability-is-there-a-duty-of-care-for-customer-information/.

44 Under the Rule 12(b)(6) paradigm, data breach plaintiffs face difficulties overcoming defenses such as lack of standing and failure to demonstrate a cognizable injury. In 2011, a class of data breach victims in Whitaker et al. v. Health Net of Cal., Inc. filed suit for a data breach that occurred when IBM lost nine servers containing 800,000 Health Net customers' confidential information. The plaintiffs contended that they had standing to sue because of the threat of loss. The judge rejected plaintiffs' argument, and dismissed the lawsuit because "the threat plaintiffs allege [was] wholly conjectural and hypothetical." *See* The Typical Data Breach Lawsuit and How to Protect Your Company, InsideCounsel (Oct. 2014), http://www.mvalaw.com/news-publications-347.html.

45 In the wake of the Ashley Madison breach, in which self-proclaimed hacktivists released the personal, financial, and social information of about 30 million users of the website, various class actions have been filed against Ashley Madison alleging more than $500 million in damages. *See* Kim Zetter, *Ashley Madison Hit with $500 Million in Lawsuits* (Aug. 25, 2015, 3:30 PM), http://www.wired.com/2015/08/ashley-madison-hit-500-million-lawsuits/.

46 Doe v. Avid Life Media Inc., No. 15-CV-01347, Dkt. No. 1, at 33–35 (C.D. Cal. Aug. 24, 2015); Stein, *supra* note 43.

47 Doe v. Avid Life Media Inc., No. 15-CV-01347, Dkt. No. 1, at 33–35 (C.D. Cal. Aug. 24, 2015).

48 Stein, *supra* note 43.

49 *Id.*

At the time of this writing, the Target and Ashley Madison lawsuits are ongoing, and there remains significant uncertainty on this issue. In opposition to this new type of tort, a Pennsylvania trial court recently dismissed a class action lawsuit brought on behalf of more than 62,000 employees and former employees of the University of Pittsburgh Medical Center (UPMC), whose confidential personal identifying information was stolen from UPMC's computer system.[50] The court refused to find "that the courts should impose a new affirmative duty of care that would allow data breach actions to recover damages recognized in common law negligence actions."[51] Moreover, the *UMPC* court not only found that there are no generally accepted reasonable care standards concerning data protection obligations, but also held that the use of "'expert' testimony and jury findings" is not a "viable method for resolving the difficult issue of the minimum requirements of care that should be imposed in data breach litigation, assuming that any minimum requirements should be imposed."[52]

Although the Target, Ashley Madison, and UPMC lawsuits are not directly related to the legal profession, their outcomes could significantly impact the standard of care expected of law firms with respect to information security. These decisions are likely to be invoked soon, as it is only a matter of time before some court is faced with a precedent-setting legal malpractice claim involving a data breach.

A 2014 study by insurance broker Ames & Gough found that half of the leading legal malpractice insurers surveyed have had a lawyers' professional liability insurance claim arising from a cyber or network security event.[53] Of the insurers with these claims, the majority traced the breach to a lost or stolen laptop.[54] For the remainder, a combination of employee error, hackers, and disgruntled employees led to a breach.[55] These security breach claims can be extremely costly, and may not always be covered by the traditional professional liability policies held by law firms. In the face of all the uncertainty concerning limits of liability for data breaches, and the potentially massive dollar amounts involved, client lawsuits pose a significant risk to law firms that have inadequate information security.

1.2.3 Clients Can Be Liable for Their Law Firm's Inadequate Security

When a breach or incident at a law firm involves a client's data, the client may also be liable to third parties affected by the breach. This client liability may be via vicarious liability, or via direct liability for failure to exercise due diligence in

---

50 Dittman v. UMPC, No. GD-14-003285 (Allegheny Cty. Ct. C.P. May 28, 2015); Colleen Maranges, Bergerman LLP, *Court Refuses to Recognize Negligence Claim for Data Breach* (June 26, 2015), http://www.lexology.com/library/detail. aspx?g=83dc337e-1326-473e-91d2-ade1a657f4d1.
51 Dittman, *supra* note 50.
52 *Id.*
53 Ames & Gough, *Law Firms Seeing Rise in Malpractice Claims Severity* (July 3, 2014), http://www.claimsjournal.com/news/ national/2014/07/03/251303.htm.
54 *Id.*
55 *Id.*

vetting the law firm before sharing personal data with it. Indeed, in *In re GMR Transcription Services, Inc.*, the FTC brought an action under Section 5 of the FTC Act ("unfair or deceptive acts or practices in or affecting commerce") against a company that failed to "adequately verify that their service provider . . . implemented reasonable and appropriate security measures to protect personal information."[56] The FTC also found fault with the terms of the contract with the service provider, and the steps the company took to verify that the service provider was adequately protecting data.[57] Given *GMR*, clients will likely increase their scrutiny of their law firms' security systems to avoid potential liability. Law firms that do not meet client standards will not get hired.

There is also a potential conflict of interest if a law firm represents a client in any FTC investigation, any other regulatory action, or any lawsuits emerging from a breach of the law firm's security. For example, the client might want to emphasize how the law firm did not accurately represent its practices when the client conducted a due diligence investigation of the firm's data protection capabilities. The firm might be reluctant to fall on its sword to protect the client's reputation because it could implicate the firm's reputation, causing the client to go to a competitor law firm to represent it in connection with the incident.

1.2.4 Breach Mitigation and Investigation Costs

On top of all the costs discussed in this chapter, a law firm facing a breach will also face the costs of investigating and mitigating the breach itself. Although the costs arising from any single data breach are unpredictable, the average total organizational cost of a data breach in the United States in 2015 was $6.53 million.[58] Of this $6.53 million average, the four primary cost centers of a data breach are: (1) detection and discovery in the form of digital forensic investigations and audit services; (2) escalation, including crisis management and communication to executive managers; (3) notification costs in the pursuit of regulatory compliance; and (4) *ex post facto* response costs in the form of remediation activities, legal expenses, and identity protection services for affected consumers.[59]

In addition to these process-related activities, affected firms may also experience opportunity costs associated with a security event, in the form of turnover of existing clients and diminished ability to acquire future clients.[60] Often, these lost business costs may be greater than any one of the process-related expenses described earlier. In 2015, the average lost business cost worldwide for

---

56 *In re* GMR Transcription Services, Docket No. C-4482, https://www.ftc.gov/system/files/documents/cases/140821gmrdo. pdf; https://www.ftc.gov/system/files/documents/cases/140821gmrcmpt.pdf.
57 *Id.*
58 Ponemon Institute, *2015 Cost of Data Breach Study: Global Analysis* 7 (May 2015), http://www-01.ibm.com/common/ssi/cgi-bin/ssialias?subtype=WH&infotype=SA&htmlfid=SEW03053WWEN&attachment=SEW03053WWEN.PDF (last accessed Sept. 28, 2016).
59 *Id.* at 25.
60 *Id.* at 26.

organizations resulting from a data breach was the highest cost component, averaging $1.57 million.[61]

1.3   Conclusion

Any company is a potential target for a data breach, but law firms are particularly attractive targets for cyber criminals, hacktivists, or other malicious actors, due to the sensitive client data they hold and their relative lack of security. The consequences for law firms that have been breached can be extremely costly and may include ethics violations, lawsuits, reputational damage, and breach mitigation and investigation costs. Although law firms are beginning to recognize their vulnerability to cyber threats, they have generally been slow to respond to potential threats or take steps to reduce that vulnerability. One of the keys to formulating an adequate protection system is for the law firm first to understand the nature of cyber threats, a topic covered in later in the book.

---

61 *Id.* at 17.

2

THE TEN COMMANDMENTS OF CYBERSECURITY

Daniel Garrie

Imagine that your most valuable client's information and records are stolen. The firm is at a complete loss on what to disclose to this individual and other clients. While the information technology (IT) department and managing partners are scrambling to figure out what to do, they soon realize all of their firm's records are missing and someone is demanding the firm pay a ransom in exchange for its release. Now imagine further that the firm has no alternative but to pay the demand (in Bitcoins) to ensure the security of its clients.

One has to look no further than the Panama Papers and other headlines to realize how quickly and easily our digital platforms can be used against us. Although the Internet has delivered on its promise of global access and efficiency, it also accelerates and scales up the darker forms of human activity: theft, fraud, extortion, blackmail, espionage (state and corporate), terrorism, insider trading, property destruction and criminal mischief. Soon, the Internet of Things (IoT) will even more seamlessly connect our devices to everything we need—as well as everything we need to fear.

As we continue to learn, the Internet was built for connectivity and speed, not security and protection. For criminals, rogue states, and mischievous actors, the digital world has become the "promised land"—low risk and high reward—offering a borderless reach, assured anonymity, and defenseless victims who, under the current state of the law, are largely not allowed to fight back.

Foreign governments, state-sponsored actors, criminals, terrorists, and lone actors are increasingly targeting our data systems and information networks. The finances, trade secrets, and operations of our enterprises, as well as the identities and privacy of our citizens, are at constant risk. Networks that control critical corporate and governmental infrastructure (power grids, manufacturing plants, communications, health and transportation systems) are being probed for vulnerabilities with an eye toward future infiltration and disruption. The federal government—as well as our leading military and law enforcement agencies—have been repeatedly targeted by cyber criminals. Hackers in China and Russia are targeting U.S. defense contractors. North Korea's alleged cyberattack on Sony Pictures in 2014 destroyed data, disabled thousands of computers, and disrupted the executive suite. Distributed denial-of-service attacks have been launched against governmental agencies, the media, utilities, banks, hospitals, and manufacturing firms, to name just a few.

With more than 100 million Americans' personal data compromised in recent years—including credit card information and medical records—it is no surprise that 9 out of 10 Americans say they feel they have lost control of their personal information. These cyber threats are among the most urgent risks to America's economic and national security and the personal safety of its citizens.

As America's cyber adversaries have grown more sophisticated and active, emboldened by their successes and the absence of consequences, the need to be proactive, nimble, and resilient has increased. In this environment, it is easy for even the most sophisticated enterprises to feel overwhelmed. The federal government, which is obligated to protect the information provided to it by the American people, has a unique responsibility to lead. The fact is, though, that even the U.S.

government does not have in place all the tools it needs, and, in many areas, it lacks even the safeguards that many businesses require.

This book offers a great amount of detail, but the following "commandments" are proven and commonsense steps that can be taken immediately.

2.1 Develop and Practice Strong Cyber Hygiene

- Conduct full background checks of personnel to mitigate "insider" threats.
- Implement robust passwords or other advanced means of multifactor authentication.
- Ensure security of computing and communication devices, especially when traveling abroad.
- Train employees on email etiquette and "spear-phishing" schemes.
- Keep personnel up-to-date as to relevant incidents, causes, and consequences.
- Increase and demonstrate cybersecurity common sense as part of performance reviews.
- Utilize surveillance and malware detection and "detonation" software.
- Assess the security needs for encrypted phones, laptops, and smart devices.

2.2 Know and Secure Vendors' Networks

- Limit access in accordance with need.
- Conduct due-diligence investigations into the backgrounds of vendors with access. Enterprise security is only as strong as its weakest link.
- Review existing contract language. Understand vendors' cybersecurity protocols.
- Contractually bind vendors to security standards and protocols.
- Identify, rank, engage, and audit third-party vendors in accordance with geography and business importance. Vendors must be willing to become partners in maintaining your security.
- Require vendors that provide critical data to disclose cyber incidents within 72 hours of occurrence.

2.3   Identify and Protect the "Crown Jewels"

- Identify and separately protect critical data and systems (such as client data, Internet protocol, business strategy, market-sensitive information, and internal communications).
- Verify and update processes with the executive management team.
- Implement and regularly update appropriate controls, systems, and processes to protect systems.
- Verify, validate, and regularly test security systems to ensure the continued protection of critical data in the most effective manner.

2.4   Practice Your Incident Response Plan

- Engage the senior partners, as well as your business, legal, marketing, insurance, human resources, and technology departments, to develop a cross-functional incident response plan and team.
- Retain outside technical, legal, and public relations experts to be on call for the inevitable cyber incident.
- Identify appropriate contacts within law enforcement and applicable regulators *before* a cyberattack.
- Focus on range, motivations, and objectives of potential attacks (e.g., theft, denial of service, ransom, publication).
- Comply with privacy laws, and work with counsel to protect the confidentiality of the firm's work.

2.5   Create and Develop a Global Communications and Messaging Framework

- Ensure that any communications plan covers all relevant constituencies: associates, clients, and third-party vendors.

- Identify all regulators (federal, state, foreign) that will expect disclosure.
- Identify media, social media, and source channels for disseminating company information.
- Retain messaging experts to ensure a coordinated response when it is needed.

2.6 Test the Incident Response Plan and Update Regularly

- Utilize a third-party firm to conduct annual penetration tests to identify weaknesses in IT networks, infrastructure, and employee practices.
- Report the results to the executive management team on a regular basis.
- Modify the plan to reflect the results of testing.

2.7 Develop a Robust Cyber Threat Monitoring and Sharing Team

- Monitor cyber threats both internally and externally, and regularly probe systems for weaknesses.
- Monitor the Internet, social media, and dark web for stolen data and information on key executives and business operations.
- Test employee practices and compliance with security procedures.
- Participate in industry cyber threat sharing platforms, and ensure an organizational ability to act on the intelligence provided.

2.8 Evaluate Cybersecurity Insurance

- Assess the full range of risks and costs from disruption of services, data leaks, and data ransom and extortion schemes.

- Ensure that insurance coverages map to the cybersecurity controls, processes, vendors, and protocols in any incident response plan.
- Stay abreast of the market. Cyber insurance is still in its infancy and continues to evolve; coverage and pricing remain works-in-progress.
- Regularly review policies for gaps, newly available coverage, and price competitiveness.
- Verify and validate that key partners have coverage. A vendor that is hacked can lead to your organization being compromised.

2.9 Engage Privacy and Cybersecurity Expertise for All Priority Jurisdictions

- Maintain industry contacts for information and threat sharing, including best practices and solutions.
- Use industry leverage to petition the government for needed information, assistance, and liability safe harbors.
- Maintain and update this information on a regular basis.
- Consult privacy counsel to ensure that cybersecurity solutions do not violate local laws.

2.10 Maintain Government Relationships

- Know the key agencies and personnel in the jurisdictions in which you do business. The government can be a critical partner in prevention as well as in response. Their expertise and intelligence can be invaluable.
- The time to forge such relationships is *before* a crisis, not after a cyber-security breach.

CHAPTER

3

A SURVEY OF
CYBER THREATS AND
THEIR CONTEXT

Daniel Garrie, David Lawrence, and
Tim Murphy
Contributing Authors: Matthew H.
Lawrence, and Alex Tarnow

3.1   Introduction

This chapter serves as an introduction to the range of cyberattacks that law firms have experienced—and will continue to confront. As part of this process, we outline the rationale for why the digital communications and client files of law firms constitute high-value targets to a wide range of diversely motivated actors, many of whom are armed with increasingly sophisticated technologies (as well as proven low-tech methods) for penetrating a firm's systems. In doing so, we seek to provide context for the continued thinking about and weighing of a risk-based approach to law firm security and data protection protocols.

At the outset, it is critical that law firms recognize the breadth and depth of the methods that cyberattackers use, their long-term incentives for targeting law firms,[1] and the range of consequences to a firm of a successful attack.

Principally, cyberattackers will have two central objectives: (1) to gain administrator or specific user access to a firm's computer systems, or (2) to cause physical or virtual damage to a firm's computer or data storage systems.

The first goal, achieving access, allows cybercriminals to possess a client's data and communications, and would generally enable a sufficiently sophisticated actor to transfer, alter, or delete this information, often without detection.[2] The second goal, causing physical or virtual damage to a firm's systems, constitutes a malicious and destructive act upon the enterprise[3] that generally requires no special access, because the attacks are either external or "insider" driven (e.g. a denial-of-service attack), or exploitative (e.g. attacking an unpatched operating system). Significantly, both forms of attacks can be deployed to steal confidential and

---

1 AMERICAN BAR ASSOCIATION, CYBERSECURITY LEGAL TASK FORCE SECTION OF SCIENCE & TECHNOLOGY LAW, REPORT TO THE HOUSE OF DELEGATES: RESOLUTION 109 (August 2014) at 4, http://www.americanbar.org/content/dam/aba/administrative/house_of_delegates/resolutions/2014_hod_annual_meeting_109.authcheckdam.pdf ("The threat of cyberattacks against law firms is growing. Lawyers and law offices are facing unprecedented challenges from the widespread use of electronic records and mobile devices. There are many reasons for hackers to target the information being held by law firms. They collect and store large amounts of critical, highly valuable corporate records, including intellectual property, strategic business data, and litigation-related theories and records collected through e-discovery.").

2 RAYMOND R. PANKO, BUSINESS DATA NETWORKS AND TELECOMMUNICATIONS (2003) ("The hacker is now in a position to wreak havoc in the system by means such as reading or altering sensitive information, changing or deleting key files, wiping out the hard drive, and using the compromised target to launch attacks against other targets."). While this access can be actively used to cause harm to a firm, it is also possible to use that access to passively ingest a firm's, or client's, sensitive data. Imagine a law firm that has a robust patent prosecution practice. If a cybercriminal wanted to engage in corporate espionage, it is unlikely it would be able to access a company's research, but once that information is sent to the law firm to prepare the patent application, it might be in significant jeopardy if the law firm does not have proper cybersecurity processes in place.

3 Al Bento & Regina Bento, *Empirical Test of a Hacking Model: An Exploratory Study*, 14 COMM. ASS'N FOR INFO. SYS. 672, 621 (Dec. 13, 2004), http://aisel.aisnet.org/cgi/viewcontent.cgi?article=3291&context=cais&sei-redir=1&referer=http%3A%2F%2Fscholar.google.com%2Fscholar%3Fq%3Dhacking%2Badministrator%2Blevel%2Baccount%26btnG%3D%26hl%3Den%26as_sdt%3D0%252C33#search=%22hacking%20administrator%20level%20account%22 ("When hackers are unable to achieve control of the target, they often express their frustration by launching Denial-of-Service (DoS) attacks (such as *Smurf, Fraggle* and *Syn*) that disrupt services or make them inaccessible to legitimate users, networks, and systems.").

market-sensitive information, as well as to hold data and systems hostage as part of an extortion scheme that requires a ransom to be paid (ransomware).[4]

Cyberattacks can be launched directly against a firm's systems, or by exploiting employees, clients, vendors, and suppliers; for example, through a firm's providers of software, data storage, human resource (HR) materials, and e-discovery.[5] In sum, law firms must understand that they are neither immune nor unique from other enterprises in the following regard. Their security chain will be only as strong as its weakest internal and external links.

As targets, however, law firms do have a special allure for cybercriminals. Inherently, they will always be high-value targets due to their possession of information that is core to the relationship between clients and their counsel. This includes confidential and sensitive communications, trade secrets, financial data, and intellectual property (IP), as well as market-sensitive information about litigation, governmental investigations, mergers, and acquisitions.

Irrespective of the nature and purpose of the attack, firms must anticipate the wide-ranging potential harms to and contagions of commercial, legal, financial, and reputational matters that come from being "hacked." By its very nature, the damage from an attack can be highly consequential and long term: to client relationships, day-to-day operations, and hard and soft dollar costs, as well as to internal and public confidence in a firm's planning and continuity.

Inevitably, a breach will also implicate difficult cost-benefit (and hindsight) analyses about the need for enhanced security, client and regulatory disclosure, governmental cooperation, media response, remediation, and enterprise resiliency. A successful attack on a law firm draws quick and repeated inquiries from clients, regulators, and the media. Attacks on law firms are of great interest to these constituencies (as well as to a firm's competitors and the public at large), not only because of the highly sensitive nature of attorney-client matters—and the often embarrassing secrets revealed—but also because many firms have developed extensive "best" practices in advising their clients on the very issues of cybersecurity, data privacy, information protection, crisis management, and contingency planning. This is an irony that has not been lost on the diverse community of hackers who seek to target law firms.

The nature, timing, coordination, and messaging of a firm's response to a breach is therefore critical. Prior planning and preparation will always be essential. It is of further significance that, to date, insurance carriers do not recognize the "all-in" costs of a successful attack upon a law firm as an insurable risk.

---

4 Jason Proctor, *Ransomware Hackers Pose Threat to B.C. Law Firms—British Columbia*, CBC NEWS, http://www.cbc.ca/beta/ news/canada/british-columbia/ransomware-hackers-pose-threat-to-b-c-law-firms-1.2898490.

5 *See* Phil Huggins, *Supplier Security*, MANAGING PARTNER 17 (Mar. 20, 2015).

3.2 The State of Our Digital Union: Necessary Context for Adopting a Risk-Based Approach

As we now know all too well, the Internet was constructed for universal connectivity and accessibility, not with an eye toward security and containing the darker sides of human behavior.[6] Although the Internet has delivered on its promise of social and economic progress, it also will continue to deliver unparalleled opportunities to those seeking to scale up global conflict, terrorism, criminal activity, state and industrial espionage, and vandalism. In the near future, the Internet of Things (IoT) will not only accelerate new ways for businesses to provide even greater access and efficiencies, but also offer bad actors scalable means to further compromise enterprise and personal security.[7]

Increasingly, rogue governments, state-sponsored actors, criminals, terrorists, and lone actors are targeting global data systems and information networks. Irrespective of where data is held, the finances, trade secrets, and operations of our enterprises, as well as the identities and privacy of our citizens, are at constant risk. On a daily basis, denial-of-service and data theft attacks are launched against governmental agencies, the media, utilities, banks, hospitals, retailers, manufacturers, and professional service firms, to name only a few.[8]

Networks that control and support corporate and governmental infrastructures (power grids, manufacturing plants, and communications, health, finance, and transportation systems) are being probed for vulnerabilities with an eye toward future infiltration and disruption.[9] The federal government, as well as our leading military and law enforcement agencies, has been repeatedly targeted by cybercriminals, including the intrusion last year into the Office of Personnel Management during which the personal information of millions of current and former federal employees was stolen.[10] Hackers in China and Russia continue to target leading firms throughout the private sector, as well as governmental agencies.[11] North Korea's alleged cyberattack on Sony Pictures in 2014 destroyed data, disabled thousands of computers, and disrupted the entire executive-suite layer of that

---

6 Shahida Sweeney, *Internet Not Designed for Security, Warns International Expert*, CIO, http://www.cio.com.au/article/569270/internet-designed-security-warns-international-expert/.

7 Robert Plant, *Here's Why the Internet of Things Could Be a Security Nightmare*, WALL STREET JOURNAL, http://blogs.wsj.com/experts/2016/02/23/heres-why-it-should-be-scared-of-the-internet-of-things/.

8 Kim Zetter, *The Biggest Security Threats We'll Face in 2016*, SECURITY WIRED, http://www.wired.com/2016/01/the-biggest-security-threats-well-face-in-2016/.

9 Grant Gross, *Cyberattack Could Knock Out Huge Chunk of U.S. Electric Grid*, Apr. 14, 2016, http://www.computerworld.com/article/3056617/security/cyberattack-could-knock-out-huge-chunk-of-us-electric-grid.html.

10 Kate Vinton, *21.5 Million Americans Were Compromised in OPM's Second Breach*, FORBES, (July 19, 2015), http://www.forbes.com/sites/katevinton/2015/07/09/21-5-million-americans-were-compromised-in-opms-second-breach/?ss=Security&utm_source=twitter&utm_medium=social&utm_content=Oktopost-twitter-profile&utm_campaign=Oktopost-2015-07%20General%20Campaign#302475676916.

11 Barrie Barber, *Cyber Hackers from China, Russia Target Area Defense Firms*, http://www.mydaytondailynews.com/news/news/local-military/cyber-hackers-target-area-defense-firms/nqsGX/.

company.[12] In 2016, Iranian operatives were criminally charged with hacking into New York's water systems.[13]

On October 21, 2016, a cyberattack denied millions of Internet users access to websites including Twitter, Reddit, and Netflix by an attack on Dynamic Network Services Inc. (Dyn).[14] The number of points of access to launch such an attack had been increased dramatically through the expansion of the Internet of Things (IoT) that includes smart devices, web cameras, appliances and other nonsecure connections to the Internet.[15]

With more than 100 million Americans' personal data compromised in recent years—including credit card, bank, tax, and medical records—it is no surprise that 9 out of 10 Americans say they feel they have lost control of their personal information.[16] These cyber threats are among the most urgent risks to America's economic and national security and the personal safety of its citizens.

As cyber adversaries have grown more sophisticated and active, emboldened by their successes and the absence of consequences, the need for enterprises to be proactive, nimble, and resilient has increased. In this environment, it is easy for even the most sophisticated firms to feel overwhelmed. No single enterprise or source possesses the answers.

The federal government, which is obligated to protect the information provided to it by the American people, has a unique responsibility to lead. The fact is, though, that even the U.S. government does not have in place all the tools it needs, and in many areas it lacks safeguards that many businesses require.[17]

Lessons have been learned from both our successes and failures, so it is essential for firms to continue to share hard-earned collective wisdom.[18] For this reason, various industries, including the financial and legal sectors, have recognized the need to form information-sharing groups to disseminate information about cyber threats and other vulnerabilities.[19] In the future, businesses will be better able to share information with each other and coordinate their efforts through such programs as the newly created Cybersecurity Information Sharing Act.

---

12 Bob Orr, *Why the U.S. Was Sure North Korea Hacked Sony*, CBS (Jan. 29, 2015), http://www.cbsnews.com/news/why-the-u-s-government-was-sure-north-korea-hacked-sony/.

13 Erik Larson et al., *U.S. to Charge Iran in Cyber Attacks Against Banks, New York Dam—Sources*, REUTERS (2016), http://www.reuters.com/article/us-usa-iran-cyber-iduskcn0wp2nm.

14 Haley Sweetland Edwards, *How Webcams Helped Bring Down the Internet, Briefly*, TIME (October 25, 2016),

15 *Cyber attacks take down major websites*, CRAIN'S CHICAGO BUSINESS (October 21, 2016), www.chicagobusiness.com/article/20161021/NEWS08/161029970.

16 Dan Kedmey, *9 in 10 Americans Feel They've Lost Control of Their Personal Data*, TIME (Nov. 12, 2014), http://time.com/3521166/privacy-personal-data-report/.

17 *U.S. Government "Worse Than All Major Industries" on Cybersecurity*, REUTERS (Apr. 15, 2016), http://www.nbcnews.com/tech/tech-news/u-s-government-worse-all-major-industries-cyber-security-n556461.

18 *See* David Lawrence et al., *"Ten Commandments" of Cyber Security Can Enhance Safety*, KNOWLEDGE@WHARTON, http://knowledge.wharton.upenn.edu/article/how-the-ten-commandments-of-cyber-security-can-enhance-safety/.

19 The effort is coordinated by the Financial Services Information Sharing and Analysis Center, which oversees the legal group and similar entities that focus on other industries, such as retail. The group includes Sullivan & Cromwell, Debevoise & Plimpton, Paul Weiss Rifkind Wharton & Garrison, Allen & Overy, and Linklaters. It will be affiliated with the financial industry's forum for cyber threat discussions, called the Financial Services Information Sharing and Analysis Center (FS-ISAC), according to William Nelson, CEO of FS-ISAC. Christine Simmons & Nell Gluckman, *Law Firms to Form Cybersecurity Alliance*, THE AMERICAN LAWYER (Mar. 4, 2015), http://www.americanlawyer.com/id=1202719660496/Law-Firms-to-Form-Cybersecurity-Alliance?slreturn=20160319022150.

President Obama has repeatedly warned of the existential nature of our cyber exposures.[20] To this end, he recently announced the formation of a bipartisan Commission on Enhancing National Cybersecurity to focus on long-term solutions.[21] This commission will be composed of top business, strategic, and technology experts from inside and outside the government, and will provide specific recommendations for bolstering cybersecurity awareness and protections across the public and private sectors over the next decade.[22]

While this is a significant step toward recognizing and responding to our exposures, the commission's first report was presented on 1st December 2016. Fortunately, in the interim, when it comes to understanding our global state of preparedness and our ability to respond, there are some consensus views to inform *all firms* about the nature of these exposures:[23]

- The immense security costs now imposed upon public and private enterprises solely to stay in business effectively represent the single greatest protection tax in modern history.
- Cyber risk is now a systemic threat to national security, economic sustainability, safety, public confidence, and the freedoms that constitute our way of life. It has led to the greatest theft and transference of money, information, intellectual property, and state secrets in modern history.
- There are only three types of operating enterprises left in the world (including law firms): Those that have been hacked; those that are going to be hacked; and those that already have been hacked, but don't yet know it.
- The consensus on the annual cost of cyberattacks to the global economy is around $445 billion, but the "whisper" number of true damages dwarfs this estimate. Many successful intrusions are never detected. Other attacks go unreported due to national security considerations and business concerns over client relationships, litigation, and reputational harm.
- The occurrence of a large catastrophic and systemic attack is no longer a matter of if, only when and how costly: to life, property, reputations, the economy, and our overall sense of confidence and security.
- If you can imagine it, hackers can do it. And even if you can't imagine it, they have—and are working on it.
- Only a small fraction of the threat surfaces to the public through headlines and episodic disclosures. Rest assured, there is no shortage of plans or talent for launching systemic strikes against critical infrastructure—defense, power, transportation, telecom, medical, and finance systems. There are even applications (apps) for performing such attacks available on the dark web.

20 Barack Obama, *Protecting U.S. Innovation from Cyberthreats*, WALL STREET JOURNAL, Feb. 9, 2016, http://www.wsj.com/articles/protecting-u-s-innovation-from-cyberthreats-1455012003.
21 Roberta Rampton, *Obama Names Cyber Experts from Business, Academia to New Panel*, REUTERS, Apr. 13, 2016, http://www.reuters.com/article/us-usa-cyber-obama-idUSKCN0XA2O1.
22 *Id.*
23 David Lawrence et al., *We Don't Need a Crisis to Act Unitedly against Cyber Threats*, KNOWLEDGE@WHARTON, June 1, 2015, http://knowledge.wharton.upenn.edu/article/we-dont-need-a-crisis-to-act-unitedly-against-cyber-threats/.

- Officials fear that it may take a cyber 9/11 event before we wake up and acknowledge the magnitude of this threat. By then, broad-scale and irreparable harm will have occurred, and we may be locked into a zero-sum blame game.

- Cybersecurity is not a technology issue in need of a patch. Technology and its portals are merely the newest means for a widening range of individual, group, and state-sponsored actors to achieve familiar ends. In reality, it is about fraud, theft, state and industrial espionage, extortion, illicit finance, geopolitical conflict, terrorism, economic disruption, human rights violations, and vandalism. There is no simple fix.

- Most consequential threats emanate from a relatively discrete group of states, state-sponsored actors, and state-protected groups. Long-term solutions will have to reflect geopolitical realities.

- Those behind cyberattacks may be criminals, spies, terrorists, "hacktivists," or enemy states, but they are rational actors. The infamous 1930s bank robber, Willie Sutton, reportedly offered a simple explanation as to why he robbed banks: "It's where the money is." Whether the hacker is an outsider breaking in or an insider attacking from within, our connected networks offer the keys to the castles that contain, among other assets, our money, state and military secrets, operational systems, IP, business strategies, market-sensitive information, private communications, personal identities, legal advice, and reputations.

- Cybercrime remains a virtually perfect crime and act of war. It is low risk and high reward. It is agile, cheap, and remotely scalable. It morphs and innovates in ways that leave enforcement officials fighting yesterday's battles with yesterday's weapons. Victims have little or no recourse. Cybercrime does not fit within our current perspective on and process for dealing with domestic and international crime. There are no laws, treaties, or boundaries to limit tactics, weapons, and targeting of civilians. Easily cloaked and launched from safe havens, cybercrime carries little risk of detection, prevention, apprehension, or punishment. With so much to gain and so little to lose, why stop?

- Cyberattack victims unfairly shoulder the blame. In the Alice-in-Wonderland aftermath of cyberattacks, the perpetrators are often beyond the law and the victimized enterprise stands trial. As defendants, they are convicted of knowing that they were attractive, inviting the assault, and then failing to fend off their attackers.

- Our lack of coordination is inconsistent with democratic models for security. Global security has always required partnerships between governmental bodies and an informed and committed citizenry. Unfortunately, even the seemingly simple decision to report an attack to authorities involves a complex calculus about likely costs and uncertain benefits. Critical issues about confidentiality, privacy, information sharing, and safe-harbor notifications have not yet been sufficiently addressed. International treaties will have to be enacted and enforced.

■ Even the most sophisticated and costly efforts at prevention and detection have proven only partially effective; more useful in delaying the inevitable or deflecting the contagion to another enterprise that offers less resistance. Institutions are asking themselves, "How fast and nimble do I have to be to outrun this bear?" In the short term, the answer is, perhaps "Just faster than the other guys." In the longer term, the bear is still out there.

■ In cyberspace, supply-chain security matters. As noted earlier, a firm's information security is only as strong as its weakest link with access.

■ Our current balkanized approach to security fits a popular definition of insanity: We are doing the same thing over and over again, without even expecting a different result. No single entity, sector, or nation can manage this risk on its own. Robust procedures and protections for shared knowledge and resources must be an essential component of a cybersecurity strategy.

■ Insurance can only provide a partial answer. The insurance market is still in its infancy. Policies generally have low limits and numerous exclusions. To increase the amount and scope of coverage, carriers would need better actuarial data and intelligence regarding the cyber risk profiles of the companies they insure, as well as the steps that can be taken to mitigate the risks.

3.3   The Threats Landscape for Law Firms

Unfortunately, the legal disclaimer that attaches to the marketing of mutual funds—*past performance may not be indicative of future returns*—does not apply to our cyber exposures. To the contrary: When it comes to cyberattacks, even if history does not repeat itself exactly, it rhymes close enough.

While the number of hackers and cybercriminals has increased substantially over the last several years,[24] the fundamental approaches they utilize to compromise the integrity of law firm systems have not changed because, essentially, the core elements of computer technology have not changed. Because core methodologies have remained the same for years, enhanced "hacking tools" have been

---

24 *The Rise of the Hacker*, THE ECONOMIST, Nov. 7, 2015, http://www.economist.com/news/business/21677632-rise-hacker.

developed. These easily accessible sets of software have enabled even novice hackers to implement very sophisticated cyber hostilities.

Thus, it is essential for law firms to realize that, even if they believe themselves to be low profile—for a variety of reasons[25]—they will be attractive and susceptible to a wide range of actors seeking entrance to their information. Because law firms act as warehouses of sensitive and personally identifiable client data, they must recognize that, in many ways, they are the perfect victims: high-impact, high-vulnerability, silent sufferers.[26]

- Law firms are repositories of communications and other sensitive information about clients, which, in the wrong hands, can be readily used for illegal financial and competitive gain. This includes information about IP, trade secrets, finances, mergers, acquisitions, commercial strategies, and governmental investigations.
- Historically, firms have not been front-line targets for cyberattacks. Accordingly, as a general matter, they have not invested as heavily as other enterprises in security resources and personnel.
- Law firms are understandably reluctant to disclose the possibility of a breach to authorities or outside parties, lest they lose the confidence and trust of their clients.[27]

As a result, the Federal Bureau of Investigation (FBI) and other authorities have issued a series of alerts to warn law firms and their clients about the increasing occurrence and potential of attacks.[28] Indeed, recent events prove what law enforcement officials have been warning companies about for years. As hacking tools and hackers for hire proliferate in certain corners of the Internet, it has become easier for criminals to breach computer networks as a way to further a range of crimes, from insider trading to IP and identity theft to extortion.

In 2015, the American Bar Association reported in its Legal Technology Survey that 1 in 4 firms with at least 100 attorneys have experienced a data breach.[29] The breaches were blamed on hacker penetrations, website attacks, "phishing" schemes, and stolen or lost smartphones or computers.[30] In March of 2016, it was reported that cyber thieves had broken into two of the prominent law firms that represent

---

25 For example, parties to matrimonial proceedings may unlawfully access their former spouse's computer or phone. *See* Henry Gornbein, *Divorce, Hacking, and Criminal Prosecution*, HUFFINGTON POST, Jan. 12, 2011, http://www.huffingtonpost.com/henry-gornbein/divorce-hacking-and-crimi_b_205257.html.

26 Drew T. Simshaw, *Legal Ethics and Data Security: Our Individual and Collective Obligation to Protect Client Data*, 32 AM. J. TRIAL ADVOC. 549, 550 (2015).

27 Indeed, one of the hardest questions for law firms is the determination of when they are required to publicly disclose a data breach to a client and regulators. Forty-seven U.S. states have their own breach-notification laws, forcing law firms and other companies to navigate a patchwork of different rules. *See* John Clabby & Joseph Swanson, *Developments in Cybersecurity: Privacy Laws, Hacking Beyond Customer Data, and Communicating with Corporate Boards*, JD SUPRA, Jan. 3, 2016, http://www.jdsupra.com/legalnews/developments-in-cybersecurity-privacy-99147/.

28 Matthew Goldstein, *Law Firms Are Pressed on Security for Data*, DEALBOOK, Mar. 26, 2014, http://dealbook.nytimes.com/2014/03/26/law-firms-scrutinized-as-hacking-increases/?_php=true.

29 Melissa Maleske, *1 in 4 Law Firms Are Victims of a Data Breach*, LAW360 (Sept. 22, 2015), http://www.law360.com/articles/705657/1-in-4-law-firms-are-victims-of-a-data-breach.

30 *Id.*

Fortune 500 companies and banks on Wall Street.[31] Presently, U.S. authorities reportedly are investigating the data breaches at Weil Gotshal & Manges LLP and Cravath Swaine & Moore LLP.[32]

Most notoriously, in April 2016, public reports disclosed a massive leak of millions of documents and records from Panama City-based law firm Mossack Fonseca, which exposed the business, financial, and tax dealings of thousands of world leaders, public figures, and popular celebrities, as well as their global networks of friends, family members, and advisors. It has been described as the greatest data breach in history, at least of those publicly reported and within the private sector.

The implications of the Mossack Fonseca breach and the ensuing disclosures (the "Panama Papers") are still playing out legally, politically, and in the court of public opinion—and will for years to come. Depending upon regional geopolitics, authorities around the world are either now gathering evidence for potential criminal cases against the firm and its clients, or attempting to control ("spin") the discussion about the significance of this information.

Putting aside questions about who was responsible for this hack and the motivations therefor, experts quickly reached important conclusions about the nature of the attack[33]:

- The breach was long-standing (occurring over more than a year) and was not discovered by the firm until public disclosures of the records.
- The outflow of client-sensitive information was voluminous (dating back to the 1970s and estimated at 4.2 million emails, 3 million database files, 2.1 million PDFs, 1.1 million images, 320,166 text files, and 2,242 files in other formats).
- The dissemination was continuous and widespread. There was a global appetite and capacity to analyze and further publicize the data as "news worthy" (an effort that is still ongoing).
- The consequences to the firm and its clients will be long term; investigations have been opened in numerous jurisdictions and public disclosures are continuing.
- Most relevantly, Mossack Fonseca was not unique as a firm in relying upon antiquated and vulnerable information technology (IT) platforms, lax data and encryption protections, and outdated security access protocols.

According to authorities, the growing attacks on law firms also reflect the enhanced ability of actors to scour the digital landscape for sophisticated types of information and tools. In February 2016, a posting appeared on an underground Russian website called DarkMoney.cc, in which the person offered to sell his hacking services to other would-be cyber thieves and identified specific

31 Nicole Hong & Robin Sidel, *Hackers Breach Law Firms, Including Cravath and Weil Gotshal*, WALL ST. J., Mar. 29, 2016, http://www.wsj.com/articles/hackers-breach-cravath-swaine-other-big-law-firms-1459293504.

32 *Id.*

33 *See* James Temperton & Matt Burgess, *Panama Papers: The Security Flaws at the Heart of Mossack Fonseca*, WIRED UK, Apr. 6, 2016, http://www.wired.co.uk/news/archive/2016-04-06/panama-papers-mossack-fonseca-website-security-problems.

law firms as potential targets.[34] Of note, YouTube also hosts videos that offer hacking tutorials.[35]

Law firm hackers, like commercial fishermen casting wide nets, often seek to gather large amounts of information indiscriminately and then analyze it later to see how it could be of value. This, in turn, can make it even more difficult to determine the actors responsible and the ultimate objectives of their attacks.

Understandably, the risks to law firms have raised obvious concerns among clients, many of whom have now taken matters into their own hands. Many clients are now asking for certifications about security, whereas others are conducting their own assessments of the firms they hire. Even major corporate clients that might not independently question their law firm's cybersecurity practices are increasingly being obligated to by governmental agencies like the Securities and Exchange Commission's Office of Compliance Inspections and Examinations (OCIE).[36] The State of New York has recognized the need for enhanced cybersecurity by being the first state to implement mandatory cybersecurity requirements on financial institutions. The regulation will require third-party vendors, such as law firms, to be compliant with cybersecurity best practices.[37]

In response to this new phenomenon, some law firms now affirmatively disclose that they are compliant with cybersecurity standards such as ISO 27001.[38] Other law firms even view their investments in cybersecurity as offering a potential competitive advantage to attract clients.[39]

Notwithstanding the material risks to attorney-client relationships—and the protection of communications, IP, business strategies, public market transactions, and sensitive governmental affairs—to date the legal industry has generally operated within a set of cybersecurity guidelines that has yet to give clear guidance about basic standards and best practices. (Note, though, that the ABA Model Rules of Professional Responsibility were updated, especially in Model Rules 1.1 and 1.6, to address cybersecurity.)[40] Also, the Florida Supreme Court has recognized the need for increased awareness of cyber technology and security by requiring technology-related CLE courses.[41]

---

34 *See generally* Hong & Sidel, *supra* note 29.

35 Laurie Segall, *YouTube's "RAT" Problem*, CNN, Jul. 29, 2015, http://money.cnn.com/2015/07/29/technology/youtube-ratting-problem/index.html.

36 Kenneth N. Rashbaum et al., *Cybersecurity: Business Imperative for Law Firms*, New York Law Journal, Dec. 10, 2014, http://www.newyorklawjournal.com/id=1202678494487?keywords=Kenneth+N.+Rashbaum&publication= New+York+Law+Journal.

37 Meghan Tribe, *As Cybersecurity Hurdles Loom, Smaller Firms Face Big Challenges*, The American Lawyer, Sept. 27, 2016, http://www.americanlawyer.com/id=1202768670107/As-Cybersecurity-Hurdles-Loom-Smaller-Firms-Face-Big-Challenges?slreturn=20160929162108

38 Mary K. Pratt, *Law Firm Makes a Case for Security Certification*, CIO, Aug. 28, 2015, http://www.cio.com/article/2969323/security/law-firm-makes-a-case-for-security-certification.html.

39 *See* ALM Media Properties, *Cybersecurity Ignorance Is Big Risk for Law Firms & Corporate Counsel, ALM Legal Intelligence Analysts Find*, ALM, Dec. 16, 2015, http://www.alm.com/press-room/cybersecurity-ignorance-is-big-risk-for-law-firms-corporate-counsel-alm-legal-intelligence-analysts-find/.

40 Model Rules of Prof'l Conduct r. 1.1, cmt. 2 (Am. Bar Ass'n 2012) ("To maintain the requisite knowledge and skill, a lawyer should keep abreast of changes in the law and its practice, including the benefits and risks associated with relevant technology"); *see also id.* at r. 1.6(c) ("A lawyer shall make reasonable efforts to prevent the inadvertent or unauthorized disclosure of, or unauthorized access to, information relating to the representation of a client.").

41 Victor Li, *Florida Supreme Court Approves Mandatory Tech CLE Classes for Lawyers*, ABA Journal (September 30, 2016), http://www.abajournal.com/news/article/florida_supreme_court_approves_mandatory_tech_cles_for_lawyers.

Inevitably, cybersecurity standards for the legal profession will change, either voluntarily (e.g. through the American Bar Association), by regulation (e.g., the Federal Trade Commission, Department of Justice, or SEC), or because of the concerns and liability claims of clients. Until appropriate guidelines are set, however, it is essential for every firm to understand and assess the nature of the exposures it faces. To this end, information sharing, benchmarking, and proactive thinking will be essential.

3.4   The Range of Specific Threats

As noted, hacks and intrusions can come from many sources and directions, including state actors, and foreign and domestic criminal networks seeking easy means to steal valuable information. Notwithstanding the origins, most cyberattacks will fall into one of two main categories: human intent or mistake, and software exploitation. The former gains access to a system by exploiting information gained through acts of commission or omission by individuals with access to the system. The latter category seeks to gain access to systems through a vulnerability in a platform's security protocols or software. The specific forms of exposures that will be discussed include theft and loss of devices, employee criminality (insider threat), social engineering, privilege abuse, bypassing of security controls, network port probes, unpatched software vulnerabilities, denial-of-service attacks, group phishing, spear phishing, website exploits/browser security, bots, viruses and worms, Trojan horses, zero-day exploits, and spyware.

Again, it is important to keep in mind that attacks can be launched directly upon a firm and its personnel, or through clients, vendors, and suppliers. Firms must be particularly attuned to the controls of software suppliers, data storage providers, HR, and e-discovery platforms.

3.4.1   Theft or Loss of a Device

The most commonly reported cyber breach experienced by law firms is that related to the loss or theft of a laptop, thumb drive, smartphone, tablet, or other mobile device.[42] If the information on the device was not encrypted and contained, or offered personally identifiable information, a theft of information likely will occur. With access to office email and other law office networks, such a theft or loss provides an open door for cybercriminals to quickly steal confidential information.[43]

---

42 Steve Couch, *Law Firm Exposure to Cyber Breach Threats*, OSBA, https://www.ohiobar.org/newsandpublications/ohiolawyer/pages/law-firm-exposure-to-cyber-breach-threats.aspx.
43 *Id.*

3.4.2 Employee Criminality: The Insider Threat

Employee criminal activity (insider threat) is also a significant risk within the law firm environment.[44] The intentional theft of a laptop, client data, user identifications and passwords, or the importation of various forms of malware and spyware, can easily go undetected for a long period of time. Such conduct can originate with an employee, or can originate through outside parties who "influence" an employee who is in a compromised position (for various reasons).[45] Often, by the time such conduct is discovered, the stolen data has made its way to third parties for various purposes.[46] For this reason, it is also essential to conduct thorough and updated background checks of personnel, as part of any cybersecurity measures.

3.4.3 Social Engineering

Social engineering is defined as "an attack vector that relies heavily on human interaction and often involves tricking people into breaking normal security procedures."[47] A cyberattacker using social engineering will typically trick someone with access to the target computer system into divulging certain information (e.g., a password) that will enable the attacker to gain access to the system.[48] This technique can be used in isolation or can be combined with other modalities of cyber-hostilities to achieve the attacker's goals. The danger of social engineering cannot be overstated: A law firm can have all the best technological cybersecurity measures in place, but if an employee is tricked into revealing a password, the entire cybersecurity regime is rendered moot.

3.4.4 Insider/Privilege-Abuse Hostilities

Insider/privilege-abuse hostilities occur when an employee or contractor, who has a certain level of authorized access, exceeds the scope of that authority. In May 2014, the Ponemon Institute found that nearly half of the 693 corporations it surveyed did not have any policies for assigning privileged user access.[49] Moreover, 22% of respondents felt that risk of insider threats will continue to rise or stay the same.[50] Insider/privilege-abuse hostilities are incredibly difficult to defend against,

---

44 *Id.*

45 *Id.*

46 *Id.*

47 Margaret Rouse, *Social Engineering* (definition), Tech Target, http://searchsecurity.techtarget.com/definition/social-engineering.

48 *See generally* Sherly Abraham & InduShobha Chengalur-Smith, *An Overview of Social Engineering Malware: Trends, Tactics, and Implications*, 32 Tech. Soc'y 123 (2010); *see also* Michael Workman, *Gaining Access with Social Engineering: An Empirical Study of the Threat*, 16 Info. Sys. Sec. 315, 316 (2007).

    Social engineers often attempt to persuade potential victims with appeals to people's emotions such as excitement or fear, whereas others utilize ways to establish interpersonal relationships or create a feeling of trust and commitment. For example, they may promise a valuable prize or financial interest on a transfer bank deposit if the victim complies with a request for bank account information. The emotional aspect of the interaction distracts people and serves to interfere with the potential victim's ability to carefully analyze the content of the message. *Id.*

49 *Privileged User Abuse & the Insider Threat*, Ponemon Institute, May 2014, http://www.raytheoncyber.com/rtnwcm/groups/cyber/documents/content/rtn_257010.pdf.

50 *Id.*

as they involve parties who are trusted and authorized to access a company's computer systems.[51] As a practical matter, it is incredibly difficult to effectively monitor users who have authorized access, since those parties have regular access to confidential information.[52] Another possible complication in attempting to monitor users is the question of who, and how trustworthy, the individual performing the monitoring is. This creates a situation where monitoring has the potential to become unproductive, inefficient, and wasteful as a security procedure.[53]

3.4.5 Bypassing of Security Controls

Bypassing security controls, in the network security context, means that a hacker exploits "a flaw in a security system . . . to circumvent security mechanisms to get system or network access."[54] The key element to bypassing security controls is that the hacker, through a hardware device, program, or piece of code, can access the system being targeted without having to go through the security clearance procedures that were implemented by the developer of the system.[55] Bypass points are often referred to as *back doors* or *trap doors*.[56] Generally, back doors can be placed through two routes: (1) by the original programmer, or (2) by a hacker implementing a system compromise such as a virus or worm.[57] A company may need to create a bypass in its system to allow authorized users to circumvent normal security procedures.[58] In contrast, hackers use back doors for easier and continued access to a system after an initial compromise.[59]

Sometimes, rather than focusing on access to a computer system, hackers may only want to access the data stored within that system, and will then seek what is referred to as a *crypto bypass*. A crypto bypass is a flaw that allows data to circumvent encryption processes that would normally be required to export data and remain in plain-text form.[60]

---

51 Frank L. Greitzer et al., *Combating the Insider Cyber Threat*, 6 IEEE Security & Privacy 61, 61–64 (2002) ("The insider threat is manifested when human behavior departs from compliance with established policies, regardless of whether it results from malice or a disregard for security policies.").

52 *Combating the Insider Threat*, U.S. Comp. Emergency Readiness Team (last updated May 2, 2014), https://www.us-cert.gov/security-publications/Combating-Insider-Threat (attempting to give companies some guidance in being able to preempt, detect, and respond to insider/privilege-abuse hostilities).

53 *See* Frank L. Greitzer & Deborah A. Frincke, *Combining Traditional Cyber Security Audit Data with Psychosocial Data: Towards Predictive Modeling for Insider Threat Mitigation*, Insider Threats in Cyber Security 25 (Christian Probst et al., eds.), 2010 (proposing an alternative approach to internal threat monitoring that focuses on identifying potential insider threats before they become a problem).

54 Margaret Rouse, *Bypass* [definition], TechTarget, http://searchsecurity.techtarget.com/definition/bypass.

55 *Id.*

56 A *back door* is an undocumented "means of [accessing] a computer program that bypasses security mechanisms." Margaret Rouse, *Back Door* [definition], TechTarget, http://searchsecurity.techtarget.com/definition/back-door.

57 *Id.*

58 *Id.*

59 *Bypass Authentication*, Knox, http://knoxd3.blogspot.com/2014/01/bypass-authentication.html. Negligence, ignorance, or simple understatement of security threats often result in authentication schemes that can be bypassed by simply skipping the login page and directly calling an internal page that is supposed to be accessed only after authentication has been performed. In addition to this, it is often possible to bypass authentication measures by tampering with requests and tricking the application into thinking that the user is already authenticated. This can be accomplished by modifying the given URL parameter, by manipulating the form, or by counterfeiting sessions. *Id.*

60 Rouse, *Bypass, supra* note 54.

3.4.6 Network Port Probes

A *port* is "nothing more than an integer that uniquely identifies an endpoint of a communication stream."[61] The easiest way to conceptualize a port is like a phone number extension, except that every phone number uses the exact same extensions (e.g., extension 100 gets you the master voice mailbox on every 200 number around the globe). A computer can have up to 65,535 ports,[62] with each being dedicated to a specific function. Ports also work to divide computer processes, since only one process (e.g., email) can operate on a given port. A hacker who performs a network port scan essentially sends a series of messages to every port on a computer system in an attempt to discern which processes correspond to which ports. This gives the hacker an idea of where a computer system may be most vulnerable. For example, a hacker may use a port scan to discover that an email port has no password protection, and then seek to exploit that weakness in a potential attack. It is important to understand that even though a port scan may not directly cause harm to a computer system, it is a critical reconnaissance step that will inform how a hacker will carry out an attack, and what sorts of cyber-hostilities the hacker is likely to employ.

3.4.7 Unpatched Software Vulnerabilities

An *unpatched software vulnerability* "is a security flaw, glitch, or weakness found in software or in an operating system (OS) that can lead to security concerns" through the use of an exploit by a hacker.[63] There is a constant struggle going on between software and operating system developers, who try to create a product without flaws, and hackers, who are constantly searching for any imperfection they can use to exploit the software and gain access to the computer system.

There are many known types of software vulnerabilities,[64] and more are being discovered. An example of one of the most common vulnerabilities is a buffer overflow, which is useful in understanding how this type of cyberhostility functions. [65] A buffer overflow "occurs when a program or process tries to store more data in a buffer (temporary data storage area) than it was intended to hold. Since buffers are meant to contain a limited amount of data, the extra information—which has to go somewhere—can overflow into adjacent buffers, corrupting or overwriting the valid data held in them."[66] Cybercriminals will attempt to exploit a buffer overflow in order to gain unauthorized access to a law firm's computer

---

61 *Glossary of Security Terms*, SANS, http://www.sans.org/security-resources/glossary-of-terms.

62 Margaret Rouse, *Port* [definition], TECHTARGET, http://searchnetworking.techtarget.com/definition/port.

63 *Gateways to Infection: Exploiting Software Vulnerabilities*, TRENDMICRO, http://about-threats.trendmicro.com/RelatedThreats. aspx?language=tw&name=Gateways+to+Infection%3A+Exploiting+Software+Vulnerabilities.

64 *Common Weakness Enumeration*, CWE-2000: COMPREHENSIVE CWE DICTIONARY, https://cwe.mitre.org/data/slices/2000.html.

65 *Gateways to Infection*, *supra* note 63.

66 Margaret Rouse, *Buffer Overflow* [definition], TECHTARGET, http://searchsecurity.techtarget.com/definition/buffer-over-flow; *see also Gateways to Infection*, *supra* note 63.

system.[67] Buffer overflows, and other software vulnerabilities, are typically the result of poor software construction, but fortunately, they are not permanent. A company can apply a software "patch"[68] to fix whatever poor lines of code led to the vulnerability.

Vulnerabilities are found in nearly every substantial piece of software, including operating systems, which is why companies are constantly looking for vulnerabilities and releasing patches. For example, on the second Tuesday of every month, Microsoft releases patches for all newly identified vulnerabilities. This tradition has come to be known as "Patch Tuesday."[69] Once Microsoft releases its patch to the public, users are expected to update their systems with the new patches.[70] These patches remedy whatever vulnerability was detected in the software. However, they are effective only if they are installed, and unfortunately, many users do not actively update their software with the newest patches on a regular basis. This creates a far bigger threat than just the latent vulnerability itself. A patch, in the hands of a cybercriminal, is an easy-to-use instruction manual for how to exploit the software vulnerabilities found in unpatched systems.

3.4.8   Denial of Service Attacks

A *denial of service attack* (DoS) is defined as "the prevention of authorized access to a system resource or the delaying of system operations and functions."[71] DoS attacks attempt to overload a computer system by forcing the improper allocation of resources through bulk accessing of a network connection.[72] Imagine someone ringing your front door bell and then running away. While you are answering the door, you are unable to do anything else. This is the basis of a DOS attack. In the world of high-speed communications, a hacker can knock on your digital door millions of times a second, and force your computer system to do nothing but answer the door, leaving it no time to perform legitimate functions, such as email.[73]

---

67 Rouse, *supra* note 66. Although it may occur accidentally through programming error, buffer overflow is an increasingly common type of security attack on data integrity. In buffer overflow attacks, the extra data may contain codes designed to trigger specific actions, in effect sending new instructions to the attacked computer that could, for example, damage the user's files, change data, or disclose confidential information. Buffer overflow attacks are said to have arisen because the C programming language supplied the framework, and poor programming practices supplied the vulnerability.

68 Margaret Rouse, *Patch (fix)* [definition], TechTarget, http://searchenterprisedesktop.techtarget.com/definition/patch.

69 Margaret Rouse, *Patch Tuesday* [definition], TechTarget, http://searchsecurity.techtarget.com/definition/Patch-Tuesday.

70 *Id.*

71 *Glossary of Security Terms*, SANS, http://www.sans.org/security-resources/glossary-of-terms.

72 *See Understanding Denial-of-Service Attacks*, U.S. Comp. Emergency Readiness Team, https://www.us-cert.gov/ncas/tips/ST04-015. In a denial-of-service attack, an attacker attempts to prevent legitimate users from accessing information or services. By targeting your computer and its network connection, or the computers and network of the sites you are trying to use, an attacker may be able to prevent you from accessing email, websites, online accounts (banking, etc.), or other services that rely on the affected computer.

73 *Id.* ("By sending many, or large, email messages to the account, an attacker can consume your quota, preventing you from receiving legitimate messages.").

3.4.9   Group Phishing

Phishing is an attempt, usually made through email, to steal your personal information, perpetrated by masquerading as a legitimate entity.[74] Hackers often send these fake emails by the thousands, which is referred to as *group phishing*. A phishing email will generally claim that the sender is a well-known organization, which the target may or may not have a relationship with, that needs your personal information, such as credit card number, social security number, and/or usernames and passwords. This information is not generally collected in the email; rather, the message almost always contains a link asking the target to access a website in order to relay the information.[75] Importantly, because group phishing relies on numbers, time is of the essence to hackers, because the most recently stolen identities fetch the highest prices.[76]

3.4.10   Spear Phishing

Unlike group phishing, *spear phishing,* as its name suggests, is a targeted, individually designed, phishing attempt to gain access, or spread malware, to a specific system. The goal of a spear phishing attack is typically not to steal an identity, but rather to steal intellectual property, financial data, trade or military secrets, or other confidential data.[77] Hackers may use any kinds of means available to make their phishing attempt as effective as possible. For example, the FBI has warned of spear-phishing scams where the emails appeared to be from the National Center for Missing and Exploited Children.[78] These attacks require only a momentary lapse in judgment as a result of an emotionally charged email, which makes spear phishing incredibly dangerous and incredibly difficult to guard against.

3.4.11   Website Exploits/Browser Security

Web browsers, such as Internet Explorer, Mozilla Firefox, and Apple Safari (to name a few), are ubiquitous on all computers that an organization would use.[79] Hence, they have become an increasingly popular choice of attack routes for hackers,[80] as these browsers usually have not been properly configured to maximize

---

74 *What Is Phishing?*, PHISHTANK, https://www.phishtank.com/what_is_phishing.php; *see also* Margaret Rouse, *phishing* [definition], TECHTARGET, http://searchsecurity.techtarget.com/definition/phishing.

75 *Online Fraud: Phishing*, NORTON, http://us.norton.com/cybercrime-phishing.

76 *See Phishing: A Very Dangerous Cyber Threat*, INFOSEC INST. (Dec. 13, 2012), http://resources.infosecinstitute.com/phishing-dangerous-cyber-threat/ ("The total loss for various organizations comes to $2.1 billion over the last 12 months. RSA estimates that there have been nearly 33,000 phishing attacks each month worldwide this year; countries such as Canada have registered an increase of 400 percent in the number of attacks.").

77 *Id.* ("Spear phishing attempts are not typically initiated by 'random hackers' but are more likely to be conducted by perpetrators out for financial gain, trade secrets or military information.").

78 Darrell Foxworth, *FBI Warns of Spear-Phishing E-Mail with Missing Children Theme*, FED. BUREAU OF INVESTIGATION (Aug. 26, 2013), http://www.fbi.gov/sandiego/press-releases/2013/fbi-warns-of-spear-phishing-e-mail-with-missing-children-theme ("The subject of the e-mail is 'Search for Missing Children,' and a zip file containing three malicious files is attached. E-mail recipients should never open attachments or click links in suspicious e-mails.").

79 *Securing Your Web Browser*, U.S. COMP. EMERGENCY READINESS TEAM, https://www.us-cert.gov/publications/securing-your-web-browser.

80 *Id.*

security. "Often, the web browser that comes with an operating system is not set up in a secure default configuration. Not securing a web browser can lead quickly to a variety of computer problems ranging from spyware being installed to intruders taking control of the computer."[81]

3.4.12   Bots/Command & Control Centers

"A bot (short for "robot") is a program that operates as an agent for a user or another program or simulates a human activity."[82] Bots can be used to perform a wide range of functions that a human would otherwise perform, ranging from automated tasks to providing information.[83] The purpose of these functions is generally to collect information, as is the case with web crawlers, but bots can also be used to interact automatically with web interfaces such as Internet messaging.[84]

Bots can be used for either good or malicious purposes. An example of a good bot is Googlebot, a program created by Google in order to index all websites on the Internet.[85] Malicious bots attempt to access computer systems, and engage in self-propagation in order to infect many systems. These systems are then linked back to a command and control (C&C) center for the hacker to use them all as a network of compromised devices known as a "botnet."[86]

Using a botnet, hackers can use a multitude of bots to engage in flood-type attacks against their targets. A wide gamut of malware programs is included, making this type of cyberattack very flexible. This method enables bots to log keystrokes, collect passwords, capture and analyze packets, gather financial information, launch DOS attacks, relay spam, and open back doors on the infected host.[87] Because bots are so versatile, they can easily be modified within hours of

---

81 *Id.* ("Attackers focus on exploiting client-side systems (your computer) through various vulnerabilities. They use these vulnerabilities to take control of your computer, steal your information, destroy your files, and use your computer to attack other computers. A low-cost way attackers do this is by exploiting vulnerabilities in web browsers.").
This problem is made worse by a number of factors, including the following nine items:
    (1) Many users have a tendency to click on links without considering the risks of their actions.
    (2) Web page addresses can be disguised or take you to an unexpected site.
    (3) Many web browsers are configured to provide increased functionality at the cost of decreased security.
    (4) New security vulnerabilities are often discovered after the software is configured and packaged by the manufacturer.
    (5) Computer systems and software packages may be bundled with additional software, which increases the number of vulnerabilities that may be attacked.
    (6) Third-party software may not have a mechanism for receiving security updates.
    (7) Many websites require that users enable certain features or install more software, putting the computer at additional risk.
    (8) Many users do not know how to configure their web browsers securely.
    (9) Many users are unwilling to enable or disable functionality as required to secure their web browser.
82 Margaret Rouse, *Bot (robot)* [definition], TECHTARGET (May 26, 2015), http://searchsoa.techtarget.com/definition/bot.
83 *What Is the Difference: Viruses, Worms, Trojans, and Bots?*, CISCO, http://www.cisco.com/web/about/security/intelligence/virus-worm-diffs.html [hereinafter *What Is the Difference?*]; *see generally* Markus Jakobsson & Zulfikar Ramzan, CRIMEWARE: UNDERSTANDING NEW ATTACKS AND DEFENSES (2002).
84 *What Is the Difference*, *supra* note 83.
85 *Googlebot*, BOTOPEDIA, http://www.botopedia.org/user-agent-list/search-bots/googlebot.
86 Nyakundi Elijah, *Computer Viruses and Their Effects*, NYASOFT (Feb. 1, 2015), http://nyasoft.blogspot.com/2015/02/computer-viruses-and-their-effects.html; Chunyong Yin et al., *Botnet Detection Based on Correlation of Malicious Behaviors*, 6 INT'L J. HYBRID INFO. TECH. 291, 293 (2013), http://www.sersc.org/journals/IJHIT/vol6_no6_2013/26.pdf ("Bot infection usually occurs through trapped files, e-mail attachments or web pages. However, trend in bot technology includes a blending of Trojan-horse, virus, worm, and backdoor functionality.").
87 *What Is the Difference?*, *supra* note 83.

their identification by anti-malware companies.[88] Furthermore, bots can take advantage of back doors that have been created by worms and viruses, which gives them the potential to infect even the most secure computer systems.[89]

3.4.13   Viruses/Worms

A computer *virus* "is a program or programming code that replicates by being copied or initiating its copying to another program, computer boot sector or document."[90] Viruses have the capability to spread from computer to computer, and from network to network, leaving a trail of infected systems as they travel. Viruses can have a wide variety of effects, ranging in severity from causing annoying effects, to damaging data or software, to causing denial-of-service conditions.[91] Most viruses are code that is added onto an executable file, which means that a virus can lie dormant in a system, but not be active or able to spread until the host file is executed.[92] Once the host file is executed, the virus is activated.[93] Viruses often do not prevent the host file from running as usual,[94] but some viruses are coded in such a way as to delete a computer's files, including the host file, upon their execution.[95]

A computer *worm* "is a self-replicating virus that does not alter files but resides in active memory and duplicates itself."[96] Computer worms are similar to viruses in that they replicate functional copies of themselves and can cause the same type of damage.[97] Whereas viruses require the spreading of an infected host file, worms are stand-alone software and do not require a host program or human to help with their propagation.[98] In order to spread, worms must exploit vulnerability in a computer system or use social engineering to exploit the users of a target system.[99] Worms function by taking advantage of file or information transport features in a computer system, which allow the worm to travel unaided.[100]

3.4.14   Trojan Horses

A *Trojan horse* "is a program in which malicious or harmful code is contained inside apparently harmless programming or data in such a way that it can get control and

---

88 *See* Ken Dunham & Jim Melnick, Malicious Bots: An Inside Look into the Cyber-Criminal Underground of the Internet 2 (2002).
89 *Id.*
90 Margaret Rouse, *Virus* [definition], TechTarget, May 26, 2015, http://searchsecurity.techtarget.com/definition/virus.
91 *What Is a Computer Virus or a Computer Worm?*, Kaspersky, https://usa.kaspersky.com/internet-security-center/threats/computer-viruses-vs-worms#.WBe3StUrLIU ("Computer worms can exploit network configuration errors (for example, to copy themselves onto a fully accessible disk) or exploit loopholes in operating system and application security. Many worms will use more than one method in order to spread copies via networks.").
92 *What Is the Difference?, supra* note 83.
93 *Id.*
94 *See* Alan Solomon, *All About Viruses*, VX Heaven, http://vxheaven.org/lib/aas10.html.
95 *Id.*
96 Margaret Rouse, *Worm* [definition], TechTarget, May 26, 2015, http://searchsecurity.techtarget.com/definition/worm.
97 *Computer Worms*, Tech-FAQ, http://www.tech-faq.com/computer-worm.html (last updated Nov. 26, 2013).
98 *Id.*
99 *What Is the Difference?, supra* note 83.
100 *Id.*

do its chosen form of damage."[101] The danger of Trojan horses is that the software, to a user, will look legitimate, when the user has actually been tricked into loading and executing a malicious piece of code.[102] Trojan horses can have a wide variety of effects, including irritating users (e.g. pop-up windows), damaging the computer system (e.g. deleting files or spreading other malware), or developing a back door, which a hacker can later use to gain easy access to the computer system.[103]

3.4.15   Zero-Day Exploits

An *exploit* is when a hacker uses a piece of software, a command, or a methodology to take advantage of a particular security vulnerability.[104] An exploit only confirms whether a vulnerability exists, meaning it is not an inherently malicious endeavor, though in the hands of a bad actor it can be used to devastating effect.[105] Additionally, exploits are a common component found in malware.

To combat exploits, security vendors study known exploits and identify them based on their content and behavior while executing.[106] These vendors then categorize exploits based on identified indicators of compromise (IOCs),[107] which are included in "Known Signature" databases. These databases are continually updated with the newest identified exploits, but they are helpless against a *zero-day exploit*, which is an exploit "that takes advantage of a security vulnerability on the same day that the vulnerability becomes generally known."[108] These exploits are essentially impossible to detect until they have been caught, identified, analyzed for new IOCs, and added to known signature databases.[109]

3.4.16   Spyware

Spyware is "any technology that aids in gathering information about a person or organization without their knowledge."[110] Spyware can take many different forms.

---

101 Margaret Rouse, *Trojan horse* [definition], TechTarget, May 26, 2015, http://searchsecurity.techtarget.com/definition/Trojan-horse.

102 *Crimeware: Trojans and Spyware*, Norton, http://us.norton.com/cybercrime-trojansspyware. Increasingly, Trojans are the first stage of an attack and their primary purpose is to stay hidden while downloading and installing a stronger threat such as a bot. Unlike viruses and worms, Trojan horses cannot spread by themselves. They are often delivered to a victim through an email message where it masquerades as an image or joke, or by a malicious website, which installs the Trojan horse on a computer through vulnerabilities in web browser software such as Microsoft Internet Explorer. *Id.*

103 "Trojan horses are broken down in classification based on how they breach systems and the damage they cause." Vangie Beal, *Trojan Horse*, Webopedia, http://www.webopedia.com/TERM/T/Trojan_horse.html (providing an analysis of the various classifications of Trojan horse).

104 Margaret Rouse, *Exploit* [definition], TechTarget, May 26, 2015, http://searchsecurity.techtarget.com/definition/exploit.

105 *What Is the Difference?, supra* note 83.

106 *See generally* Leyla Bilge & Tudor Dumitras, *Before We Knew It: An Empirical Study of Zero-Day Attacks in the Real World*, in Proc. of the 2012 ACM Conference on Computer & Comm. Security 233–44 (2012).

107 An IOC is an artifact observed on a network or in an operating system that indicates a computer intrusion with high confidence. Typical IOCs are virus signatures and IP addresses, MD5 hashes of malware files or URLs, or domain names of botnet command and control servers.

108 Margaret Rouse, *Zero-Day Exploit* [definition], TechTarget, July 2010, http://searchsecurity.techtarget.com/definition/zero-day-exploit.

109 Elizabeth Palermo, *What Is a Zero-Day Exploit?*, Tom's Guide (Nov. 22, 2013, 4:56 PM), http://www.tomsguide.com/us/zero-day-exploit-definition,news-17903.html ("The most dangerous varieties of zero-day exploits facilitate drive-by downloads, in which simply browsing to an exploited Web page or clicking a poisoned Web link can result in a full-fledged malware attack on your system. Such attacks exploit vulnerabilities within a Web browser's software, or within third-party browser plug-ins.").

110 Margaret Rouse, *Spyware* [definition], TechTarget, http://searchsecurity.techtarget.com/definition/spyware.

For example, spyware can appear as programs that monitor what a user does online (sometimes referred to as a *spybot*), thereby gathering information without having to be installed on the computer system. Often, these types of spyware are not necessarily used for malicious purposes, but rather to gather information about users in order to sell the aggregated information to advertisers or other interested parties.[111] Spyware can also be placed locally onto a computer as a software virus or as the result of installing a new program.[112] Not all data-collecting programs are spyware, as users not infrequently agree to allow software that they are installing to monitor some of their data; however, to be proper, the user must know what data is being collected and with whom it is being shared.[113] Spyware, unlike the data-collection programs discussed earlier, is installed without the users' consent, and generally without the users being aware that they are downloading the software. Often, spyware can be unintentionally downloaded by as simple an action as clicking an option in a deceptive pop-up window.

3.5   Conclusion

Cyber threats are among our most significant and rapidly growing exposures to a rapidly expanding universe of incentivized actors and conspirators: organized criminals, state and state-sponsored actors, terrorists, and hackivists, to name a few. New forms of cyberhostilities arise daily, and new technologies for launching these attacks will continuously develop and evolve.

Unfortunately, until political and law enforcement solutions also evolve, law firms will remain primarily responsible for their own defense. As a result, it is now incumbent upon all law firms to understand why they represent a potentially attractive target, as well as the varied and multifarious nature of the threats. To this end, knowledge sharing and benchmarking will be essential components in the formulation of an effective, risk-based approach to protecting the security and confidentiality of client relationships.

Although the discussion in this chapter is not an exhaustive or comprehensive list or description of the threats that exist in the cyber realm and their intricacies, we hope it will serve as a useful introduction to the most common and prevalent threats that law firms are likely to face, and to the ways in which they act.

---

111 *Id.*

112 *Id.*; *see also* Beal, *Spyware, supra* note 103 ("Spyware is similar to a Trojan horse in that users unwittingly install the product when they install something else. A common way to become a victim of spyware is to download certain peer-to-peer file swapping products that are available today.").

113 Beal, *supra* note 103 ("Licensing agreements that accompany software downloads sometimes warn the user that a spyware program will be installed along with the requested software, but the licensing agreements may not always be read completely because the notice of a spyware installation is often couched in obtuse, hard-to-read legal disclaimers.").

CHAPTER

4

WHAT IT TAKES TO FRUSTRATE THE HACKER KNOCKING AT YOUR DOOR

Bill Spernow, Daniel Garrie, and Greg Kelley

It is often said that water takes the path of least resistance. This is equally true of hackers seeking to break into law firm computer systems. This chapter discusses methods and practices to frustrate these hackers.

 ## 4.1   Don't Be the Low-Hanging Fruit

What many businesses today do not realize is that everyone is a target.[1] You may be a target because of who you do business with, information you have, or the simple fact that you are on the Internet. So, how do you go about protecting yourself? One of the easiest ways is to prevent yourself from being one of the many low-hanging fruits. What does that mean? This chapter discusses ways to avoid being an easy target.

 ## 4.2   Proper Password Management Is Essential to Security

One of the first and best ways to avoid being low-hanging fruit is proper password management. To understand password management, let's understand how passwords are stored in a Windows environment. In Windows, the password is not stored in plain text; instead, the hash of a password is stored. Some of you reading this might have heard the word *hash* in the context of computer forensics; the term is used similarly here.[2] To create a hash, the password is put through a mathematical formula; the result is a series of letters and numbers that represent the password. The way the formula works means that you can't take a hash and turn it back into a password. So, when you enter your password into your Windows computer, that password is put through the same hash formula and the result is compared to the stored hash of your password. If the hashes match, then the password you entered is considered to match the stored password and you are allowed to log into or onto your computer.

Windows allows both uppercase and lowercase letters, numbers, and punctuation symbols to be included in a password. With that set of characters, there

---

1 Kim Zetter, *Everyone Has Been Hacked. Now What?*, WIRED (May 4, 2012), http://www.wired.com/2012/05/everyone-hacked/.
2 Alan G. Konheim, *Hashing for Storage: Data Management*, in HASHING IN COMPUTER SCIENCE: FIFTY YEARS OF SLICING AND DICING (2010).

are 6,634,204,312,890,625 possible different passwords if one restricts the length of the password to eight characters. Hackers are often left to "brute-force" crack a password, which means that they have to try all of those combinations until they are successful. If hackers could enter a password every second, it would still take them 210 million years to guess. So you think you are safe? Not really. In 2012, Jeremi Gosney of Stricture Consulting Group created a computer that was able to guess 350 billion passwords per second.[3] As a result, he could crack any eight-character Windows password in less than six hours. Not so safe now, are we? Well, consider this: If you used 10 characters for our passwords—a mere 2 more characters—Gosney's machine would take five and a half years to crack them.

Of course, Mr. Gosney's research was done in 2012. Machines and password-cracking methods have evolved since then. Still, realize that to be successful, password-cracking routines need to try different passwords over and over. Windows has a built-in prevention mechanism to prevent anyone from repeatedly trying passwords. You can set Windows to lock an account after any number of consecutively entered bad passwords.[4] A good rule of thumb is five bad passwords in a row. That means after five guesses, the account is locked. When the account is locked, it no longer allows someone to log into the account. That action has two results. First, the hacker cannot make any more password guesses until the account is unlocked. Second, the person who (legitimately) uses the account immediately finds out that they cannot use it anymore. This person reports the lock to the IT department, which then is alerted to the possibility that someone is trying to hack the account.

Another great weapon against brute-force attacks is to change your password frequently.[5] If a hacker is trying to brute-force attack your password and you change the password, in essence that causes the hacker to have to start all over again from the beginning in guessing passwords. Changing passwords monthly is a good idea, but can sometimes be a bit much for most users. A change every 90 days should strike a good balance between being a nuisance and practicing good password management.

Proper password management also means training your users to use good passwords. So far we have been talking about brute-force attack: guessing all combinations of letters and numbers. Another, sometimes easier method, is what is called a *dictionary attack*.[6] Hackers are known to start guessing passwords by trying words in the dictionary. Sometimes that will include foreign-language dictionaries as well. Think you are smart by changing the letter "I" to a "1" or an "S" to a "$" in your password? That is called password "munging." Hackers compensate for munging nowadays as well. Best advice here? Forget words in the dictionary.

3 Dan Goodin, *25-GPU cluster cracks every standard Windows password in <6 hours*, Ars Technica (Dec. 9, 2012), http://arstechnica.com/security/2012/12/25-gpu-cluster-cracks-every-standard-windows-password-in-6-hours/.

4 *Account lockout threshold*, Microsoft: TechNet, July 17, 2014, https://technet.microsoft.com/en-us/library/hh994574.aspx.

5 Melissa Cocks, *The Importance of Changing Passwords*, NSK, Oct. 2, 2009, http://blog.nskinc.com/topic/data-security/IT-Services-Boston/The-Importance-of-Changing-Passwords.

6 Dan Goodin, *Why Passwords Have Never Been Weaker—and Crackers Have Never Been Stronger*, Ars Technica, Aug. 20, 2012, http://arstechnica.com/security/2012/08/passwords-under-assault/.

Unfortunately, with complex passwords, users often find themselves at a loss to remember the passwords. As a result, many resort to writing down passwords on a sticky note and putting that note on their monitors. If an organization allows that activity to occur, it might as well return to the use of "1234" as a password. The solution for remembering passwords is a password management application.[7] Many password management applications are available, and many of them are free. Some are web based so that users can access their passwords from multiple locations. The use of a password-protected Word document or Excel spreadsheet is also acceptable.

Some organizations still tolerate the most egregious violation of sound security hygiene: password sharing.[8] The biggest problem with this practice is that it removes all accountability for actions in an environment. If multiple people know passwords to one's account, it is exceedingly difficult to properly ascribe blame if that account is then used in an unauthorized fashion. All too often, computer forensic investigations grind to a screeching halt because it is determined that multiple people had access to the account in question and therefore it was impossible to determine who was responsible for the offending action. Some organizations feel the need to share passwords with their IT department. That practice too is unnecessary. Proper planning would allow IT to get into any device through the ability to reset a password.

Proper password management extends to mobile devices. While "bring your own device" (BYOD) is prevalent today, that doesn't stop a company from extending its password policies to those mobile devices.[9] In fact, since version 2003 Microsoft Exchange has had a feature built in that allows a company to force mobile devices to be encrypted, require a password, require a password of a certain length, and change that password.[10] So, needless to say, password management can and should be implemented on all mobile devices.

One other thing to keep in mind is that brute-force password cracking works best when the database containing the hashes is stolen. Once stolen, the hashes can be brute-force cracked offline without any detection. Therefore, proper protection of your computers to prevent the stealing of hashes is important (this is discussed later).

To summarize, implement and practice the following password policies:

1. Ignore words from the dictionary
2. Use passwords at least 10 characters in length; the bigger the better.
3. Implement a lockout policy in your environment to catch brute-force attempts.

---

7 April Glaser, *You Need a Password Manager. Here Are Some Good Free Ones*, WIRED, Jan. 24, 2016, http://www.wired.com/2016/01/you-need-a-password-manager/; David Silver et al., *Password Managers: Attacks and Defenses*, USENIX, Aug. 2014, https://www.usenix.org/system/files/conference/usenixsecurity14/sec14-paper-silver.pdf.

8 Monica Whitty et al., *Individual Differences in Cyber Security Behaviors: An Examination of Who Is Sharing Passwords*, 18 CYBERPSYCHOL. BEHAV. SOC. NETWORKS 3 (Jan. 2015), http://www.ncbi.nlm.nih.gov/pmc/articles/PMC4291202/.

9 Nate Lord, *BYOD Security: Expert Tips on Policy, Mitigating Risks, & Preventing a Breach*, DIGITAL GUARDIAN, Jan. 12, 2016, https://digitalguardian.com/blog/byod-security-expert-tips-policy-mitigating-risks-preventing-breach.

10 *Id.*

4. Change your passwords every 90 days.
5. Do not ignore or exclude mobile devices.
6. Do not ignore or exclude administrative accounts running on servers.

4.3 Firewalls: Regulating Who and What Can Access Your System

Now that we have talked about passwords, let's discuss another area where you can keep from being the low-hanging fruit. Organizations large and small should implement a firewall and put some very simple, basic, effective controls in place.

What is a firewall? Basically, a *firewall* is a device that sits between your network and the Internet. A firewall acts as a gateway or a traffic cop, monitoring communication going between your environment and the rest of the world.[11] A firewall can deny traffic, allow traffic, or just monitor and log traffic. Some are simple: plug them in, make some configuration changes, and let them go. Others are more complex, requiring hours to properly configure.

One common misstep that many people make is neglecting to implement the same password controls on the firewall. The most egregious of violations is when people do not change the out-of-the-box password for the administrative account. In November of 2014, an article in *Network World* discussed a website that broadcasted more than 73,000 Internet-accessible cameras.[12] How were the hackers able to do that? They just used the default passwords for each camera, connected, and started broadcasting. A properly functioning firewall would block the hacker from broadcasting anything. However, if the default password on a firewall is not changed, the hackers will instead use that account to give themselves an open door to come into your network and steal whatever they want.

After changing your default password, the next step to consider with firewalls is stopping traffic coming into your environment. The stopping or allowing of traffic is usually done by disabling or enabling different ports. Everyone is familiar with an Internet Protocol (IP) address.[13] IP addresses are used by any device (such as your computer) that is connected to the Internet (or any network) to communicate with other devices. Think of an IP address as a phone number or house address. However, each device also listens on specific ports for communication.[14]

---

11 Kenneth Ingham & Stephanie Forrest, *A History and Survey of Network Firewalls* (Technical Report TR- CS-2002-37), University of New Mexico (2002), http://www.cs.unm.edu/~treport/tr/02-12/firewall.pdf.

12 Ms. Smith, *Peeping into 73,000 Unsecured Security Cameras Thanks to Default Passwords*, NETWORK WORLD, Nov. 6, 2014, http://www.networkworld.com/article/2844283/microsoft-subnet/peeping-into-73-000-unsecured-security-cameras-thanks-to-default-passwords.html.

13 *Understanding IP Addressing: Everything You Ever Wanted to Know*, 3COM (2001), http://pages.di.unipi.it/ricci/501302.pdf.

14 *Network Port*, TECHOPEDIA, https://www.techopedia.com/definition/24717/network-port.

Web servers listen on port 80 for regular traffic and port 443 for encrypted (https://) traffic.[15] What does that mean? When a computer browses a website, it not only is communicating with the IP address of that website, but is also communicating on port 80 and port 443, depending on whether the communication is unencrypted or encrypted. If your email server is sending email to another server, it contacts that other server on port 25.

Back to the firewall. For small offices with no email servers, web servers, or other servers that need to communicate with the outside world, the setup is quite easy: Block all incoming traffic. For other environments that do have external-facing servers, such as an email server, a common practice is to start with enabling only what you need. You can stop and allow traffic not only to certain IP addresses but also to certain ports.[16] That means if you have an email server in your network, best practice is to not allow all port traffic to that server, but to allow only traffic to port 25, the port used for email traffic. A best practice in firewall setup is to open up only those IP addresses and those ports that are needed for communication and to disable everything else. Over time, a company may have to open up more ports as it increases its services, but do not neglect the concept of closing ports as time goes on and services are discontinued. If you make a switch and start using email in the cloud, turn off the traffic to your email server.

One common mistake seen in many environments is to allow traffic through the firewall directly to a server for the purpose of using Remote Desktop.[17] That policy does nothing other than open up a vulnerability that doesn't need to be there. A more appropriate method for connecting to an internal server via Remote Desktop would be to establish a virtual private network (VPN) connection instead.[18] A VPN will allow remote users to communicate on your network as if they were sitting in your office. The network traffic over a VPN is encrypted and secure. Once on a VPN, users can then connect to whatever server or computer they desire through Remote Desktop.

Firewall selection is also important. A practice seen, but not recommended, is using an email server or web server for a dual purpose as a firewall. Understand that your firewall is going to receive the brunt of network traffic and attacks.[19] If you are using your firewall as an email server as well, that extra service burden on the firewall compromises its effectiveness and can weaken your firewall and jeopardize the security of your systems. The best practice is to use a dedicated device that serves only one purpose: acting as a firewall. Preferably, the device should

---

15 *Service Name and Transport Protocol Port Number Registry*, IANA (last updated Apr. 7, 2016), https://www.iana.org/assignments/service-names-port-numbers/service-names-port-numbers.txt.

16 Ed Bott, *Lock IT Down: Block TCP/IP Ports to Increase Security*, TECHREPUBLIC, May 4, 2000, http://www.techrepublic.com/article/lock-it-down-block-tcp-ip-ports-to-increase-security/.

17 *Remote Desktop Connection*, PCWORLD, Aug. 17, 2011, http://www.pcworld.com/article/234326/remote_desktop_connection.html.

18 *Remote-Access VPNs Provide Secure Access*, CISCO, http://www.cisco.com/c/en/us/solutions/enterprise-networks/security/networking_solutions_products_genericcontent0900aecd8051f37b.html; *Virtual Private Networking: An Overview*, MICROSOFT: TECHNET, Sept. 4, 2001, https://technet.microsoft.com/en-us/library/bb742566.aspx.

19 Karen Scarfone & Paul Hoffman, *Guidelines on Firewalls and Firewall Policy*, NAT'L INST. STANDARDS AND TECH. Special Publication 800-41, Rev. 1 (Sept. 2009), http://csrc.nist.gov/publications/nistpubs/800-41-Rev1/sp800-41-rev1.pdf, at § 5.1.

have originally been designed as a firewall; this is better than taking a server and making it into a firewall.

4.4 Applying Patches: Keeping Your Software as Secure and Up-to-Date as Possible

We've discussed password policies and firewalls as some basic steps to ensure that your system will not be low-hanging fruit that is particularly appealing to hackers. Another important and easy step a company can take to help shore up its defenses is to apply updates and patches in a timely fashion. While it would be unreasonable to insist that a company apply patches as soon as they are released, especially to production servers, statistics on exploited companies show that administrators generally take way too long to apply patches. The 2015 Verizon data breach investigations report showed that 99.9% of companies that were compromised through the exploitation of a known vulnerability were actually compromised more than a year after the vulnerability was published and publicized.[20] That statistic means that administrators were waiting for more than a year to patch known vulnerabilities. That delay is clearly not best practice. The actual best practice depends on the precise nature and risk profile of the business, but a regular and timely application of patches is essential to maintaining good security hygiene.[21]

The following areas should be considered, first and foremost, when applying patches:

1. Patches to operating systems (Windows, Linux, Mac)
2. Patches to firewalls, wireless routers, and other network devices
3. Patches to user applications such as Microsoft Office, Adobe Acrobat, Adobe Flash
4. Recommended configuration changes

Item number 4 is as important as the first three, but is often overlooked. It does not require installing updated files; rather, it is usually centered on changes to a configuration. Those changes may be to the Windows Registry or an option in an application. An example is the disabling of older versions of Secure Sockets Layer, or SSL, on a web server.[22] SSL deals with encrypted communication between a client and a server. Older versions are vulnerable to some attacks.

---

20 *2015 Data Breach Investigations Report*, Verizon Enterprise Solutions, https://msisac.cisecurity.org/whitepaper/documents/1.pdf.

21 For more information, *see A Practical Methodology for Implementing a Patch Management Process*, SANS (2003), https://www.sans.org/reading-room/whitepapers/bestprac/practical-methodology-implementing-patch-management-process-1206; Rick Rosato, *Best Practices for Applying Service Packs, Hotfixes and Security Patches*, Microsoft: Developer Network, https://msdn.microsoft.com/en-us/library/cc750077.aspx.

22 *What Is SSL (Secure Sockets Layer) and What Are SSL Certificates?*, Digicert, https://www.digicert.com/ssl.html.

4.5   Perimeter Security Controls: What It Takes to Keep the Bad Guys Out

Owners of homes and businesses protect those facilities with locks, guards, alarm systems, and other forms of security. The type of protection may be as simple as a lock on a door, but quite often it involves multiple layers of security with notifications for various events. Access to gain entry into a facility is controlled by keys, codes, and identification. The more guarded the facility, the more layers in place. Your network can and should also be controlled in the same way.[23] Protecting your perimeter is an important deterrent to those who wish to gain access to your environment.

One of the most basic protections for your perimeter, as discussed previously, is a firewall, a device that usually sits between your network and the outside world. See Figure 4-1 for a rendition of a typical network with a firewall.[24]

The diagram in the figure illustrates the placement of a firewall within a network. The diagram also shows two purposes of a firewall. The first is connectivity between laptops and desktops in your environment and the Internet.[25] The second is connectivity for servers that communicate with the outside world.[26] Those types of servers may be email servers, web servers, or FTP servers, but are collectively known as *forward-facing servers*, in that they are directly accessible by others using the Internet.[27] Note that the email and FTP servers are in a separate area from the rest of the network. This placement is commonly known as a demilitarized zone (DMZ).[28] The reason for placing forward-facing servers in the DMZ is because those servers need more open communication to the outside world and are more likely to be compromised due to their accessibility from the outside world.[29] Should those servers become compromised, the rest of your network can be protected by limiting the type of network traffic that occurs between the servers in the DMZ and the rest of the computers in your environment.[30]

With its placement in your environment, the firewall is perfectly set up to be a traffic cop for communications between your network and the Internet.[31] What can that traffic cop do? First, it can limit the communications.[32] For example, your

23 John Edwards, *Security At the Edge: Locking Down the Network Perimeter*, IT SECURITY, Feb. 4, 2008, http://www.itsecurity.com/features/security-edge-020408/.

24 Margaret Rouse, *Firewall* [definition], TECHTARGET, http://searchsecurity.techtarget.com/definition/firewall.

25 *Id.*

26 *Id.*

27 *See generally Security Best Practices to Protect Internet Facing Web Servers*, MICROSOFT, http://social.technet.microsoft.com/wiki/contents/articles/13974.security-best-practices-to-protect-internet-facing-web-servers.aspx.

28 Margaret Rouse, *DMZ (demilitarized zone)* [definition], TECHTARGET, http://searchsecurity.techtarget.com/definition/DMZ.

29 *Id.*

30 *Id.*

31 Lewis & Knopf, CPAs, PC, *Computer Protection: Call a Traffic Cop*, 3 FINANCIAL RX3 (Mar. 2010), http://www.lewis-knopf.com/newsletters/financial-rx-article/computer-protection-call-a-traffic-cop/.

32 *Id.*

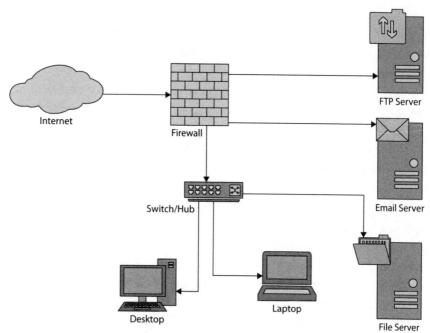

Figure 4-1 Typical network with firewall.

email server may also have a built-in web server so that employees can retrieve email via a web browser. A proper way to implement that feature is not to allow traffic over unencrypted HTTP (e.g., http://myemail.com) but only over encrypted HTTPS (e.g., https://myemail.com). The firewall can limit that traffic by allowing only HTTPS traffic to get to the web server. A properly configured firewall should be set up to enable only that traffic which is necessary and deny all other traffic. The other thing that a traffic cop can do is look for traffic that should not occur. What if your email server all of a sudden started accepting FTP requests or starting sending traffic to another FTP server? Your firewall can be configured to look for that traffic and block it. Another example would be finding unencrypted, readable data being sent over HTTPS, which is an avenue for encrypted communications. Your firewall can also act as a traffic cop by looking for traffic going to certain IP addresses or coming from certain IP addresses.[33]

Another device that can help with protecting a firm's perimeter is an intrusion detection system (IDS).[34] An IDS sits inside your network and monitors traffic for suspicious activity.[35] Think of an IDS as an antivirus (AV) application, but for network traffic. Your AV is programmed to look for applications with specific signatures or behaviors indicating that they are viruses.[36] An IDS looks for patterns or

---

33 For an example of creating these types of rules, *see Add or Edit Firewall Rule*, MICROSOFT: TECHNET, https://technet.microsoft.com/en-us/library/cc753558.aspx.

34 Matthew Berge, *What Is Intrusion Detection?*, SANS, https://www.sans.org/security-resources/idfaq/what-is-intrusion-detection/1/1; Margaret Rouse, *Intrusion Detection (ID)* [definition], TECHTARGET, http://searchmidmarketsecurity.techtarget.com/definition/intrusion-detection.

35 Berge, *supra* note 34.

36 Margaret Rouse, *Antivirus Software* [definition], TECHTARGET, http://searchsecurity.techtarget.com/definition/antivirus-software.

behaviors that would indicate someone may have hacked into your computer net-work and is stealing data.[37] An IDS system is not a replacement for a firewall, nor is a firewall a replacement for an IDS. The two devices work in tandem to block traffic and identify malicious traffic.[38]

However, just like your alarm system needs someone to respond to it, or your guards need someone to whom they would report an incident, your firewall needs somewhere to report. Better yet, your company needs to have someone monitor the firewall and potential security incidents. Monitoring of firewall and other sim-ilar logs is one of the most neglected security activities. What some organizations with all the protection in the world fail to realize is that if someone is not watching what is going on, you cannot properly respond when an incident occurs. Take the example mentioned previously regarding the blocking of certain IP addresses. How does a firm know what IP addresses to block? Monitoring of firewall or IDS systems could indicate consistent, malicious activity coming from a specific IP address. With that information, the firewall could be configured to block all traffic to and from that address.

Monitoring helps with setting a baseline of expected network traffic.[39] Cre-ation of a baseline is paramount to finding malicious activity.[40] The reason that organizations will forgo monitoring, or not monitor correctly, is that the amount of data generated by a firewall or IDS system can be daunting. For large organiza-tions, it can be downright impossible.[41] The solution is to generate a baseline of what is expected traffic.[42] A baseline will show what types of traffic one can expect in one's environment. A baseline will also provide information as to how much data will typically traverse the firewall to the outside Internet. With that informa-tion, rules can be created to identify unusual types of network traffic or large increases in traffic.[43] To illustrate this concept, let's review an organization with which we previously worked. The organization contacted us regarding a breach of data that had occurred. The investigation revealed that the stolen information was compressed into ZIP files, but then the ZIP files were renamed as JPG files. The fake JPG files were then put on the company's website and downloaded through that public-facing website. No alarms were triggered because JPG files being down-loaded from a website is quite normal. However, if the client had had a trigger for very large JPG files, such as these were, then it is possible the activity could have been detected and stopped.

---

37 Berge, *supra* note 34.

38 Joel Snyder, *Do You Need an IDS or IPS, or Both?*, TECHTARGET, http://searchsecurity.techtarget.com/Do-you-need-an-IDS-or-IPS-or-both.

39 *Baseline Process Best Practices* (White Paper), CISCO, Oct. 3, 2005, http://www.cisco.com/c/en/us/support/docs/availability/high-availability/15112-HAS-baseline.html.

40 Vangie Beal, *Intrusion Detection (IDS) and Prevention (IPS) Systems*, WEBOPEDIA, July 15, 2005, http://www.webopedia.com/DidYouKnow/Computer_Science/intrusion_detection_prevention.asp.

41 Richard Bejtlich, *Top Seven Network Traffic Monitoring Challenges*, TECHTARGET, http://searchnetworking.techtarget.com/tip/Top-seven-network-traffic-monitoring-challenges.

42 *See, e.g.*, Michael Brandenburg, *How to Set a Network Performance Baseline for Network Monitoring*, TECHTARGET, http://searchnetworking.techtarget.com/How-to-set-a-network-performance-baseline-for-network-monitoring.

43 *Avoiding Network Traffic Confusion with Consistent Firewall Rules*, TECHTARGET, http://searchsecurity.techtarget.com/magazineContent/Avoiding-Network-Traffic-Confusion-with-Consistent-Firewall-Rules.

One trap that organizations commonly fall into is the "set it and forget it" mindset.[44] Security is an ever-evolving discipline. What was once considered good doctrine can become a bad practice. For example, years ago it was considered a secure practice to dispose of hard drives by using a magnet to wipe them clean.[45] With today's new hard drives, not only is that practice not considered a best practice, but magnets, except for extremely powerful ones, are ineffective in wiping hard drives.[46] The other issue with "set it and forget it" is that hackers are constantly evolving their methods and attacks.[47] With each new vulnerability that is published by Microsoft, Apple, US-CERT (through the CVE list), or others, hackers take aim at the company networks to exploit those vulnerabilities. Especially in the case of a vulnerability that doesn't have a fix, or has an automated fix, the only way for a company to protect itself is to adjust its protections.

Perimeter controls should not stop at just a firewall or IDS system. The firewall is going to protect one entry point into your network. What other entry points might an organization have that need to be protected? Consider the following list[48]:

1. Mobile devices. Cell phones and tablets are quite often used outside of your network. Therefore, these devices constitute another entry point into your perimeter. Any plan dealing with perimeter protections should include defenses for these devices. Encryption (discussed later) and proper password management (previously discussed) should be considered. However, one also needs to consider limiting the type of data accessible by mobile devices, as well as mobile device management (MDM) tools that allow remote deactivation or wiping of stolen devices.

2. Wireless networks. Whether used for internal staff or guests, wireless networks are another entry point into your environment. Some companies do away with wireless networks altogether. Best practices will segment or separate guest networks from the rest of a firm's network environment, often with physically separate network cables, switches, and routers to prevent any access to the firm's environment by a wireless network. Finally, routine scanning is important to identify new wireless networks that may pop up in your environment. A cell phone or tablet acting as a wireless hot spot, when not monitored, can be a recipe for disaster.

3. Portable storage devices. Tapes, CD/DVD, and USB drives must all be considered perimeter devices, as they can contain client data and be accessed outside of your environment. Encryption of these devices is discussed later, but some firms choose to restrict their use altogether by employing technological restrictions on their use.

---

44 Fred Donovan, *The Days of a "Set It and Forget It" Approach to Endpoint Security Are Over, Says ESG*, Fierce IT Security, Jan. 13, 2015, http://www.fierceitsecurity.com/story/days-set-it-and-forget-it-approach-endpoint-security-are-over-says-esg/2015-01-13.
45 Craig Wright, *Overwriting Hard Drive Data*, SANS, Jan. 15, 2009, https://digital-forensics.sans.org/blog/2009/01/15/overwriting-hard-drive-data/.
46 *Id.*
47 *Hackers Are Evolving*, Comms Bus., Dec. 14, 2015, http://commsbusiness.co.uk/features/hackers-are-evolving/.
48 For a deeper analysis of new points of entry that affect perimeter security, *see* Axel Buecker et al., *Understanding IT Perimeter Security*, IBM, 2008, http://www.redbooks.ibm.com/redpapers/pdfs/redp4397.pdf.

4.6   Encryption

Encryption is a technology that has gotten more use recently but is still underutilized. In encryption, data is put through a formula that codes (encrypts) the data with a key.[49] The key is usually password protected. The larger the key, the more difficult it becomes to brute-force decrypt the data.[50] The key is usually pseudo-random generated through an algorithm built into the encrypting application.[51] There are multiple applications that perform encryption and various uses of encryption. However, there are two basic types of encryption: symmetric key encryption and public key encryption.

Symmetric key encryption is what is used in applications such as True Crypt, VeraCrypt, and Microsoft's BitLocker. In symmetric key encryption, the data is encrypted and decrypted with the same key.[52] Therefore, parties that communicate using symmetric key encryption must both have the same key.

Public key encryption has its biggest implementation with the program Pretty Good Privacy (PGP). In public key encryption, the data is encrypted with a key that is shared publicly,[53] but the data cannot be decrypted with that key. Instead, the data has to be decrypted with a private key which is held by the recipient of the data. Let's explain this process a little further. Say Company A and Company B want to use public key encryption to exchange data. Each company would provide the other company with its public key. That would allow each company to encrypt data being sent to the other company. However, if the public key was stolen, the encrypted data would still be safe, because it takes the private key (which ideally neither company would share, as neither needs to share it) to decrypt the data.

With that definition out of the way, let's discuss the various uses for encryption.

The most common use of encryption (but one that many do not realize) occurs when you are browsing a secure website, denoted by "https" at the beginning of the URL, or a secure FTP site, denoted by "ftps" at the beginning of the URL. The "s" at the end of "http" or "ftp" signals that the browser and website will use the Secure

---

49 Margaret Rouse, *Encryption* [definition], TechTarget, http://searchsecurity.techtarget.com/definition/encryption.
50 Margaret Rouse, *Brute-Force Cracking* [definition], TechTarget, http://searchsecurity.techtarget.com/definition/brute-force-cracking.
51 Rouse, *supra* note 49.
52 Margaret Rouse, *Secret Key Algorithm (Symmetric Algorithm)* [definition], TechTarget, http://searchsecurity.techtarget.com/definition/secret-key-algorithm.
53 Margaret Rouse, *Asymmetric Cryptography (Public-Key Cryptography)* [definition], TechTarget, http://searchsecurity.techtarget.com/definition/asymmetric-cryptography.

Sockets Layer (SSL) protocol.[54] SSL uses the public key encryption method just described.[55] It is important, however, when browsing secure websites, that your browser reports that the certificate is valid. Websites create or purchase certificates from a small group of certificate authority (CA) organizations.[56] Organizations should make sure to use SSL when possible to prevent various attacks. SSL is commonly used for email access over a website or on FTP sites for downloading of encrypted data. If your FTP server does not support "ftps," then you should consider encrypting the contents of the files being transferred (as is discussed later in this chapter).

For secure email communications, encryption is vitally important. Secure email communication can be done in one of two ways. The first method is the use of a provider.[57] The recipient of a secure email communication will get an email that provides a link to log into a website. Of course, the website communicates via SSL as described earlier. Once logged in, the recipient can read the secure message and then reply to the sender, securely. The second method for secure email communications is the implementation of PGP.[58] PGP works by the two parties exchanging their public keys. Each party encrypts its messages using the recipient's public key. The recipient then decrypts the message using its own private key.

Years ago, full disk encryption was not popular, as the process was very resource intensive and thus encrypted hard drives would run slower. With today's faster processors, increased memory, and more streamlined encryption processes, omitting encryption of your devices is not recommended.[59] Multiple versions of Microsoft Windows come with BitLocker already built in.[60] BitLocker is a full disk encryption scheme that makes use of the Trusted Platform Module (TPM) chip. The TPM chip helps with encryption by, among other things, storing the encryption keys.

Disk encryption should not be restricted to just your computers. USB devices used for transferring data to others should also be encrypted.[61] Consider that the majority of the documents an attorney will exchange with others are likely to be confidential, contain personally identifiable information (PII), or contain other sensitive data.[62] You can label documents "confidential" or "attorney's eyes only" all you want, but if the drive on which the data is stored gets lost or stolen, it really isn't confidential anymore. Encrypting the data is rather easy. VeraCrypt is the successor to TrueCrypt, a popular free encryption application that no longer has a support structure and for

---

54 Margaret Rouse, *Secure Sockets Layer (SSL)* [definition], TECHTARGET, http://searchsecurity.techtarget.com/definition/ Secure-Sockets-Layer-SSL.

55 *Behind the Scenes of SSL Cryptography*, DIGICERT, https://www.digicert.com/ssl-cryptography.htm.

56 Margaret Rouse, *Certificate Authority (CA)* [definition], TECHTARGET, http://searchsecurity.techtarget.com/definition/ certificate-authority.

57 Eric Geier, *How to Encrypt Your Email*, PCWORLD, Apr. 25, 2012, http://www.pcworld.com/article/254338/how_to_ encrypt_your_email.html.

58 Margaret Rouse, *Pretty Good Privacy (PGP)* [definition], TECHTARGET, http://searchsecurity.techtarget.com/definition/ Pretty-Good-Privacy.

59 *Full-Disk Encryption (FDE)*, WHATIS, http://whatis.techtarget.com/definition/full-disk-encryption-FDE.

60 *See BitLocker Drive Encryption Overview*, MICROSOFT, https://technet.microsoft.com/en-us/itpro/windows/keep-secure/ bitlocker-overview.

61 *Encrypt Your Thumb Drive*, WIRED, https://technet.microsoft.com/en-us/library/ff404223.aspx.

62 David G. Ries, *Safeguarding Confidential Data: Your Ethical and Legal Obligations*, 36 LAWPRACTICE 4 (July/Aug. 2010), http:// www.americanbar.org/publications/law_practice_home/law_practice_archive/lpm_magazine_articles_v36_is4_pg49.html.

which updates are therefore no longer available.[63] VeraCrypt is free and rather easy to use. Best practices for using VeraCrypt start by creating an encrypted container on a drive. You can put the VeraCrypt application on the unencrypted part of the drive. Your sensitive documents are then put in the encrypted part. Sending data in this fashion allows one to rest easy, knowing that if the drive is lost or stolen in transit, the encrypted documents on the drive are safe. The encrypted data is protected by a password, which is usually transmitted via email after the drive reaches its destination. Do not put the password on the drive or include a memo with the drive that contains a password. Doing so defeats the purpose of encrypting the data.

Mobile devices such as cell phones and tablets often have encryption built in.[64] In fact, for the past few years, all new iPhones released had their data automatically encrypted.[65] All a user needed to do was implement a PIN for access to the phone and the encryption protection would be complete. With Android phones, encryption is a simple task that usually takes less than an hour to implement. Due to the fact that millions of cell phones are stolen yearly, and those cell phones likely contain your sensitive data in the form of messages and documents, cell phone encryption is a no-brainer.

One may want to consider encrypting sensitive data on servers in your environment. Depending on the type of data and the requirements for holding that data, encryption may be an option. The protection chosen depends on one's requirements and goals for encryption. If the goal of encryption is to prevent stolen devices from being accessible, full disk encryption will provide that protection.[66] Content on devices that are locked, logged out, or turned off will be inaccessible to anyone who does not have the proper credentials to decrypt the data. But consider a server containing data with various levels of confidentiality: That server is constantly on and accessible by those with the proper credentials. Therefore, full disk encryption would not be helpful in protecting the data. However, sensitive data such as personnel records or confidential client information could be stored in encrypted databases. Encrypting a database applies an additional level of security. Separation of accounts used to access the server from accounts used to access the database completes this layer of protection. Should a server account become compromised, the hacker will then need to compromise an additional account to access the encrypted database.

Most forms of encryption are protected through the use of a password. As discussed previously in this chapter, proper password management is key to maintaining the effectiveness of passwords, and the same holds true here. Your encrypted data is only as safe as the password chosen to protect that encryption. Using a password of "password" or "1111" can render the encryption moot. Furthermore, with mobile devices, encryption can be made stronger by setting the mobile device

---

63 *Veracrypt*, https://veracrypt.codeplex.com/.

64 Robert Sheldon, *Mobile Data Encryption Techniques: On-Device and On-the-Go*, TechTarget, http://searchmobilecomputing. techtarget.com/tip/Mobile-data-encryption-techniques-On-device-and-on-the-go.

65 Robert Sheldon, *How Apple iOS Encryption and Data Protection Work*, TechTarget, http://searchmobilecomputing.techtarget. com/tip/How-iOS-encryption-and-data-protection-work.

66 *Full-Disk Encryption (FDE)* [definition], WhatIs, http://whatis.techtarget.com/definition/full-disk-encryption-FDE.

to wipe or reset itself after a certain number of invalid attempts (usually 10), rendering any data on the device unrecoverable.

Other types of encryption are managed with keys or certificates.[67] In larger environments, certificates are generated and used to encrypt network traffic and documents. When certificates or keys are not being used, they should be stored in a secure location. Some types of certificates, called *trusted root certificates,* are used to generate other certificates that are used for encryption. The trusted root certificates are also used to authenticate certificates.[68] Those trusted root certificates are only periodically used and are therefore often stored on encrypted drives that are then unplugged from the computer and locked in a cabinet. The reason for this added protection is that if the trusted root certificate fell into the wrong person's hands, certificates could be generated to thwart encrypted communications or perform other malicious activities.

The largest benefit of encryption is that many privacy acts consider encrypted data as data that is inaccessible. If such data is lost or stolen, when a company can prove that it was properly encrypted, usually that company does not have to report the records as being stolen.[69] The Health Insurance Portability and Accountability Act (HIPAA) considers properly encrypted data as data that has been rendered unusable, unreadable, or indecipherable to unauthorized individuals.[70]

4.7 Summary

Many organizations today are hacked, not because they were targeted by hackers, but rather because it was easy for hackers to compromise their systems. The first step to keep your firm from being hacked is to avoid being an easy target: the low-hanging fruit. Timely updating of computers, having a proper password policy, and implementing even a basic firewall all go a long way toward making sure your organization is not hacked just because it was the easiest target. The next step is creating perimeter controls to protect your firm's environment. These controls will not only make it difficult for a hacker to enter your network, they will allow for monitoring of traffic taking place between your network and the Internet. Encryption can be a very effective tool in protecting a law firm's sensitive data in the event its perimeter security measures are breached.

---

67 *See, e.g., Symantec Managed PKI for SSL,* Symantec, https://www.symantec.com/ssl-certificates/managed-pki-ssl/#.

68 *Manage Trusted Root Certificates,* Microsoft: Technet, https://technet.microsoft.com/en-us/library/cc754841.aspx.

69 *Data Breach Disclosure Regulation: Today's Challenge,* Thales e-Security, https://www.thales-esecurity.com/solutions/by-business-issue/data-breach-notification.

70 *Guidance to Render Unsecured Protected Health Information Unusable, Unreadable, or Indecipherable to Unauthorized Individuals,* HHS.gov, http://www.hhs.gov/hipaa/for-professionals/breach-notification/guidance/index.html.

CRYPTOGRAPHY

Daniel Garrie, Rick Borden, and Jeff Stapleton

5.1   Introduction

5.1.1   Why Is Cryptography Important Today?

More than ever before, personal, confidential, and other sensitive information is being transmitted over the Internet through emails, shared files, and the cloud, which are all potentially exposed.[1] Many individuals, small businesses, and large organizations today increasingly rely on technology, but do not fully understand the importance of data, software, and systems security.[2] Individuals and small businesses typically do not have information security knowledge or cybersecurity expertise. Larger organizations might not have cybersecurity expertise or sufficient funds to properly manage an information security group. Moreover, security professionals have trouble using programs and tools intended for security purposes.[3] As a result, several companies have recently suffered major data breaches resulting in high-profile litigation.[4] Damages can be massive, and additional losses can include the time and cost of credit monitoring for all customers (direct and indirect); years of systemic and obtrusive company-wide audits to identify and correct not just the source of the leak, but also other broken business processes that were discovered during the audits[5]; long-term impact to profitability/revenue projections; data theft and destruction of files, servers, and storage systems.[6] A basic knowledge of cryptography, encryption, and cybersecurity is necessary to help users understand how they are an important part of the network that keeps their own data, and the data of their employer, safe.

5.1.2   What Is Cryptography versus Encryption?

The term *cryptology* originates from ancient Greek meaning "secret" and "study," as in the discipline of covert communications. There are also the terms *cryptography*, meaning the practice of secret writing, and *cryptanalysis*, meaning the undoing of

---

1 "A major catalyst for email encryption were revelations about widespread online surveillance in documents leaked by Edward Snowden, the former National Security Agency contractor." Agence France-Presse, *NSA Spying Inspires ProtonMail End-to-End Encrypted Email Service*, May 19, 2014, http://gadgets.ndtv.com/internet/news/nsa-spying-inspires-protonmail-end-to-end-encrypted-email-service-526769; *see also* Miners, *NSA Sniffing Prompts Yahoo to Encrypt Traffic Between Its Data Centers*, Apr. 3, 2013, http://www.computerworld.com/s/article/9247410/NSA_sniffing_prompts_Yahoo_to_encrypt_traffic_between_its_data_centers.

2 *See* Garrie, *The BYOD Dilemma: How to Keep Your Assets from Turning into Liabilities*, 2014, http://blog.legalsolutions.thomsonreuters.com/wp-content/uploads//2014/02/BYOD-white-paper.pdf.

3 Sasse & Flechais, *Usable Security: Why Do We Need It? How Do We Get It?*, in SECURITY AND USABILITY: DESIGNING SECURE SYSTEMS THAT PEOPLE CAN USE 13, 14 (O'Reilly Media, 2005).

4 Sony, Target, and eBay are among the most recent victims. *See, e.g.*, Ellis, *Lawsuits Say Sony Pictures Should Have Expected Security Breach*, Dec. 20, 2014, http://www.cnn.com/2014/12/20/us/sony-pictures-lawsuits/.

5 *See* FTC Red Flags Rule, Nov. 9, 2007, http://www.ftc.gov/sites/default/files/documents/federal_register_notices/identity-theft-red-flags-and-address-discrepancies-under-fair-and-accurate-credit-transactions-act/071109redflags.pdf.

6 The event coordination site Meetup was shut down for seven days by a hack known as a distributed Denial-of-Service attack (DDOS), causing losses in the hundreds of thousands of dollars, in addition to the disruption of communities whose organizers rely on the website. *See* Newman, *Aggressive Hackers Brought Meetup Down. Here's How It Came Back*, Mar. 10, 2014, http://www.slate.com/blogs/future_tense/2014/03/10/ddos_attacks_brought_meetup_down_but_now_it_has_better_network_security.html.

secret writing. The earliest known use of cryptography was by the Egyptian priesthood circa 1900 BC who substituted their own secret symbols for hieroglyphics. Ancient cryptography such as the Caesar Cipher and pre-modern cryptography such as the Playfair cipher were manually computed by individuals. Modern cryptography, ushered in by World War II, is too complex for simple paper-and-pencil calculations and requires the processing power of computers.

We can think about *cryptography* as a specialized branch of mathematics that offers various information security controls, including data confidentiality (encryption), data integrity and authentication (message authentication), and possibly nonrepudiation (digital signatures). The term *encryption* is commonly misused as the equivalent of cryptography, but this is a misnomer and can lead to invalid assumptions. This is analogous to calling every fastener a nail when building a house, when actually nails, screws, staples, cement, tape, and glue are all used. If the architect, the general contractor, the bricklayer, the plumber, the electrician, the drywaller, and other construction workers called everything a nail, there would be mass confusion and many mistakes. Different types of cryptographic functions provide different security controls, and are sometimes used in combination with each other, so it can get complicated. Let us first provide a few definitions that are used throughout this chapter.

Cryptographic algorithms are processes of discrete steps performed by a computer to transform data, with inputs consisting of the data to be transformed and associated processing parameters which might include a *cryptographic key* and output of the transformed data. Note that not all algorithms use keys, whereas others might use one or more keys. Algorithms exist in mathematics, computer science, and many other disciplines; however, a cryptographic algorithm has more rigor and (it is hoped) fewer bugs and design flaws.

Cryptographic protocols are the ways people implement one or more cryptographic algorithms to establish cryptographic keys or exchange data securely using one or more messages over an unsecured environment (e.g., the Internet). Let's consider a simple protocol example with two people, Alice and Bob, where Alice wants to send data (here a series of questions) to Bob, who responds with an answer. However, Alice wants some assurance that the answer comes from Bob and not from anyone else—for example, Eve. Alice and Bob decide to exchange the secret number seven (7), which will be included in some form or another in the data to try to show that the data was from Alice to Bob or vice versa. They agree to set up a protocol in which any time Alice sends data to Bob, she includes a number she chooses at random. When Bob responds with the answer, he includes the product of Alice's random number and their secret number (7). Messages might look like this:

Alice's Question	Bob's Answer
5: Who won the 1965 World Series?	35: Los Angeles Dodgers
3: Who won the 1973 Super Bowl?	21: Miami Dolphins
2: Who was the drowsy dwarf?	15: Slugo

Alice sends the random numbers 5, 3, and 2 and verifies Bob's answers 35 and 21 because $5 \times 7 = 35$ and $3 \times 7 = 21$; however, $7 \times 2 = 14 \neq 15$, which was the answer she received. Thus, Alice can detect that the third message *may* not be from Bob (the drowsy dwarf might not be Slugo) because the number returned is wrong. However, this simple protocol does not actually *prove* anything: it can only indicate that the first two answers likely came from Bob and the third likely did not. Bob may have a programming error and miscalculated the third answer. Eve might have stolen the secret number, coerced Bob, or (using cryptanalysis) determined that the secret number was seven: after all, how hard can it be to factor a number that just happens to be the product of two prime numbers? The lesson here is that protocols, just like algorithms, can have bugs. They might reveal too much information about themselves, or, if the participants (Alice and Bob) do not follow the rules, the security can be compromised.

Cryptographic keys are strings of binary zeros and ones that are used with cryptographic algorithms. Keys control how the algorithm transforms input data into output data. Different keys for the same input will yield different outputs, and different inputs using the same key will likewise yield different outputs. Depending on the algorithm, keys might be a random number used with symmetric cryptography, or a mathematically generated number used with asymmetric cryptography. Generally speaking, keys must only be used by authorized entities; they must be kept secret to the extent that nobody needs to know the actual key (although we will see that for public key cryptography there is a valid exception); and keys cannot be used forever—they have a lifecycle and must be changed periodically. The lesson here is that keys must be managed properly, and that is where we get the term *key management*. Our next brief discussion of symmetric and asymmetric cryptography will be followed in more depth by the application of each in encryption.

Symmetric cryptography algorithms use the same key to perform both a function and the function's inverse. Anyone having access to the symmetric key can execute the function or its inverse, and accordingly transform data. Thus, it is imperative that only authorized individuals have access to the symmetric keys. Note that some algorithms have no inverse function, so these are sometimes called one-way functions. Symmetric keys are often called *secret* keys to distinguish them from asymmetric keys.

Asymmetric cryptography algorithms use two different mathematically related keys: one key is used to perform a function and the other key is used for the inverse function. Further, one key can be made public while the other is kept private. The public key cannot be used to determine the private key, so it can be shared with many others (this is the key secrecy exception mentioned earlier); hence we get the term *public key cryptography*. Unlike symmetric cryptography, anyone can have access to the public key without endangering the corresponding private key, and only the authorized individual needs access to the private key.

Cryptography has primarily been a tool of the military, ambassadors, and spies, through which they convey important information in a covert fashion. Military couriers would send orders to the battle front or return tactical battlefield situations to headquarters. Ambassadors might receive political instructions or return important economic information. And, of course, spies would send critical information about . . . spy stuff. If the messages were intercepted, encryption would keep the adversary from reading the information, although sometimes the fact that a secret message was sent might be just as important as the message itself.

When we think about protecting information, there are two aspects that must be considered: data in transit, and data in storage. *Data in transit* happens when information is sent over the Internet from one location to another (Alice to Bob), transmitted using a mobile device, laptop, desktop computer, network appliances, midrange servers, or even mainframes. Data transmission includes file transfers, emails, text messages, videos, voice messages, and even old-fashioned telephone calls. These transmissions might originate over cellular, Bluetooth, near field communications (NFC) or Wi-Fi, or local area network (LAN) connections. *Data in storage* happens when information is stored temporarily or permanently. For example, the sender (Alice) often stores the data on its local device, and the receiver (Bob) typically stores the data on its local device, but there are many intermediate systems across networks and the Internet that temporarily store the data in passing. Let's consider the various threats that can be deterred using cryptography.

- *Data disclosure* happens when an unauthorized individual (Eve) gets copies of personal information, either unintentionally by the sender or receiver, or intentionally by a bad actor who steals data from the sender, the receiver, or an intermediary system on the Internet.
- *Data modification* happens when an individual (Eve) changes or replaces personal information, either unintentionally by the sender, receiver, or intermediary system, or intentionally by a bad actor who changes data at the sender, receiver, or an intermediary system.
- *Entity masquerading* happens when a bad actor (Eve) intentionally sends, receives, or falsifies information on an intermediary system that appears to be from a legitimate source.

Different cryptographic algorithms and protocols can provide various security controls, including data confidentiality, data integrity, and data authentication. **Data** encryption can provide data confidentiality, preventing disclosure of data in transit or in storage. Message authentication can provide data integrity, enabling detection of modified data in transit or in storage. Digital signatures can provide both data integrity and entity authentication to avoid entity masquerading. Cryptography can also provide the foundational technology for nonrepudiation[7] (as described later in this chapter), but such services require additional legal considerations.

Symmetric cryptography cannot provide nonrepudiation because anyone with legitimate access might use the keys, so data integrity and authentication cannot be independently proved to a third party. Asymmetric cryptography can provide

7 J. J. Stapleton, Nonrepudiation, *in* Security Without Obscurity: A Guide to Confidentiality, Authentication, and Integrity (CRC Press, 2014).

nonrepudiation because only the legitimate user can access the private key. Further, the *Digital Signature Guideline (DSG)*,[8] published by the American Bar Association (ABA) Information Security Committee (ISC), essentially describes the requirements for a nonrepudiation service in terms of the sender and the receiver, to protect each other from false claims.

> Signer authentication and document authentication are tools used to exclude impersonators and forgers and are essential ingredients of what is often called a non-repudiation service in the terminology of the information security profession. A non-repudiation service provides assurance of the origin or delivery of data in order to protect the sender against false denial by the recipient that the data has been received, or to protect the recipient against false denial by the sender that the data has been sent. Thus, a non-repudiation service provides evidence to prevent a person from unilaterally modifying or terminating legal obligations arising out of a transaction effected by computer-based means.

Another quasi-cryptography subject is electronic signatures, which should not be confused with digital signatures. The Uniform Electronic Transactions Act (UETA) defines *electronic signature* as an electronic sound, symbol, or process, attached to or logically associated with a contract or other record and executed or adopted by a person with the intent to sign the record. The UETA definition is consistent with the European Union (EU) *Directive on Electronic Signatures*. Digital signatures are described in more detail later in this chapter.

5.2 Encryption

Encryption is the transformation of readable data by normal means into indecipherable data, thus providing data confidentiality. *Decryption* is the inverse function, transformation of the indecipherable back into the original readable format. Encryption algorithms have cleartext (or plaintext) data as input and ciphertext as output. Decryption algorithms have ciphertext as input and cleartext as output. For example, a sender (Alice) might encrypt a cleartext message into ciphertext and transmit the ciphertext to a recipient (Bob); then the receiver (Bob) can decrypt the ciphertext back into the original cleartext message. As another example, a user can encrypt a cleartext note into ciphertext, store the ciphertext onto a device, and then later

---

8 Information Security Committee (ISC), Electronic Commerce and Information Technology Division, Section of Science and Technology, & American Bar Association (ABA), DIGITAL SIGNATURE GUIDELINES: LEGAL INFRASTRUCTURE FOR CERTIFICATION AUTHORITIES AND SECURE ELECTRONIC COMMERCE (Aug. 1996).

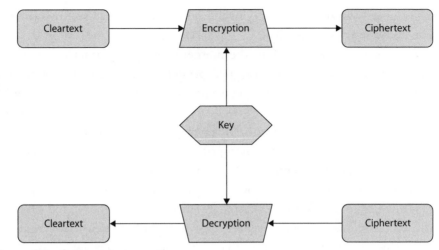

Figure 5-1 Symmetric encryption.

retrieve the ciphertext from the device and decrypt the ciphertext back into the original cleartext note. Figures 5-1 and 5-2 illustrate the overall processes.

The encryption process actually has two inputs, the cleartext and a cryptographic key; its inverse function, decryption, likewise has two inputs, the ciphertext and the same key. When the same key is used for both encryption and decryption, it is called *symmetric* encryption (shown in Figure 5-1); in contrast, when two different mathematically related keys are used, it is called *asymmetric* encryption (shown in Figure 5-2). However, symmetric and asymmetric encryption are not used interchangeably, and asymmetric encryption is not the same as *digital signatures* (discussed in Section 5.4 of this chapter). These two points are

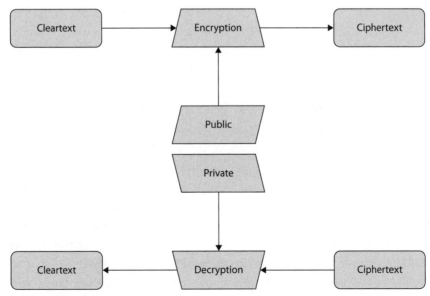

Figure 5-2 Asymmetric encryption.

often misunderstood and can lead to invalid assumptions or bad security analysis, so some discussion is worthwhile.

Without getting too deep into the mathematics of asymmetric cryptography, suffice it to say that asymmetric encryption has limitations that symmetric encryption does not. First, cleartext gets encrypted using the public key which anyone might have, but ciphertext gets decrypted using the private key which only the owner has. Second, asymmetric encryption works best with small bits of cleartext, whereas symmetric encryption works with small bits, medium messages, and large files. Third, and possibly more importantly, asymmetric cryptography consumes more computing power than symmetric cryptography. Thus, symmetric cryptography is faster, requires little memory, and takes up very little disk storage. The differences are significant enough that symmetric cryptography is used far more often than asymmetric cryptography to protect data. In fact, asymmetric encryption is so resource costly that it is typically used to protect symmetric keys rather than data (as discussed in Section 5.5 of this chapter). Meanwhile, we need to explore the risks of symmetric encryption.

5.3 Message Authentication

Message authentication is the use of symmetric cryptography to detect data modification and provide limited entity authentication. Unlike encryption, which can prevent data disclosure, message authentication can only detect; it cannot prevent an attacker from changing or replacing information. Cryptography is used to create a message authentication code (MAC) which can later be reused to verify that the data has not been attacked. *Verification* is the inverse function of the original MAC generation, but verification recreates the MAC for comparison. Figure 5-3 illustrates the overall process.

Similar to encryption, the MAC generation function has two inputs, the cleartext and a symmetric key; however, the output differs such that a MAC is produced. Unlike decryption, the MAC verification function has the cleartext and the key as inputs, and the output is a recalculation of the MAC so that the original MAC is compared to the recomputed MAC to determine if the cleartext has been changed. For example, Alice generates the MAC and sends both the cleartext and MAC to Bob. Bob then recalculates the MAC using the received cleartext and compares the newly recomputed MAC to the received MAC. If either the cleartext or the MAC have been changed during transmission, Bob's MAC will not match Alice's MAC. Unfortunately, Bob only knows the verification has failed; he does not know what actually happened.

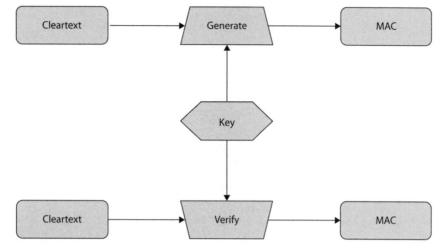

Figure 5-3 Message authentication.

Conversely, if the MAC does verify, Bob knows two things. First, he knows the cleartext has data integrity; that is, his version of the cleartext is the same as what Alice sent. Second, he can authenticate Alice, because only he and Alice have access to the symmetric MAC key, and Bob knows he did not send the cleartext to himself. However, if the symmetric MAC key was shared with anyone else, the entity authentication cannot be definitive. Also, even if the symmetric MAC key is only accessible by Alice and Bob, the entity authentication is not provable to a third party, so the message does not have *nonrepudiation*. Any crypto-savvy third party, perhaps a judge, would realize that Bob could have falsified the cleartext because the verification function calculates the MAC just like the generation function using a shared symmetric key.

5.4 Digital Signatures

A *digital signature* uses asymmetric cryptography to detect data modification and provide entity authentication. Unlike asymmetric encryption, digital signatures are generated using the private key and the digital signatures are verified using the corresponding public key. And, unlike message authentication, the private key is only accessible to the signer, whereas any verifier can have a copy of the public key. When discussing digital signatures, the preferred and technically correct terms are *sign the data* (cleartext) and *verify the signature*. Other commonly misused terms include *encryption*, *encrypt* and *decrypt* the hash, and *sign* the hash.

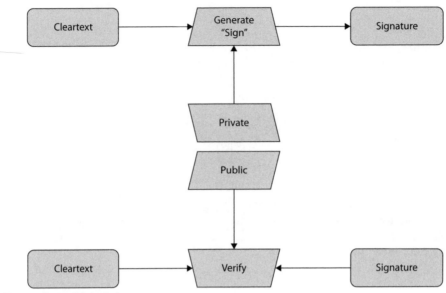

Figure 5-4 Digital signatures.

Perhaps one of the reasons for the bad terminology and loose usage is that the first commercially used asymmetric algorithm for digital signatures was RSA,[9] named for the inventors Rivest, Shamir, and Adleman. It just so happens that RSA is reversible—that is, it can encrypt with the public or private key, and the inverse can decrypt with the private or public key—but ironically it is one of the few digital signature algorithms that has this property. Most of the other digital signature algorithms can *sign* using the private key and only *verify* using the public key. Thus, it is more correct to just use the terms *sign the data* and *verify the signature*, which sidesteps having to think about the underlying cryptography and avoids bad assumptions.

Regardless, another point of confusion is that digital signatures always include a hash algorithm, which is not shown in Figure 5-4 simply because the hashing function is part of the signature generation and signature verification processes. The cleartext is always hashed before the private key is used to create the signature and before the public key is used to verify the signature. This is true for all digital signature algorithms, so the hash algorithm can just be considered part of the overall cryptographic process. Basically, we know the hash is there, but for most discussions it can be presumed and simply ignored.

Similar to message authentication, one party signs the data, and another party verifies the signature. For example, Alice generates the signature using her private key and sends both the cleartext and signature to Bob. Bob then verifies the signature using Alice's public key. If either the cleartext or signature have been changed during transmission, the verification will fail, but Bob only knows it failed; he does not know what actually happened. The important fact to realize is that Bob does not have any keys besides Alice's public key, and Alice can provide

9 Rivest, Shamir, & Adleman, *A Method for Obtaining Digital Signatures and Public-Key Cryptosystems*, COMMUNICATIONS OF THE ACM, Feb. 1978, 120–26.

her public key to dozens or thousands of individuals without endangering her private key.

Conversely, if the digital signature does verify, Bob knows three things. First, he knows the cleartext has *data integrity*—that his version is the same as what Alice sent. Second, he can authenticate Alice, because only Alice has access to her private key. Third, and most importantly, he knows Alice cannot deny signing the cleartext, since again she is the only one with access to the private key. Because (allegedly) only Alice has access to the private key, the integrity and authentication are provable to a third party, which gives us a foundation for *nonrepudiation*.

5.5   Key Management

All symmetric and asymmetric keys have a common management lifecycle,[10] as shown in Figure 5-5. Basically, only the time frames differ depending on how keys are utilized. The lifecycle stages (generation, distribution, storage, backup and recovery, revocation expiration, and termination) always occur in a specific order, but not all stages are always needed. In general, unless security controls are in place for each lifecycle stage, any key is susceptible to compromise that affects encryption, message authentication, or digital signatures. The lesson here is that adequate security controls must be in place for each stage of the lifecycle; however, some stages might be under the control of different individuals, groups, or even applications, so interoperability and cooperation are essential among the various participants.

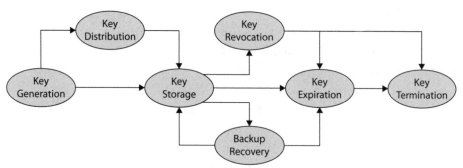

Figure 5-5 Key management lifecycle.

---

10 AMERICAN NATIONAL STANDARD X9.79 PUBLIC KEY INFRASTRUCTURES (PKI), Part 4: Asymmetric Key Management, aligns numerous International Standards Organization (ISO), Accredited Standards Committee (ASC X9), and National Institute of Standards and Technology (NIST) key management lifecycle models.

5.5.1   Key Generation

Key generation happens when symmetric keys are randomly generated or asymmetric private and public key pairs are mathematically computed. When asymmetric keys are generated, part of the key generation process includes getting a public key certificate from an organization called a certificate authority (CA), part of an overall public key infrastructure[11] (PKI). The role of the CA is to authenticate the requestor (Alice) and issue a certificate that can be trusted by a relying party (Bob). A basic certificate contains many data fields, including the key pair owner's name (Alice), the key pair owner's public key, the CA name that issued the certificate, the CA digital signature (so the CA also has its own asymmetric key pair), and a certificate validity date.

5.5.2   Key Distribution

Key distribution occurs when one or more keys have to be shared among two or more participants. For example, if Alice generates an encryption key, she needs to establish the key with Bob. As another example, if Bob generates a message authentication key, he needs to exchange the key with Alice. In both examples, symmetric keys need to be securely distributed between Alice and Bob so Eve cannot intercept the keys. For digital signatures, Alice needs to share her public key certificate with Bob, but does not need to worry about Eve.

Keys might be transmitted (*key transport*) from Alice to Bob, or mutually derived (*key agreement*) by Alice and Bob using cryptographic methods; the preferred generic term to address both methods is *key establishment*. Alternatively, when a key is generated, stored, and used at the same location, such as for file encryption, key distribution might not be needed. Thus, for some keys the lifecycle might jump from generation directly to storage without distribution.

5.5.3   Key Storage

Key storage happens after generation or distribution when keys are used for their intended purpose, such as encryption, message authentication, or digital signatures. The keys must be protected from disclosure, modification, replacement, and unauthorized access. Controls also have to be implemented so keys are only used for their intended purpose and cannot be accidentally or intentionally misused. Furthermore, keys cannot be used forever; all keys expire, upon which their use ends. Coordinating key change among multiple participants can be challenging.

For example, when Alice and Bob change their encryption key, some messages might be processed out of order, such that the old key and new key are both active. Consider when Alice encrypts and sends ten messages, the first five encrypted with the old key and the next five encrypted with the new key. Consequently, Bob might receive or process the messages in a different order, such that he needs to know which key to use for decryption. Otherwise, if Bob uses the incorrect key,

---

11 J. J. Stapleton & W. Clay Epstein, Security without Obscurity: A Guide to PKI Operations (CRC Press, 2016).

the decryption will result in invalid cleartext, and depending on the nature of the cleartext and the processing rules, might result in a message error or an application error; or worse, the error might go undetected and cause a processing error. Key synchronization errors are often difficult to detect or diagnose.

Access controls protecting cryptographic keys vary based on the product. The strongest method is to use specialized cryptographic hardware that never allows cleartext keys outside its security boundary and also performs the cryptographic algorithms and protocols inside its cryptographic boundary. Another method, when using cryptographic software, requires an end user to enter a password that is used to dynamically generate the cryptographic key so it is never stored on disk, but only appears in computer memory. An even weaker method, when using software, stores the key in a system file that is merely protected using password-based access controls. Whatever the method, once keys are securely stored with appropriate access controls and used in accordance with their purpose, the next stages (backup and recovery, revocation, and expiration) have to be considered.

5.5.4   Key Backup and Recovery

Key backup and recovery might be needed for some keys when operational outage due to a disabled key is unacceptable. Copies of keys can be stored safely in the unlikely event of an application failure that corrupts or erases keys; a key can be restored in a timely manner as part of the application recovery process. For example, if Alice's message authentication key fails because her computer crashes, she can restore the key after her computer is replaced. Thus, she can recover the key and continue exchanging messages with Bob.

However, keys do not always have to be recovered, and in some cases it is better when keys are *not* recoverable. For example, if Alice's digital signature private key fails, she could recover the key and continue to sign messages for Bob to verify using her public key certificate. However, the backup copy of Alice's private key poses an unacceptable risk because if it was ever compromised, then Eve could generate counterfeit signatures. Thus, if Alice's computer crashes, she would generate a new key pair, get a new certificate, and provide the certificate to Bob.

Conversely, the certificate authority that issued Alice's public key certificate would back up its private certificate signing key. From an operational perspective, the CA might have issued thousands of certificates used by millions of relying parties, so it would be better for the CA to keep using the same private key rather than have to generate new keys and redistribute its own certificate to those millions of relying parties.

5.5.5   Key Revocation

Key revocation might be needed, before the key expires, to prevent its use. Revoked keys should not be used, so applications need a method to validate key status. Further, because all keys have an expiration date, revoked keys still expire. For example, if a certificate revocation list (CRL) is used to track revoked certificates, once the certificate expires per its validity date, the certificate no longer has to be kept on the CRL. This is true for all keys: revoked or expired keys should not be used, including those in backup, as revoked or expired keys should not be restored.

There are many business, operational, and security reasons to revoke keys. For example, from a security perspective, if a key is known or suspected to be compromised, it should be revoked. From an operational perspective, if an application is decommissioned, the key should be revoked to avoid its misuse. When a business ceases operations, an employee departs or is dismissed, or an individual dies, the key should likewise be revoked. Revocation is typically associated with expiring certificates but in fact any key can and should be revoked. Another control to protect against accidently using revoked keys is to *terminate* the key.

5.5.6 Key Expiration

Key expiration is the stage when the useful lifetime of a key has ended. For example, Alice should not encrypt data using a key that has expired; however, Bob might need to decrypt previously encrypted data using an expired key. Likewise, Alice should not use an expired message authentication key, but Bob might need to verify a previously generated MAC. Thus, the same symmetric key can have different time frames depending on its cryptographic function versus its inverse function. Similarly, Alice should not sign messages using her private key when the corresponding public key has expired per its certificate validity date. However, Bob might need to use an expired certificate to verify an older signature. Thus, knowing when a message gets signed is extremely important. Once expired keys no longer have to be used, keys can then be properly *terminated* to avoid misuse or reuse by anyone.

5.5.7 Key Termination

Key termination is the process to systematically destroy all copies of expired keys to prevent reuse or recovery. Symmetric keys must be deleted so they cannot be used. Asymmetric private keys must be deleted when certificates are revoked. Public key certificates are typically not erased, because without the corresponding private key, the public key is relatively benign. Also, there might be hundreds or thousands of certificate copies at unknown locations, so deleting them all is not realistic. Key termination includes all types of media, including stored files, printed paper, and peripherals such as smartcards and USB memory sticks. Practically speaking, a key inventory is needed so that terminated keys can be tracked.

5.6   Other Crypto Considerations

5.6.1   Vendor Selection

The fundamental problem with purchasing cryptography solutions is that an organization cannot buy what does not exist. Unless an organization is crypto savvy and willing to acquire patent licenses and then design, develop, and maintain its own custom solutions, there is always a worrisome dependency on commercially available products. Granted, this is true for most technologies, but as this chapter has pointed out, there are numerous concerns in proper use of cryptography and secure management of cryptographic keys. The buyer might blissfully trust its vendor, hoping the seller knows far more about cryptography, key management, business processes, and application environments than does the client—or the buyer can be proactive. The buyer understands its business processes, its regulatory atmosphere, and its application environment far better than anyone else. Thus, the buyer needs to determine its own security requirements and educate itself about cryptography and key management.

Organizations need to stipulate their security requirements, evaluate products based on relevant criteria, and determine the product (or products) that are the best fit. Because vendors must sell products to many clients across different industries, they cannot afford to build custom solutions. Rather, vendors often rely on industry security standards to determine requirements. Therefore, it is in an organization's own self-interest to influence standards so that vendors will build products that it can rely upon. Nonetheless, claims of compliance with standards must be validated—the mantra here is: *verify, then trust*. Unfortunately, many standards bodies do not have compliance programs, so, although the standards are worthwhile, conformity is not so easily measured.

The lesson here is to understand your security requirements and recognize that today, while cryptography is an essential ingredient within any product, it is not the only thing needed. For example, even an encryption product that provides good cryptographic algorithms and protocols with secure key management processes still has to have well-defined roles and responsibilities with appropriate separation of duties, including different access controls for end users, application administrators, system administrators, and key management officers. Thus, an organization must establish its cryptographic evaluation criteria when selecting vendor products.

5.6.2   Jurisdictional Law

The remarks that it's a small world and the digital age is making it smaller every day imply that cryptography is a universal language for everyone to just get along.

However, this is not actually the case: many international and national jurisdictions have different laws and regulations when it comes to allowing cryptography. For example, in U.S. history preceding the millennium, cryptography was listed as auxiliary military equipment, the export and import of which was controlled by the Department of State. During the first decade of the 2000s, control over nonmilitary exports was shifted to the Department of Commerce, with restrictions imposed by the Office of Foreign Assets Control (OFAC). Legal issues must be considered when cryptographic products cross jurisdictional borders, whether they are for personal use, products for general use, products for resale, and occasionally encrypted data. Some algorithms are restricted, some key sizes are limited, and sometimes keys are required to be escrowed.

There is also the related issue of data recovery. When data is encrypted (ciphertext), it is considered to be unreadable (cleartext) unless the key is accessible for decryption, so access to the key becomes a control factor. However, key escrow is not necessarily the answer, as the goal is to get the data and not necessarily the key. For example, if Alice encrypts data using a key she shares with Bob, an authorized third party might need to read the data. Alice's employer might need to ensure that she is not exposing sensitive data to Bob, or perhaps law enforcement is investigating Bob and needs to see the cleartext. An invalid assumption is that the third party needs access to the key shared by Alice and Bob; in fact, it just needs access to the cleartext, which can be achieved in various ways.

- A copy of the cleartext could be escrowed before Alice does the encryption or after Bob does the decryption.
- Alice might separately encrypt the data, using two different keys, one for Bob and another for the third party.
- Alice might encrypt the data using a key she shares with a proxy service and the proxy service might decrypt and re-encrypt the data using a key shared with Bob.

Thus, imposing encryption restrictions is an unnecessary action. Key management methods are available to provide data escrow (not necessarily key escrow) to satisfy third-party access.

5.7   Conclusion

For symmetric cryptography to work, the sender (Alice) and receiver (Bob) need to use the same cryptographic key. So, the problems include how a user stores a key, how a user shares a key, and how a user generates a key. For encryption, if the key is compromised—that is, if an unauthorized individual (Eve) gets access to the symmetric key—then copies of the ciphertext can be decrypted. Alice and Bob may think their messages are safe, but if Eve knows or has access to the key, she can decrypt ciphertext copied from the Internet. Alarmingly, Eve might collect encrypted messages between Alice and Bob for weeks, months, or years in the hopes of getting the key. For message authentication, if the MAC key is compromised—that is, if an unauthorized individual (Eve) gets access to the symmetric key—then messages can be modified. Bob might think the message is from Alice because the MAC verifies, but he cannot detect that Eve changed the message and replaced the legitimate MAC with her own using their key. Thus, a compromised key negates both data integrity and entity authentication.

Eve might also be able to intercept the symmetric key when exchanged between Alice and Bob. Because the same key must be used, somehow Alice and Bob need to establish the symmetric key in a secure fashion such that Eve cannot capture the key. There are many good ways to securely exchange keys, including manual processes, using other key encryption keys (KEK) to exchange symmetric data encryption keys, and asymmetric keys to establish symmetric encryption keys. Conversely, there are many bad ways to exchange keys. The best practice is to use products and follow procedures that comply with industry security standards, such as those published by the International Standards Organization (ISO[12]), the American National Standards Institute (ANSI[13]), the Accredited Standards Committee X9 for the financial services industry (ASC X9[14]) and the National Institute for Standards and Technology (NIST[15]).

For asymmetric cryptography to work, the sender (Alice) needs to protect her private key and the receiver (Bob) needs to validate Alice's certificate. If Alice's private key is not securely stored, Eve might make a copy without Alice's knowledge. If access to Alice's private key is not controlled, Eve might not steal the key but just guess the password and use Alice's key. In either scenario, Eve could generate a digital signature that Bob would verify and a third party would presume to be valid. Further, if Bob ever challenged Alice over a digital signature, Alice might claim Eve had compromised her private key (whether it actually happened or not), and deny signing the cleartext. Again, digital signatures can only provide a technical foundation for nonrepudiation services, but other controls would also be needed.

Information security controls (confidentiality, integrity, authentication, and nonrepudiation) provided by cryptography (encryption, message authentication, digital signatures, and key management) are part of a larger picture: cybersecurity. Cyber threats are on the rise worldwide, with business and governmental leaders declaring them a

---

12 www.iso.org.
13 www.ansi.org.
14 www.x9.org.
15 www.nist.org.

major priority.[16] The field of cryptography is vast, and this chapter can only touch on the surface concepts, but that does not lessen the importance of security for all users of the Internet and mobile devices. Best practice in crypto-cybersecurity is constantly evolving as the give-and-take continues between hackers and network defense systems, so it is important to stay updated and informed. Many excellent guides to Internet security and encryption exist, with more detail and examples than we are able to provide here. Gaining some knowledge, however slight, of the systems that come into play every time you hit "send" on an email or download a file can only be beneficial, and we hope that this chapter may encourage you to do further research in the field.

5.8 Chapter Glossary

Asymmetric cryptography—Algorithms that use two different but mathematically related keys; one key is used to perform a function and the other key is used for the inverse function.

Cryptographic algorithms—Processes performed by a computer to transform data, with inputs (data, parameters) and outputs of the transformed data.

Cryptographic key—String of binary zeros and ones used with cryptographic algorithms that control how the algorithm transforms input data into output data.

Cryptographic protocols—Implementation of one or more cryptographic algorithms to establish cryptographic keys or exchange data securely over an unsecured environment.

Cryptography—Specialized branch of mathematics that offers data confidentiality (encryption), data integrity and authentication (message authentication), and nonrepudiation (digital signatures).

Data encryption—Transformation of readable data (cleartext) into indecipherable data (ciphertext), thus providing data confidentiality.

Digital signature—Asymmetric cryptography to detect data modification and provide entity authentication.

Key management—Secure supervision of cryptographic keys throughout their lifecycle.

Message authentication—Symmetric cryptography to detect data modification and provide limited entity authentication.

Public key cryptography—Asymmetric cryptography where public keys distributed as digital certificates are used for digital signature verification, data encryption, or key management schemes, and where the corresponding private keys are used for digital signature generation, data decryption, or key management.

Symmetric cryptography—Algorithms that use the same key to perform both a function and the inverse of that function.

---

16 *See, e.g.,* Garrie, *Cybersecurity Becoming Real Issue for Boards of Directors,* Daily J., Jun. 2, 2014; Barlyn, *Wall Street watchdog to bolster reviews of brokerage security,* Reuters, Oct. 29, 2014, http://www.reuters.com/article/2014/10/29/us-finra-cybersecurity-examinations-idUSKBN0II2DA20141029.

CHAPTER

6

ISO STANDARDS

Daniel Garrie

6.1   Introduction

It is indisputable that in today's world of widespread cyberattacks, law firms must establish effective cybersecurity procedures and practices. While there is no definitive best standard, a leading option is the ISO 27000-series standards promulgated by the International Organization for Standardization (ISO).

The three standards in the series that we will be examining in this chapter are: 27000:2016, *Information technology—Security techniques—Information security management systems—Overview and vocabulary*[1]; 27001:2013, *Information technology—Security techniques—Information security management systems—Requirements*[2]; and 27002:2013, *Information technology—Security techniques—Code of practice for information security controls.*[3]

Law firms have begun looking to adopt these information security management standards in order to secure both their own and their clients' data,[4] as well as to market their security infrastructure as a selling point to potential clients.[5] For example, the law firm Shook Hardy & Bacon spent nearly $100,000 and several years in order to implement an ISO 27001-compliant data security framework.[6] The result of these efforts has strengthened its position in the market and led to prospective clients bringing their business to the firm.[7]

6.1.1   Overview of the ISO

The ISO, which comprises 162 national standards bodies, develops "voluntary, consensus-based, market relevant International Standards that support innovation and provide solutions to global challenges."[8] It was founded in 1946, and promulgated its first standard in 1951.[9] The ISO has developed more than 19,000 international standards in fields ranging "from technology, to food safety, to agriculture and healthcare."[10] The ISO has also been integral in developing standards for information security

---

1 ISO/IEC 27000:2016, http://www.iso.org/iso/home/store/catalogue_tc/catalogue_detail.htm?csnumber=66435.

2 ISO/IEC 27001:2013, http://www.iso.org/iso/home/store/catalogue_tc/catalogue_detail.htm?csnumber=54534.

3 ISO/IEC 27002:2013, http://www.iso.org/iso/home/store/catalogue_tc/catalogue_detail.htm?csnumber=54533.

4 *Safe and Secure: Cyber Security Practices for Law Firms*, CNA Professional Counsel, https://www.cna.com/web/wcm/connect/61aec549-ac28-457b-8626-aa791c782459/Safe_Secure_Cyber_Security_Practices.pdf?MOD=AJPERES.

5 Michael A. Riley & Sophia Pearson, *China-Based Hackers Target Law Firms to Get Secret Deal Data*, Bloomberg, Jan. 31, 2012, 4:37 PM, https://ccazblog.files.wordpress.com/2013/09/china-based-hackers-ta.pdf ("some law firms are now using [security accreditation] as a selling point to clients").

6 Mary Pratt, *Law Firm Makes a Case for Security Certification*, CIO, Aug. 28, 2015, http://www.cio.com/article/2969323/security/law-firm-makes-a-case-for-security-certification.html.

7 *Id.*

8 *About ISO*, ISO, http://www.iso.org/iso/about.htm.

9 *Id.*

10 *Id.*

management. These standards are often used as the basis for an accreditation, which is performed by independent, neutral, third-party auditors.[11]

The ISO 27000-series standards play a pivotal role in offering broad guidance to all organizations as to how they should deal with information security issues in a comprehensive and methodical way.[12] Additionally, ISO 27001's focus on risk assessment allows for the implementation of the standard to "keep pace with changes to the security threats, vulnerabilities and business impacts" of an organization.[13] This ensures that organizations that implement the standard can always work to address new threats as time goes on. With all of that being said, though, these standards do not explicitly dictate which steps an organization must take in order to secure its information systems; rather, organizations "are free to choose whichever specific information security controls are applicable to their particular information security situations, drawing on those listed in the standards and potentially supplementing them with other *a la carte* options (sometimes known as extended control sets)."[14]

6.2   ISO 27001

ISO 27001 defines its scope as outlining "the requirements for establishing, implementing, maintaining and continually improving an information security management system within the context of the organization. [ISO 27001] also includes requirements for the assessment and treatment of information security risks tailored to the needs of the organization."[15] This section explores key elements of the ISO 27001 standard and considers how law firms can use that standard to develop and implement cybersecurity regimens that should provide a good deal of protection, and shelter them from liability in the event that a data breach does occur.[16] The goal of the standard is for an organization to be able to: (1) establish security objectives; (2) identify security needs; (3) implement a security program; and (4) ensure compliance.[17]

---

11 For a more thorough examination of the certification (accreditation) process, *see* Section 6.3, *infra*.

12 Dejan Kosutic, *What Is Cybersecurity and How Can ISO 27001 Help?*, 27001 ACADEMY, Oct. 25, 2015, http://advisera.com/27001academy/blog/2011/10/25/what-is-cybersecurity-and-how-can-iso-27001-help/.

13 ISO/IEC 27001, IsecT, http://www.iso27001security.com/html/27001.html.

14 *Id.*

15 ISO/IEC 27001:2013, §1.

16 Nell Gluckman, *To Satisfy Clients, Law Firms Submit to Cybersecurity Scrutiny*, AM LAW DAILY, Mar. 12, 2015, http://www.americanlawyer.com/id=1202720468020/To-Satisfy-Clients-Law-Firms-Submit-to-Cybersecurity-Scrutiny-?slreturn=20160028023722.

17 David Bodenheimer & Cheryl Falvey, *Cybersecurity Standards and Risk Assessments for Law Offices: Weighing the Security Risks and Safeguarding Against Cyber Threats*, CROWELL MORING, https://www.crowell.com/files/Cybersecurity-Standards-and-Risk-Assessments-for-Law-Offices.pdf.

6.2.1 Establishing Security Objectives

The goal of implementing an information security measure is to protect one of the following: (1) data confidentiality,[18] (2) data integrity,[19] or (3) data availability.[20] Information security professionals often refer to these three goals as the *CIA triad*, each of which is discussed in this subsection.[21]

6.2.1.1 Data Confidentiality

Achieving data confidentiality means that sensitive data is not accessed by unauthorized people. The only way to achieve this goal is through the restriction of access to data.[22] The challenge information security professionals face is how access can be restricted from the unauthorized people while still allowing the right people to access the data, which can possibly implicate the availability of data (discussed later).

One of the first steps that an organization should take in establishing its security objectives is to classify its confidential data to ensure that the correct balance of protection and availability is present.[23] A common breakdown for data classification is: (1) restricted data,[24] (2) private data,[25] and (3) public data.[26] Although care should be taken with all confidential data, this stratification allows proportionate measures to be put into place for each category.[27]

6.2.1.2 Data Integrity

Maintaining data integrity involves "maintaining the consistency, accuracy, and trustworthiness of data over its entire life cycle."[28] If an organization can ensure the integrity of its data, it can know that the data has been accessed and modified only by those who are authorized to do so.[29] It is an essential element of being able to be confident in one's data. From a law firm's perspective, lawyers must know that all of the data they surround themselves with is both accurate and trustworthy.

---

18 *Confidentiality* is defined in 44 U.S.C. § 3542(b)(1) as "preserving authorized restrictions on access and disclosure, including means for protecting personal privacy and proprietary information."
19 *Integrity* is defined in 44 U.S.C. § 3542(b)(1) as "guarding against improper information modification or destruction, and includes ensuring information nonrepudiation and authenticity."
20 *Availability* is defined in 44 U.S.C. § 3542(b)(1) as "ensuring timely and reliable access to and use of information."
21 Jim Breithaupt & Mark Merkow, *Information Security Principles of Success*, PEARSON, Jul. 4, 2014, http://www.pearsonitcertification.com/articles/article.aspx?p=2218577&seqNum=3.
22 *Confidentiality, integrity, and availability (CIA triad)* [definition], TECHTARGET: WHATIS, http://whatis.techtarget.com/definition/Confidentiality-integrity-and-availability-CIA (hereinafter *CIA Triad*).
23 *Guidelines for Data Classification*, CARNEGIE MELLON UNIVERSITY, http://www.cmu.edu/iso/governance/guidelines/data-classification.html.
24 "Data should be classified as Restricted when the unauthorized disclosure, alteration or destruction of that data could cause a significant level of risk to [an organization]." *Id.*
25 "Data should be classified as Private when the unauthorized disclosure, alteration or destruction of that data could result in a moderate level of risk to [an organization]" *Id.*
26 "Data should be classified as Public when the unauthorized disclosure, alteration or destruction of that data would results [sic] in little or no risk to [an organization]." *Id.*
27 Chris Rodgers, *Data Classification: Why Is It Important for Information Security?*, SECURESTATE, Apr. 3, 2012, https://www.securestate.com/blog/2012/04/03/data-classification-why-is-it-important-for-information-security.
28 *CIA triad, supra* note 22.
29 *Integrity* [definition], TECHTARGET, http://searchdatacenter.techtarget.com/definition/integrity.

Imagine if every item in a lawyer's calendar was shifted a week back. It might take some time to discover that simple alteration, but irreparable harm may have wreaked on both the client and the firm in the interim.

Two primary avenues must be pursued when an organization seeks to protect the integrity of its data. The first is to implement a system for monitoring potential breaches and correcting, whenever possible, any data that is imperiled by such a breach. The second is to implement a rigorous security regimen that will prevent breaches, to the extent that this is possible.[30]

6.2.1.3 Data Availability

In addition to ensuring the confidentiality and integrity of its data, an organization must be able to maintain the availability of that data. Data availability is ensured by "rigorously maintaining all hardware, performing hardware repairs immediately when needed, and maintaining a correctly functioning operating system environment that is free of software conflicts."[31] In addition to maintaining hardware and software, a central tenet of data availability is that redundancy is necessary to overcome even catastrophic disasters. Redundancy can take many forms, from failover,[32] to RAID,[33] to maintaining an offsite backup of critical data.[34] An important consideration when choosing offsite backup is how readily that data can be accessed in the event of a disaster. Take, for example, a hurricane that knocked the power out in New York. If a law firm backed up its data to a center in Kansas, that same hurricane would prevent the lawyers from getting to Kansas in order to access the data, thus rendering an otherwise effective redundancy irrelevant.

These courses of action are necessary for ensuring uninterrupted access to an organization's data, but organizations often have to choose between them, and the only way to do so is to understand the types of threats that the data may face. Bad actors have already learned that law firms, which rely heavily on readily accessible data, are particularly vulnerable to this threat, and have begun to attack firms by targeting data accessibility.[35] When the international hacking collective called Anonymous launched an attack against a law firm, which resulted in the firm's

---

30 Vince Farhat et al., *Cyber Attacks: Prevention and Proactive Responses*, PRACTICAL LAW COMPANY (2011), https://www.hklaw.com/files/Publication/bd9553c5-284f-4175-87d2-849aa07920d3/Presentation/PublicationAttachment/1880b6d6-eae2-4b57-8a97-9f4fb1f58b36/CyberAttacksPreventionandProactiveResponses.pdf.

31 *CIA triad, supra* note 22.

32 "Failover is a backup operational mode in which the functions of a system component (such as a processor, server, network, or database, for example) are assumed by secondary system components when the primary component becomes unavailable through either failure or scheduled down time." *Failover* [definition], TECHTARGET, http://searchstorage.techtarget.com/definition/failover.

33 "RAID (redundant array of independent disks; originally redundant array of inexpensive disks) provides a way of storing the same data in different places (thus, redundantly) on multiple hard disks." *RAID* [definition], TECHTARGET, http://searchstorage.techtarget.com/definition/RAID.

34 *CIA triad, supra* note 22.

35 Martha Neil, *Unaware "Anonymous" Existed Until Friday, Partner of Hacked Law Firm Is Now Fielding FBI Phone Calls*, ABA JOURNAL, Feb. 6, 2012, http://www.abajournal.com/mobile/article/unaware_that_anonymous_hacking_group_existed_until_friday_law_firm_partner/; *see also* Scott Shane, *F.B.I. Admits Hacker Group's Eavesdropping*, N. Y. TIMES, Feb. 3, 2012, http://www.nytimes.com/2012/02/04/us/fbi-admits-hacker-groups-eavesdropping.html?_r=0 (law firm website defaced and then taken down).

web host's servers being "wiped clean of all client email," the firm was rendered entirely unable to effectively represent its clients during the downtime.[36]

Threats facing law firms can range from unreliable server performance that results from improper maintenance; to natural disasters (e.g., fire) that can destroy the primary data locations; to malicious activities, such as DDOS attacks[37] that prevent access to the data.

6.2.2   Identifying Security Needs

To identify the security needs of a law firm, it is necessary to undertake a thorough dissection of the firm's existing information technology and security systems.[38] The goals of this dissection are threefold: "(1) Understand what data must be protected, (2) Identify possible threats to that data, and (3) Forecast the possible consequences of a successful attack on the data in question."[39]

ISO 27001 can be of great service in identifying and achieving these goals.[40] Other procedures for identifying data assets can be as simple as interviewing various employees who control information technology systems at various points in a piece of data's lifecycle.[41] An early, thorough interview can be immensely helpful when determining the idiosyncrasies of an organization, which makes the remaining steps far easier.

Once an organization's data assets are clearly identified, it is then necessary to classify the data to better understand what security requirements will be needed.[42] This is an important step for an organization to take because:

> [b]y classifying data, [an organization] can prepare generally to identify the risk and impact of an incident based upon what type of data is involved. The classifications . . . give a basis for determining the impact based upon the level and type of access to data. Together, data classification and level of access drive the business impact which will determine the response, escalation and notifications of incidents.[43]

Being able to determine this information allows an organization to consider what types of threats each class of data may be exposed to. It is important to

---

36 Scott Shane, *F.B.I. Admits Hacker Group's Eavesdropping*, N. Y. TIMES, Feb. 3, 2012, http://www.nytimes.com/2012/02/04/us/fbi-admits-hacker-groups-eavesdropping.html?_r=0.

37 "A distributed denial-of-service (DDoS) attack is one in which a multitude of compromised systems attack a single target, thereby causing denial of service for users of the targeted system. The flood of incoming messages to the target system essentially forces it to shut down, thereby denying service to the system to legitimate users." Margaret Rouse, *Distributed Denial-of-Service Attack (DDoS)* [definition], TECHTARGET, http://searchsecurity.techtarget.com/definition/distributed-denial-of-service-attack.

38 *Cyber Risk Assessment and Management*, STAYSAFEONLINE, https://staysafeonline.org/re-cyber/cyber-risk-assessment-management/.

39 *Id.*

40 ISO/IEC 27001:2013, § 4.2.1.

41 *Every Company Needs to Have a Security Program*, APPLIEDTRUST, https://www.appliedtrust.com/resources/security/every-company-needs-to-have-a-security-program.

42 Chris Rodgers, *Data Classification: Why Is It Important for Information Security?*, SECURESTATE, Apr. 3, 2012), https://www.securestate.com/blog/2012/04/03/data-classification-why-is-it-important-for-information-security.

43 *Id.*

recognize that threats to data can come in countless forms, ranging from active attacks,[44] to passive attacks,[45] and even to accidental threats.[46] Understanding what threats an organization's data faces allows that organization to properly identify what steps must be taken to develop meaningful information security procedures and practices.

Once an organization has properly identified and classified its data, as well as what threats that data may face, it must begin to analyze the risks associated with those threats, specifically the potential impact of the threat that has been recognized.[47] This step is critical because it essentially allows an organization to add the previous steps together into a single metric: *risk*. An organization can understand its risk only after it understands its data assets, potential threats, and the harms that may materialize as a result of those threats actually occurring.

The final concern an organization must consider in identifying its security needs is what steps it should take to mitigate the harm that may result from a threat actually occurring.[48] This mitigation can be either technical or procedural, or, in the case of small-impact threats, it can be a conscious decision to accept the harm and take no action. These choices must be carefully considered by the organization, but once the decisions are reached, the organization will have a comprehensive identification of all of its security needs.

6.2.3   Implementing a Security Program

Once an organization has identified relevant risks and chosen appropriate mitigation options, the next step is to implement an information security management system (ISMS).[49] ISO 27001 is the 27000-series standard that governs the implementation of an ISMS. Due to the breadth of its applicability, ISO 27001 does not give explicit instructions on implementing an ISMS, but rather "includes suggestions for documentation, internal audits, continual improvement, and corrective and preventive action."[50] Organizations that choose to adopt ISO 27001 are free to choose whichever specific information security controls are applicable to their information security situations, drawing on those listed in the standard's appendix[51] and potentially supplementing them with other *a la carte* options (sometimes known as *extended control sets*).[52]

---

44 *Active Attack* [definition], TECHTARGET: WHATIS, http://whatis.techtarget.com/definition/active-attack.
45 *Passive Attack*, TECHTARGET: WHATIS, http://whatis.techtarget.com/definition/passive-attack.
46 Scott Cole, *Accidental Insider Threats and Four Ways to Prevent Them*, TECHTARGET, http://searchsecurity.techtarget.com/tip/Accidental-insider-threats-and-four-ways-to-prevent-them.
47 PROCEEDINGS OF THE SEVENTH INTERNATIONAL NETWORK CONFERENCE (INC 2008).
48 *Id.*
49 "An information security management system (ISMS) is a set of policies and procedures for systematically managing an organization's sensitive data. The goal of an ISMS is to minimize risk and ensure business continuity by pro-actively limiting the impact of a security breach." *Information Security Management System (ISMS)* [definition], TECHTARGET, http://searchsecurity.techtarget.in/definition/information-security-management-system-ISMS.
50 *Id.*
51 ISO/IEC 27001:2013, Annex A.
52 ISO/IEC 27001, ISECT, http://www.iso27001security.com/html/27001.html.

Implementing an ISMS requires the implementation of training and awareness programs for both personnel and management regarding the ISMS.[53] Untrained personnel often pose the greatest risk to an organization's information security systems.

There is a well-established three-step process for training employees: (1) Define which knowledge and skills are required; (2) perform trainings to reach the desired level of knowledge and skill; and (3) measure whether each individual has achieved that desired level of knowledge and skill.[54] The first step develops directly from the security needs that have been identified earlier, and the third requires regular contact and employee oversight, but the second step is the one that provides for the actual training of employees.[55] There are many resources that can be utilized to train employees, from having them attend formal courses,[56] to disseminating literature, or even hiring training consultants.[57] In addition to formal training, it is very important for an organization to raise a general awareness about the ISMS that is being implemented.[58]

6.2.4 Ensuring Compliance

ISO 27001 also lays out a framework for monitoring and improving security practices at an organization throughout the life of an ISMS.[59] The framework is quite extensive, but there are several distinct practices that an organization should follow in order to properly ensure its compliance with the ISMS: (1) execute monitoring and reviewing procedures, (2) regularly review the effectiveness of the ISMS, (3) continually re-evaluate the risk, (4) perform periodic audits, and (5) continually strive for improvement.[60]

The procedures for monitoring and review should be tailored to promptly detect errors in processing, quickly identify security breaches, allow management to determine the effectiveness of controls, and determine the effectiveness of reactions to security incidents.[61] Furthermore, in reviewing these processes, an organization should take into account the objectives of the security program, assess whether or not the selected controls are appropriate and effective, and consider any feedback received from the various stakeholders.[62]

As an organization monitors possible threats, it should also review risk assessments at regular intervals, as well as after any major organizational changes.

---

53 Dejan Kosutic, *How to Perform Training & Awareness for ISO 27001 and ISO 22301*, 27001 Academy, May 19, 2014, http://advisera.com/27001academy/blog/2014/05/19/how-to-perform-training-awareness-for-iso-27001-and-iso-22301/.

54 *Id.*

55 *Id.*

56 *See, e.g., Information Security Training Courses ISO/IEC 27001*, BSI, http://www.bsigroup.com/en-US/ISO-IEC-27001-Information-Security/Training-courses-for-ISO-27001/.

57 *See, e.g., ISO Consultancy*, http://www.itgovernance.co.uk/iso27001_consultancy.aspx.

58 Kosutic, *supra* note 53.

59 ISO 27001, § 4.2.3.

60 ISO 27001, § 4.2.4.

61 Rhand Leal, *How to Perform Monitoring and Measurement in ISO 27001*, 27001 Academy, June 8, 2015, http://advisera.com/27001academy/blog/2015/06/08/how-to-perform-monitoring-and-measurement-in-iso-27001/.

62 *Id.*

This review should take into account any changes to the threat, technology, and/ or regulatory environment in which an organization may find itself.

In sum, ISO 27001 directs organizations to seek to continually improve their information security processes and procedures. To that end, it directs organizations to regularly implement identified improvements in the ISMS, communicate these improvements to all stakeholders, and ensure that improvements are geared toward the stated objectives of the ISMS.[63]

6.3   ISO Scope and Certification

As useful as the ISO standards are for organizations, certification is essential because it enables a firm to clearly convey its compliance with the standards to potential clients and colleagues. Furthermore, certification helps ensure that an organization meaningfully monitors its own compliance and creates a strong incentive for the firm to maintain close adherence to the standards. As discussed earlier, the ISO is a body dedicated to the development and evaluation of standards, but it is not a certification body. This means that neutral third parties must be brought in to verify an organization's compliance with the standards,[64] and often consultants are hired to help prepare an organization for the certification audit.

6.3.1   Auditing an Organization's Compliance

There are many domestic and international bodies, both accredited and unaccredited, which an organization can hire to certify its compliance with the ISO standards.[65] These auditing bodies do not help an organization plan and implement an ISMS, but rather are brought in after an ISMS is established to verify that the organization is compliant with the standards. These bodies develop their procedures pursuant to the ISO's Committee on Conformity Assessment (CASCO) standards.[66] CASCO offers a mandatory minimum for what an ISO certification must be, but bodies can differentiate their standards. In performing an audit, the auditor

---

63 *Stages of the Development of International Standards*, ISO, https://web.archive.org/web/20071005165948/http://www.iso.org/ iso/standards_development/processes_and_procedures/stages_description.htm.

64 *Certification…*, ISO, http://www.iso.org/iso/home/standards/certification.htm.

65 Examples of these bodies are: (1) ANAB (ANSI-ASQ National Accreditation Board), (2) UKAS: United Kingdom Accreditation Service, (3) JAB: Japan Accreditation Board, (4) DAkkS: German Accreditation. Almerindo Graziano, *Choosing the Right Accreditation Body for Your ISO27001 Compliance*, Aug. 15, 2015, https://www.linkedin.com/pulse/choosing-right-certification-body-your-iso27001-almerindo-graziano.

66 *Id.*

will look at certain "documented information" items,[67] for both fit and purpose.[68] Choosing an independent auditor is a very important decision, but it only becomes relevant after an organization has developed and implemented its ISMS.

6.3.2   Preparing to Obtain an ISO Certification

While an organization can attempt to implement the necessary framework in order to get ISO certified by itself, it is almost always the case that an organization will retain an outside company to help aid it in the process of developing and implementing an ISMS. These companies differentiate themselves through any one (or more) of the following factors: objectives, cost, qualifications, staffing, location, and fit.[69] Beginning with objectives, an organization must consider what its short- and long-term ISMS goals are and see if there are consulting companies that can help it become ISO 27001 certified, as well as plan for its future beyond a simple certification.[70] Cost, qualifications, and staffing are all related to each other, meaning that if an organization is willing to pay, it can get large numbers of highly qualified people—but, generally speaking, an organization must determine its needs and budget accordingly. For example, the qualification and staffing needs of a sole practitioner who deals with personal injury cases may be vastly different from those of a multinational firm that deals with highly sensitive financial and employment data. Location can also be a potentially important element: Because the consulting company will be working closely with the organization, it would generally make sense to pick a consultant that is geographically near the organization—but only if it meets the key criteria listed earlier. *Fit* is a catch-all

---

67 See *ISO/IEC 27001:2013 Information technology—Security techniques—Information security management systems—Requirements (second edition)*, INFORMATION SECURITY STANDARDS, http://iso27001security.com/html/27001.html.

The following are the mandatory documents:
1. ISMS scope (per clause 4.3)
2. Information security policy (clause 5.2)
3. Information security risk assessment process (clause 6.1.2)
4. Information security risk treatment process (clause 6.1.3)
5. Information security objectives (clause 6.2)
6. Evidence of the competence of the people working in information security (clause 7.2)
7. Other ISMS-related documents deemed necessary by the organization (clause 7.5.1b)
8. Operational planning and control documents (clause 8.1)
9. The results of the risk assessments (clause 8.2)
10. The decisions regarding risk treatment (clause 8.3)
11. Evidence of the monitoring and measurement of information security (clause 9.1)
12. The ISMS internal audit program and the results of audits conducted (clause 9.2)
13. Evidence of top management reviews of the ISMS (clause 9.3)
14. Evidence of nonconformities identified and corrective actions arising (clause 10.1)
15. Various others: Annex A, which is normative, mentions but does not fully specify further documentation, including the rules for acceptable use of assets, access control policy, operating procedures, confidentiality or nondisclosure agreements, secure system engineering principles, information security policy for supplier relationships, information security incident response procedures, relevant laws, regulations and contractual obligations plus the associated compliance procedures and information security continuity procedures.

ISO 27001, § 4.2.1.

68 *Information Security Management System (ISMS)* [definition], TECHTARGET, http://searchsecurity.techtarget.in/definition/information-security-management-system-ISMS.

69 John Verry, *6 Factors for Choosing the Right ISO 27001 Consulting Firm*, PIVOTPOINT SECURITY, Feb. 18, 2014, http://www.pivotpointsecurity.com/blog/how-to-choose-the-right-iso-27001-consulting-firm/.

70 This can range from considering what an organization's long-term information governance goals are, to considering additional regulatory or legal factors in the implementation of an ISMS.

term that stands for the proposition that an organization should only hire a company with which it feels it can work productively, because ultimately that is the only way to ensure that the organization will stick to the ISMS that is prepared. The choice of consulting firm is incredibly important, and an organization should spend the time and resources necessary to ensure that it is making the right choice. This does not mean that an organization should seek the most expensive consultant, but rather that, in order to get the best outcome management and the information technology (IT) department should collaborate to determine the actual needs of the law firm.

6.3.3 Scope of an ISMS

Mere certification of compliance with ISO 27001, however, does not provide the full picture of a company's information security management practices. The scope of a certification allows an organization to define the data that will be protected in the organization at a given time.[71] The scope of a certification is one of the most critical elements in the entire certification process, because it defines what is subject to the ISMS—and that can vary greatly. For example, an organization can be fully compliant with ISO 27001, but only for a small portion of its information technology systems, which limits the applicability of the ISMS and thus the certification in its entirety.[72] The scope of an ISMS is considered so critically important that a document outlining the scope of the ISMS is a mandatory requirement to obtain an ISO certification.[73]

Even though the ISO 27001 certification is intended for implementation on an enterprise-wide level,[74] Section 4.3 allows an organization to define its own scope for an ISMS in each of its departments.[75] This flexibility enables an organization to perform a phased implementation of its ISMS, which is, often, a more feasible option for an organization than a single organization-wide implementation, which can be cost prohibitive.[76]

6.3.4 ISO 27001's Statement of Applicability

In addition to the scope of an ISO certification, an organization must prepare a *Statement of Applicability*, which is also a mandatory requirement under ISO 27001, Section 6.[77] While there is no explicit definition of a Statement of Applicability, the term "refers to the output from the information security risk assessments and, in

---

71 Dejan Kosutic, *How to Define the ISMS Scope*, ADVISERA 27001 ACADEMY, http://advisera.com/27001academy/knowledge-base/how-to-define-the-isms-scope/.
72 *Id.*
73 *Supra* note 52.
74 *Id.*
75 *Id.*
76 *Planning For and Implementing ISO 27001*, 4 ISACA (2011), http://www.isaca.org/Journal/archives/2011/Volume-4/Pages/Planning-for-and-Implementing-ISO27001.aspx
77 *See* ISO 27001, § 6.1.

particular, the decisions around treating those risks."[78] This means that an organization must specify which security measures it intends to use and in what ways those measures will be implemented.[79] Often, organizations use a matrix to match identified risks with the security measures that will be used to address them.[80] The matrix generally uses ISO 27002 as a guide for identifying risk controls, but any consistent framework is sufficient to achieve the goal.

The scope of a certification and the Statement of Applicability are critical elements of an organization's ISMS. Third parties use these documents to contextualize and understand an organization's ISO 27001 certification and get a broader sense of that organization's information security practices and circumstances.[81] These documents enable an organization to provide clear assurances to potential clients, partners, and other third parties so that those groups can comfortably rely on the organization's ability to keep their data secure. This assurance process is increasingly becoming more important for both large, institutional clients, and savvier, smaller clients when they look for a law firm.[82]

6.4   Conclusion

ISO standards, particularly ISO 27001, can be a great resource for organizations that are taking steps to secure their information security systems. As clients begin to focus on the security of their data, law firms will need to look to widely accepted standards, such as ISO 27001, in order to convince their clients of their ability to protect the clients' interests. Even though certification is currently optional, not pursuing it may soon be damaging to the business interests of law firms. The flexibility of the ISO 27001 certification, which comes from the scope of the certification as well as the Statement of Applicability, allows the standards to be adopted by a wide range of firms, ranging from sole practitioners to large multinational shops.

---

78 *Id.*

79 Dejan Kosutic, *The Importance of Statement of Applicability for ISO 27001*, Advisera 27001 Academy, http://advisera.com/27001academy/knowledgebase/the-importance-of-statement-of-applicability-for-iso-27001/.

80 *Id.* ("The information security control objectives and controls from [ISO 27002] are provided as a checklist at Annex A in order to avoid 'overlooking necessary controls'"). Organizations may use a different framework, such as NIST SP800-55, the ISF standard, BMIS and/or COBIT, or a custom approach. *See infra* Chapter 4.

81 Kosutic, *supra* note 79:

If an organization's ISO/IEC 27001 scope only notes "Acme Ltd. Department X", for example, the associated certificate says absolutely nothing about the state of information security in "Acme Ltd. Department Y" or indeed "Acme Ltd." as a whole. Similarly, if for some reason management decides to accept malware risks without implementing conventional antivirus controls, the certification auditors may well challenge such a bold assertion but, *provided* the associated analyses and decisions were sound, that alone would not be justification to refuse to certify the organization since antivirus controls are not in fact mandatory.

82 Matthew Goldstein, *Law Firms Are Pressed on Security for Data*, N.Y. Times: Dealbook, Mar. 26, 2014, http://dealbook.nytimes.com/2014/03/26/law-firms-scrutinized-as-hacking-increases/?_r=1.

DEFENDING AGAINST THREATS THROUGH INFORMATION SHARING

Cindy Donaldson and Bill Nelson

It wasn't that long ago that defending a bank's assets meant adding a rider with a shotgun to the stagecoach or closing the door and spinning the dial on a Mosler bank vault. But over the past few decades, as banking has gone digital, banks have had to evolve their cyber defenses rapidly to mitigate the risk of attacks in the virtual world. The legal services industry handles valuable assets as well, trusted with equally important data and intellectual property on behalf of clients. Therefore, the legal services industry is quickly embracing new approaches to combat evolving threats, including actively sharing information on threats and vulnerabilities within its own community.[1]

7.1 Legal Services: A Big Target for Hackers

As described throughout this book, clients entrust their law firms with many types of sensitive data that those law firms are obligated to protect. Sensitive data that firms may handle include[2]:

- Information about pending mergers or acquisitions
- Information subject to attorney-client privilege
- Intellectual property and business intelligence
- Corporate documents containing business information such as finances or information about client employees
- Information related to potential criminal activities or civil actions
- Strategic information that could be used in legal proceedings
- Personally identifiable information (PII) such as social security numbers and personal health information (PHI); some firms may also handle credit cardholder data
- Information relating to bids and appeals on government contracts

Today's cybercriminals, hacktivists, and even nation state entities have learned that law firms are a veritable gold mine of valuable information that can be used for a variety of nefarious purposes, from espionage to theft to ransom to harming reputations.

---

1 Failure to safeguard information is a violation of the Rules of Professional Conduct and the Personal Information Protection and Electronic Documents Act.
2 *See* Ch. 1.

7.2 Attacks Are Getting More Frequent and More Sophisticated

Unfortunately, the sophistication and frequency of attacks is increasing. There are numerous tactics that malicious cyber actors use to target institutions. The following are some of the types of threats that law firms face[3]:

- Targeted spear-phishing campaigns and "whaling" campaigns, which are spear-phishing campaigns targeting VIPs and top executives
- Ransomware attacks, which use malware that restricts access to a computer or system and demands that a ransom be paid
- Distributed denial-of-service (DDOS) attacks, which can impair critical services on networks or computer systems
- Destructive malware attacks, which destroy data or can even cause physical damage to computer hardware
- Insider threats, including "social engineering" attacks that deceive employees into revealing sensitive information

7.3 There Is Hope: Law Firms Should Prepare and Share

Although performing risk assessments, developing risk prevention plans, and implementing incident response plans are all critical to defending against cyber threats, information sharing is another key aspect of cybersecurity that can benefit all members of a given sector. *Information sharing* is part of a community defense strategy whereby multiple firms share cyber threat information to collectively improve their knowledge of threats in the community and better prepare for them. Firms can determine ahead of time when, what, and how to share sensitive information regarding cyber and physical threats, as well as mitigation strategies. By pooling their collective data, expertise, and wisdom, individual members of a community each contribute to the security and well-being of the community as a whole. Information sharing can result in improving decision making, avoiding redundant effort, and promoting alignment with the most up-to-date best practices. This type of sharing is usually facilitated by an information-sharing entity called an information sharing and analysis center (ISAC) or information sharing and analysis organization (ISAO). ISAOs are industry-specific and enable member

---

3 *See* Ch. 2.

organizations to properly and effectively share information within a community to respond to the latest threats and vulnerabilities.

The importance of information sharing was highlighted by President Obama's 2015 executive order promoting private-sector cybersecurity information sharing. The order calls for the Secretary of Homeland Security to strongly encourage the development and formation of ISAOs.[4]

7.4 The Legal Services Information Sharing and Analysis Organization

In August 2015, the Legal Services Information Sharing and Analysis Organization (LS-ISAO) was launched, and many eligible law firms began participating immediately. In fact, members not only began participating, but also started sharing information about cyber threats and vulnerabilities. The LS-ISAO is a member-driven organization and has created a trusted community among eligible law firms while building upon existing security-focused practices in the legal industry.

Part of the reason that the LS-ISAO has been able to get up and running so quickly is that it chose to partner with the Financial Services Information Sharing and Analysis Center (FS-ISAC). The FS-ISAC was formed in 1999 and is known as one of the most mature information-sharing organizations, serving 7,000 members around the world as of 2016. FS-ISAC has been praised as "a key resource on cyber threats for the financial sector and has built a high level of trust over the years."[5] The FS-ISAC is a 501(c)(6) nonprofit organization and is funded entirely by its member firms and sponsors.

The FS-ISAC serves as an independent, trusted third party that facilitates sharing of actionable threat, vulnerability, and incident information in a nonattributable and trusted manner among members, the financial services sector, and industry and governmental partners. In 2014, the objective to assist other sectors was incorporated into FS-ISAC's Strategic Plan, both to provide support for the "greater good" of information sharing and also to support the sharing of information across other sectors, if other sectors desire to do so.

The LS-ISAO is leveraging the experience and infrastructure that the FS-ISAC has established, enabling the legal sector to focus on improving its defenses rather than the operation of an ISAO. This collaboration enables faster implementation of capabilities and the ability for the LS-ISAO to focus on its core mission of actionable sharing among members. In the future, the LS-ISAO will also potentially be

---

4 Exec. Order No. 13,691 (Feb. 13, 2015). Retrieved from https://www.whitehouse.gov/the-press-office/2015/02/13/executive-order-promoting-private-sector-cybersecurity-information-shari. In fact, the Department of Homeland Security is actively assisting ISAOs and ISACs through a strengthened cyber information-sharing program. *See* https://www.dhs.gov/ciscp.

5 GAO, *Bank and Other Depository Regulators Need Better Data Analytics and Depository Institutions Want More Usable Threat Information*, July 2, 2015, http://www.gao.gov/products/GAO-15-509.

able to take advantage of new solutions and technologies developed by the FS-ISAC and DTCC, including Soltra Edge, a threat intelligence-sharing platform.[6]

At the time of the release of this book, an LS-ISAO member must be a law firm duly licensed or registered with each regulatory body that it is subject to where it needs to be so licensed, with at least a majority of its lawyers admitted to practice working in and authorized to practice law in the United States, United Kingdom, or Canada (however, these requirements are subject to change by a majority of the members). To apply, a firm submits an application and is vetted against these criteria. If approved and the firm agrees to the subscriber agreement, the firm submits a subscription fee and becomes an LS-ISAO member. Currently, benefits include:

- Participation on an intelligence-sharing list server providing relevant and actionable threat alerts, vulnerabilities, and advisories from vendors and government agencies
- Access to a list of participating law firms
- Receipt of a monthly LS-ISAO report
- Monthly member meeting
- Member submission capability, which allows the members to submit information directly to an independent party
- Crisis notification and coordination
- Participation in member surveys
- Participation in LS-ISAO events

Sharing information is not mandatory, but is encouraged. To ensure that the information shared is protected, each member agrees to comply with the LS-ISAO Traffic Light Protocol, which is a method for protecting information in information sharing. The originator of the information assigns a "classification" using the colors of a traffic light, and that classification determines if and how the information can be shared with others.

LS-ISAO members are currently receiving relevant and actionable threat information alerts, vulnerabilities, and advisories. Recently, an intelligence report identified several law firms as targets for cybercriminal activity, and LS-ISAO was able to quickly respond and disseminate the intelligence to each firm individually. In the event of a crisis, a crisis notification system is also in place to bring the members together to address their needs. As the LS-ISAO grows, it will likely engage in threat automation and threat exercises, and in general its level of sophistication will increase to combat increasingly sophisticated threats.

Firms can share all types of information that may be beneficial to the community. If desired, law firms can share threat indicators about cyber threats such as malicious sites, known malware, denial-of-service attacks, and/or phishing, as well as information about software vulnerabilities pertinent to the legal industry. Information and analysis sharing help law firms understand the changing threat

---

6 Soltra, *Soltra Launches New Membership Program for Soltra Edge Users* [press release], Sept. 9, 2015, https://www.fsisac.com/sites/default/files/news/Soltra%20Press%20Release%20Membership%20Model%20FINAL%203.pdf.

environment, develop stronger controls, and respond more effectively to threats and attacks. Information about physical threats, ranging from hurricanes to geopolitical intelligence, can be shared as well. In fact, physical security is becoming increasingly integrated with cybersecurity, as cyberattacks have the potential to cause serious physical damage and physical intrusions can severely compromise cybersecurity.[7] Whether isolated or integrated, understanding both cyber and physical threats assists with protecting a law firm's business, its clients' businesses, and its response to incidents.

Depending on the type of information, LS-ISAO members can share information just between two specific members, between larger "circles of trust" (groups comprised of multiple firms), or with the entire community (if appropriate). Following the Traffic Light Protocol, the member providing the information determines how that information is distributed. A member can submit with attribution or anonymously to an LS-ISAO security analyst, as well as directly to another member. Generally speaking, as an ISAO matures, the circles of trust foster collaboration among certain groups with common interests, such as organizations that work in certain industries or organizations that have similar functional needs (e.g., business resiliency or compliance and audit).

ISAOs also typically put in place mechanisms for properly sharing information between the private sector and governmental entities, including law enforcement and the intelligence community. As one of the sources of information for intelligence, the government also shares information that can be useful for combating threats. The LS-ISAO is able to leverage the FS-ISAC's established processes for receiving and analyzing information from the government.[8]

The information shared within the LS-ISAO is put into a centralized, highly secure repository of threat indicators. Over time, this becomes a knowledge base that can help firms understand what types of threats and attacks are trending and evolving and how the firms' cyber defenses should evolve as well. Collective intelligence is gathered from various open-source websites. When appropriate, information is put into an alert and distributed to the membership. Submissions are made directly to an LS-ISAO analyst, either over the telephone or via email, or members can submit anonymous submissions directly through an LS-ISAO portal. In any event, the analyst gathers the information from the submission, scrubs it for attribution, and sends it to the originator for final approval before disseminating it to the membership.

In a short amount of time, the LS-ISAO has grown substantially. It is already sharing timely, relevant, actionable cyber and physical security information and analysis among law firms to help protect the community from cyber and physical threats. This has resulted in greater resilience, integrity, and stability of LS-ISAO members and improved their ability to provide services critical to the community. For additional information, visit www.ls-isao.com.

---

7 E.g., Stuxnet.
8 As noted earlier, the DHS is actively assisting ISAOs and ISACs through a strengthened cyber information and sharing program. *See* https://www.dhs.gov/ciscp.

8

HOW LAW FIRMS MAY USE THE CYBERSECURITY FRAMEWORK FOR CRITICAL INFRASTRUCTURE

Daniel Garrie and Rick Borden

Companies, especially those in regulated industries or where large amounts of personal information are processed, are under increasing pressure to ensure the safety of their supply chain. A number of large breaches have occurred through compromise of vendors. Law firms, because of their access to clients and those clients' most important information, are increasingly being seen as threat vectors. In financial services alone, the Office of the Comptroller of the Currency, the Securities and Exchange Commission (SEC), the Consumer Financial Protection Bureau (CFPB), the Commodity Futures Trading Commission (CFTC), and the New York Department of Financial Services, among others, have emphasized the importance of management of third-party risk. Law firms have to be able to show that they have the security policies and procedures in place to appropriately protect their clients' information.

There are many standards relating to policies and procedures for information security (IS) programs. Many companies have historically relied on the International Standards Organization (ISO) 27001/27002 (ISO 27001) standards as the basis for their information security policies. However, U.S. government contractors are required by the agencies to which they provide products or services to comply with the Federal Information Security Management Act (FISMA), enacted in 2002 and updated in December of 2014.[1] FISMA designates the National Institute of Standards and Technology (NIST) as having the responsibility for developing detailed security standards for federal computer systems.[2] Since 2002, NIST has been developing cybersecurity standards, constantly revising these standards to address the ever-changing cyber threats. Most federal agencies, and their contractors, are required to follow the NIST *Special Publication 800-53* rev. 4 (NIST 800-53) standard.

In February 2013, President Obama issued Executive Order (EO) 13636, "Improving Critical Infrastructure Cybersecurity," directing NIST to work with stakeholders to develop a voluntary framework for reducing cyber risks to critical infrastructure. On February 12, 2014, NIST issued version 1 of the Framework for Improving Critical Infrastructure Cybersecurity (the Framework). Applicable infrastructure under the EO includes utilities providing energy and water as well as sectors covering transportation, financial services, communications, health care and public health, food and agriculture, chemical and other facilities, dams, key manufacturers, emergency services, and several others. Companies covered by the EO have been requested to provide information to the federal regulator overseeing their sector as to how their policies and procedures meet the requirements outlined by the Framework.

NIST cybersecurity standards are recognized as forerunners in information security benchmarking and widely adopted both inside and outside the federal government by a variety of entities looking for cybersecurity guidance.[3] As a result, states have begun to leverage the Framework to improve the security of their infrastructures,[4] regulators have been utilizing the Framework to assess the strength of

---

1 40 U.S.C. § 11331; 44 U.S.C. § 3544; 15 U.S.C. §§ 278g-3, 278g-4. This statutory standard applies to many governmental contractors, thus extending its sphere over a portion of the private sector. 44 U.S.C. § 3544(a) and (b).

2 44 U.S.C. § 3544; 40 U.S.C. § 11331(b)(1)(C).

3 *See* Debevoise & Plimpton, *New Federal Guidance on Cybersecurity for Mobile Devices*, Feb. 9, 2015, https://www.nist.gov/news-events/news/2016/02/cybersecurity-rosetta-stone-celebrates-two-years-success.

4 http://www.naic.org/documents/committees_ex_cybersecurity_tf_final_principles_for_cybersecurity_guidance.pdf.

companies' information security policies and procedures,[5] technology companies have been developing products and services aligned with the Framework,[6] and major insurance providers have begun to offer policies tied to the Framework.[7]

It seems inevitable that the companies in critical infrastructure will start, requesting information (some already have) from those in their supply chain relating to how those entities' information security programs compare to the Framework. These vendors will in turn request similar information from their vendors, and so on. In short, the Framework is rapidly becoming the de facto document for comparison and assessment of cybersecurity programs in the United States. Law offices may find NIST to be instructive in developing an information security program.

This chapter first provides an overview of the NIST Framework, and then discusses some of the ways the NIST Framework and other NIST standards can be used by law firms. It concludes by examining some of the effects the NIST Framework has had since it was issued.

8.1 Overview of the NIST Framework

The NIST Framework consists of three primary components: (1) the Framework Core, which sets out the basic functions of a successful cybersecurity program; (2) the Framework Implementation Tiers, which provide guidance in assessing an organization's cybersecurity practices; and (3) the Framework Profiles, which help organizations develop an overview of how their cybersecurity goals fit into the overall goals, needs, and operations of the organization.[8]

8.2 The Framework Core: Functions of a Successful Cybersecurity Program

The Framework Core describes cybersecurity functions that are commonly employed across organizations to achieve specific security outcomes; it also provides examples of existing standards to facilitate implementation of those functions.[9] It essentially

---

5 FFIEC, *FFIEC Cybersecurity Assessment Tool*, June 20, 2015, https://www.ffiec.gov/pdf/cybersecurity/FFIEC_CAT_CEO_Board_Overview_June_2015_PDF1.pdf; U.S. Securities and Exchange Commission, Division of Investment Management, *IM Guidance Update: Cybersecurity Guidance* (No. 2015-02), Apr. 2015, https://www.sec.gov/investment/im-guidance-2015-02.pdf; U.S. Department of Energy, Office of Electricity Delivery & Energy Reliability, *Reducing Cyber Risk to Critical Infrastructure: NIST Framework*, http://energy.gov/oe/services/cybersecurity/reducing-cyber-risk-critical-infrastructure-nist-framework; U.S. Department of Health and Human Services, Office for Civil Rights, *Addressing Gaps in Cybersecurity: OCR Releases Crosswalk Between HIPAA Security Rule and NIST Cybersecurity Framework*, http://www.hhs.gov/hipaa/for-professionals/security/nist-security-hipaa-crosswalk/.
6 http://www-01.ibm.com/common/ssi/cgi-bin/ssialias?htmlfid=WGW03064USEN.
7 http://www.aba.com/Tools/Function/Documents/2016Cyber-Insurance-Buying-Guide_FINAL.pdf.
8 National Institute of Standards and Technology, FRAMEWORK FOR IMPROVING CRITICAL INFRASTRUCTURE CYBERSECURITY (Feb. 12, 2014).
9 https://www.nist.gov/sites/default/files/documents/cyberframework/cybersecurity-framework-021214.pdf at pp. 20–35.

answers, at a high level, a significant question: "What do we want our cybersecurity risk management program to do?" Law firms that do not have a comprehensive cybersecurity program in place may use the Framework Core to determine what their cybersecurity risk management program should achieve. Of course, any program should be adjusted in accordance with the size of and services provided by the firm.

The Framework Core addresses five basic functions to be included in an organization's cybersecurity risk management program:

- *Identification.* Understand the systems in use and engage in risk assessment and asset management.
- *Protection.* Develop safeguards for delivery of critical infrastructure services (e.g., training, data security, and access control).
- *Detection.* Perform detection and monitoring activities to identify cybersecurity events.
- *Response.* Create action plans for responding to and mitigating cybersecurity events.
- *Recovery.* Restore damaged capabilities and make improvements after an incident.

These five functions should serve as part of a guiding principle for firms; they are not intended to form a serial path or lead to a static desired end state. When addressing these functions, it is important that law firms realize that the answers to this question are ideally derived concurrently and continuously to form an operational culture that addresses the dynamic cybersecurity risk.

These five functions are divided into categories and subcategories to be as specific as possible. These subdivisions further delineate the five functions based on cybersecurity outcomes tied to programmatic needs and particular activities. Examples of categories include "Asset Management," "Access Control," and "Detection Processes." Subcategories further divide a category into specific outcomes of technical and/or management activities. They provide a set of results that, while not exhaustive, help support achievement of the outcomes in each category. Examples of subcategories include "External information systems are catalogued," "Data-at-rest is protected," and "Notifications from detection systems are investigated."

The Framework is set up to accommodate multiple standards that organizations use, including ISO 27001 and NIST 800-53, plus a number of others. Each of the specific section references within such standards are delineated such that an organization may look to the other standards for comparison. However, by including the various sections within topical areas of each of the five functions, it is easier for an organization to build, or assess the comprehensiveness of, its cybersecurity program.

These five functions contained in the Framework should be tailored to a law firm accounting for size, location, and operations of the firm. The Framework is flexible and encourages a high level of interactivity with the firm. Table 8-1 sets forth the entire Framework Core.[10]

---

10 See Framework, *supra* note 8.

Table 8-1: Framework Core: Asset Management

IDENTIFY (ID)	Asset Management (ID. AM): The data, personnel, devices, systems, and facilities that enable the organization to achieve business purposes are identified and managed consistent with their relative importance to business objectives and the organization's risk strategy.	ID.AM-1: Physical devices and systems within the organization are inventoried	• **CCS CSC** 1 • **COBIT 5** BAI09.01, BAI09.02 • **ISA 62443-2-1:2009** 4.2.3.4 • **ISA 62443-3-3:2013** SR 7.8 • **ISO/IEC 27001:2013** A.8.1.1, A.8.1.2 • **NIST SP 800-53 Rev. 4** CM-8
		ID.AM-2: Software platforms and applications within the organization are inventoried	• **CCS CSC** 2 • **COBIT 5** BAI09.01, BAI09.02, BAI09.05 • **ISA 62443-2-1:2009** 4.2.3.4 • **ISA 62443-3-3:2013** SR 7.8 • **ISO/IEC 27001:2013** A.8.1.1, A.8.1.2 • **NIST SP 800-53 Rev. 4** CM-8
		ID.AM-3: Organizational communication and data flows are mapped	• **CCS CSC** 1 • **COBIT 5** DSS05.02 • **ISA 62443-2-1:2009** 4.2.3.4 • **ISO/IEC 27001:2013** A.13.2.1 • **NIST SP 800-53 Rev. 4** AC-4, CA-3, CA-9, PL-8
		ID.AM-4: External information systems are catalogued	• **COBIT 5** APO02.02 • **ISO/IEC 27001:2013** A.11.2.6 • **NIST SP 800-53 Rev. 4** AC-20, SA-9
		ID.AM-5: Resources (e.g., hardware, devices, data, and software) are prioritized based on their classification, criticality, and business value	• **COBIT 5** APO03.03, APO03.04, BAI09.02 • **ISA 62443-2-1:2009** 4.2.3.6 • **ISO/IEC 27001:2013** A.8.2.1 • **NIST SP 800-53 Rev. 4** CP-2, RA-2, SA-14
		ID.AM-6: Cybersecurity roles and responsibilities for the entire workforce and third-party stakeholders (e.g., suppliers, customers, partners) are established	• **COBIT 5** APO01.02, DSS06.03 • **ISA 62443-2-1:2009** 4.3.2.3.3 • **ISO/IEC 27001:2013** A.6.1.1 • **NIST SP 800-53 Rev. 4** CP-2, PS-7, PM-11

8.2.1 Identify

The Framework Core begins its section on identification with "Asset Management (ID.AM)," which directs organizations to identify data assets, understand the flow of data, and prioritize their data assets based on a variety of factors. Lawyers and law firms, as well as any other organization serious about securing its data, must undertake this step in order to understand what data assets they have, as well as how data flows. Another critical element of this provision is the classification of data assets, which is a prominent consideration throughout the entire Framework Core.

The section then goes on to direct organizations to identify the business environment (ID.BE) they are operating in, specifically the organization's place in the national critical infrastructure (see Table 8-2). Furthermore, this step affords an organization an opportunity to understand the mechanics of its business and the implications that those mechanics may have on its cybersecurity policies. Furthermore, it is important to recognize that ultimately the Framework Core, while critically important to a business, is not the center of the business. It is important to identify and understand an organization's objectives and goals, in order to properly understand how the NIST Framework Core can help ensure a smooth path to achieving those goals and objectives. Law firms must understand this principle in both designing their own cybersecurity systems as well as advising clients on doing the same.

Next, the Framework Core turns to Identifying Governance (ID.GV; see Table 8-3), which directs organizations to identify and establish procedures to manage and monitor the various requirements that may inform their cybersecurity policies. This section also directs an organization to identify all of the legal and regulatory requirements it may be subjected to, and how those requirements are being managed. This step is uniquely important for law firms because it forces firms to identify the legal and regulatory requirements that they may become subject to as they are retained by various regulated entities. Furthermore, in this step a firm will begin to identify how its cybersecurity processes actually address the risks to which it is subject, which will show the gaps that will have be addressed later (per the Framework Core).

Finally, the Framework Core turns from identifying and understanding the organization to Risk Assessment (ID.RA; see Table 8-4). This critical step directs organizations to determine the threats that they may face, as well as the likelihood and impact of a given threat. This is an important step because it begins to direct an organization's focus toward the threats it may face. What is important is that in the same overarching step, organizations are determining both the threats they face, and the context of those threats (likelihood and impact). As discussed throughout this book, although law firms are a compelling target for cybercriminals, such firms cannot be expected to create perfect cybersecurity policies immediately; rather, they must prioritize elimination of the greatest risks, and go down the line thereafter. It is this process that is at the heart of a firm engaging in risk assessment.

Table 8-2: Framework Core: Business Environment

IDENTIFY (ID)	Business Environment (ID.BE): The organization's mission, objectives, stakeholders, and activities are understood and prioritized; this information is used to inform cybersecurity roles, responsibilities, and risk management decisions.	ID.BE-1: The organization's role in the supply chain is identified and communicated	• **COBIT 5** APO08.04, APO08.05, APO10.03, APO10.04, APO10.05 • **ISO/IEC 27001:2013** A.15.1.3, A.15.2.1, A.15.2.2 • **NIST SP 800-53 Rev. 4** CP-2, SA-12
		ID.BE-2: The organization's place in critical infrastructure and its industry sector are identified and communicated	• **COBIT 5** APO02.06, APO03.01 • **NIST SP 800-53 Rev. 4** PM-8
		ID.BE-3: Priorities for organizational mission, objectives, and activities are established and communicated	• **COBIT 5** APO02.01, APO02.06, APO03.01 • **ISA 62443-2-1:2009** 4.2.2.1, 4.2.3.6 • **NIST SP 800-53 Rev. 4** PM-11, SA-14
		ID.BE-4: Dependencies and critical functions for delivery of critical services are established	• **ISO/IEC 27001:2013** A.11.2.2, A.11.2.3, A.12.1.3 • **NIST SP 800-53 Rev. 4** CP-8, PE-9, PE-11, PM-8, SA-14
		ID.BE-5: Resilience requirements to support delivery of critical services are established	• **COBIT 5** DSS04.02 • **ISO/IEC 27001:2013** A.11.1.4, A.17.1.1, A.17.1.2, A.17.2.1 • **NIST SP 800-53 Rev. 4** CP-2, CP-11, SA-14

The identification phase of the Framework Core concludes with directing organizations to identify and create a Risk Management Strategy (ID.RM; see Table 8-5). This step builds on risk assessment, but takes it a step further, by now asking the organization to determine and express its tolerance for risk. Once again, the Framework Core demonstrates its applicability to all types of law firms by asking them to determine their risk tolerances. This will allow a firm to use all of the information it has collected in the prior steps to determine its risk tolerance, and to contextualize that tolerance in the type of industries and sectors that it and its clients may be working in.

8.2.2 Protect

The Framework Core next moves from identifying the threats and risks to a firm's assets to developing policies and procedures to protect those assets. This process

Table 8-3: Framework Core: Governance

IDENTIFY (ID)	Governance (ID.GV): The policies, procedures, and processes to manage and monitor the organization's regulatory, legal, risk, environmental, and operational requirements are understood and inform the management of cybersecurity risk.	ID.GV-1: Organizational information security policy is established	• **COBIT 5** APO01.03, EDM01.01, EDM01.02 • **ISA 62443-2-1:2009** 4.3.2.6 • **ISO/IEC 27001:2013** A.5.1.1 • **NIST SP 800-53 Rev. 4-1** controls from all families
		ID.GV-2: Information security roles and responsibilities are coordinated and aligned with internal roles and external partners	• **COBIT 5** APO13.12 • **ISA 62443-2-1:2009** 4.3.2.3.3 • **ISO/IEC 27001:2013** A.6.1.1, A.7.2.1 • **NIST SP 800-53 Rev. 4** PM-1, PS-7
		ID.GV-3: Legal and regulatory requirements regarding cybersecurity, including privacy and civil liberties obligations, are understood and managed	• **COBIT 5** MEA03.01, MEA03.04 • **ISA 62443-2-1:2009** 4.4.3.7 • **ISO/IEC 27001:2013** A.18.1 • **NIST SP 800-53 Rev. 4-1** controls from all families (except PM-1)
		ID.GV-4: Governance and risk management processes address cybersecurity risks	• **COBIT 5** DSS04.02 • **ISA 62443-2-1:2009** 4.2.3.1, 4.2.3.3, 4.2.3.8, 4.2.3.9, 4.2.3.11, 4.3.2.4.3, 4.3.2.6.3 • **NIST SP 800-53 Rev. 4** PM-9, PM-11

begins with Access Control (PR.AC; see Table 8-6), which directs an organization to limit both local and remote access to assets and facilities to authorized individuals only. Law firms must pay careful attention to this step because of the uniquely sensitive client information that they deal with. Though lawyers in the firm are colleagues, they must be able to set permissions on who can access certain files. Furthermore, there may be many nonlawyers on the network who should not be able to access client files. Additionally, as the practice of law evolves, remote access is becoming more and more important to attorneys, which means that access must be more carefully managed.

Table 8-4: Framework Core: Risk Assessment

IDENTIFY (ID)	Risk Assessment (ID.RA): The organization understands the cybersecurity risk to organizational operations (including mission, functions, image, or reputation), organizational assets, and individuals.	ID.RA-1: Asset vulnerabilities are identified and documented	• **CCS CSC** 4 • **COBIT 5** APO12.01, APO12.02, APO12.03, APO12.04 • **ISA 62443-2-1:2009** 4.2.3, 4.2.3.7, 4.2.3.9, 4.2.3.12 • **ISO/IEC 27001:2013** A.12.6.1, A.18.2.3 • **NIST SP 800-53 Rev. 4** CA-2, CA-7, CA-8, RA-3, RA-5, SA-5, SA-11, SI-2, SI-4, SI-5
		ID.RA-2: Threat and vulnerability information is received from information-sharing forums and sources	• **ISA 62443-2-1:2009** 4.2.3, 4.2.3.9, 4.2.3.12 • **ISO/IEC 27001:2013** A.6.1.4 • **NIST SP 800-53 Rev. 4** PM-15, PM-16, SI-5
		ID.RA-3: Threats, both internal and external, are identified and documented	• **COBIT 5** APO12.01, APO12.02, APO12.03, APO12.04 • **ISA 62443-2-1:2009** 4.2.3, 4.2.3.9, 4.2.3.12 • **NIST SP 800-53 Rev. 4** RA-3, SI-5, PM-12, PM-16
		ID.RA-4: Potential business impacts and likelihoods are identified	• **COBIT 5** DSS04.02 • **ISA 62443-2-1:2009** 4.2.3, 4.2.3.9, 4.2.3.12 • **NIST SP 800-53 Rev. 4** RA-2, RA-3, PM-9, PM-11, SA-14
		ID.RA-5: Threats, vulnerabilities, likelihoods, and impacts are used to determine risk	• **COBIT 5** APO12.02 • **ISO/IEC 27001:2013** A.12.6.1 • **NIST SP 800-53 Rev. 4** RA-2, RA-3, PM-16
		ID.RA-6: Risk responses are identified and prioritized	• **COBIT 5** APO12.05, APO13.02 • **NIST SP 800-53 Rev. 4** PM-4, PM-9

The protection section then moves on to Awareness and Training (PR.AT; see Table 8-7) as the next step of protecting assets. This is arguably the most important step in the protection of assets, because, as seen throughout this book, untrained employees pose a huge threat to organizations. Because law firms are particularly vulnerable, they must take heightened steps to train employees. Currently, hackers actively target law firm employees to obtain access to firm data and systems. The first step in the process of stopping this practice is to train all employees, and ensure that all groups within the firm understand their roles and responsibilities with respect to securing the firm.

Table 8-5: Framework Core: Risk Management Strategy

IDENTIFY (ID)	Risk Management Strategy (ID.RM): The organization's priorities, constraints, risk tolerances, and assumptions are established and used to support operational risk decisions.	**ID.RM-1:** Risk management processes are established, managed, and agreed to by organizational stakeholders	• **COBIT 5** APO12.04, APO12.05, APO13.02, BAI02.03, BAI04.02 • **ISA 62443-2-1:2009** 4.3.4.2 • **NIST SP 800-53 Rev. 4** PM-9
		ID.RM-2: Organizational risk tolerance is determined and clearly expressed	• **COBIT 5** APO12.06 • **ISA 62443-2-1:2009** 4.3.2.6.5 • **NIST SP 800-53 Rev. 4** PM-9
		ID.RM-3: The organization's determination of risk tolerance is informed by its role in critical infrastructure and sector-specific risk analysis	• **NIST SP 800-53 Rev. 4** PM-8, PM-9, PM-11, SA-14

Next, the Framework Core turns to Data Security (PR.DS; see Table 8-8), which directs organizations to manage their data in a way that is consistent with the risk strategies that were determined in the identification section. This section breaks down each type of data asset that must be protected, in the interests of ensuring the integrity of the software, firmware, and assets of an organization. Data security must be a priority for all law firms.

We next turn to developing Information Protection Processes and Procedures (PR.IP; see Table 8-9), which directs organizations to develop processes to protect data throughout its entire lifecycle. Law firms must remember that data does not only exist when it is sitting on the desktops of its attorneys. Data must be managed throughout its lifecycle, and even its destruction must be carefully protected. As long as the data exists, hackers can attempt to gain access to it; therefore, law firms must create policies and procedures ensuring the security of that data. Importantly, firms must also regularly update these policies in order to stay current with threats they may face, as well as prepare for the fallout that may come as the result of a data breach.

The penultimate step in the protection of data is the maintenance of a firm's computer systems (PR.MA; see Table 8-10). Computer systems must be regularly maintained to ensure that they are working as they are meant to be working. Of importance to law firms, there is a special focus on remote maintenance in order to ensure no unauthorized access.

Table 8-6: Framework Core: Protect

PROTECT (PR)	Access Control (PR.AC): Access to assets and associated facilities is limited to authorized users, processes, or devices, and to authorized activities and transactions.	PR.AC-1: Identities and credentials are managed for authorized devices and users	• **CCS CSC** 16 • **COBIT 5** DSS05.04, DSS06.03 • **ISA 62443-2-1:2009** 4.3.3.5.1 • **ISA 62443-3-3:2013** SR 1.1, SR 1.2, SR 1.3, SR 1.4, SR 1.5, SR 1.7, SR 1.8, SR 1.9 • **ISO/IEC 27001:2013** A.9.2.1, A.9.2.2, A.9.2.4, A.9.3.1, A.9.4.2, A.9.4.3 • **NIST SP 800-53 Rev. 4** AC-2, IA Family
		PR.AC-2: Physical access to assets is managed and protected	• **COBIT 5** DSS01.04, DSS05.05 • **ISA 62443-2-1:2009** 4.3.3.3.2, 4.3.3.3.8 • **ISO/IEC 27001:2013** A.11.1.1, A.11.1.2, A.11.1.4, A.11.1.6, A.11.2.3 • **NIST SP 800-53 Rev. 4** PE-2, PE-3, PE-4, PE-5, PE-6, PE-9
		PR.AC-3: Remote access is managed	• **COBIT 5** APO13.01, DSS01.04, DSS05.03 • **ISA 62443-2-1:2009** 4.3.3.6.6 • **ISA 62443-3-3:2013** SR 1.13, SR 2.6 • **ISO/IEC 27001:2013** A.6.2.2, A.13.1.1, A.13.2.1 • **NIST SP 800-53 Rev. 4** AC-17, AC-19, AC-20
		PR.AC-4: Access permissions are managed, incorporating the principles of least privilege and separation of duties	• **CCS CSC** 12, 15 • **ISA 62443-2-1:2009** 4.3.3.7.3 • **ISA 62443-3-3:2013** SR 2.1 • **ISO/IEC 27001:2013** A.6.1.2, A.9.1.2, A.9.2.3, A.9.4.1, A.9.4.4 • **NIST SP 800-53 Rev. 4** AC-2, AC-3, AC-5, AC-6, AC-16
		PR.AC-5: Network integrity is protected, incorporating network segregation where appropriate	• **ISA 62443-2-1:2009** 4.3.3.4 • **ISA 62443-3-3:2013** SR 3.1, SR 3.8 • **ISO/IEC 27001:2013** A.13.1.1, A.13.1.3, A.13.2.1 • **NIST SP 800-53 Rev. 4** AC-4, SC-7

Table 8-7: Framework Core: Awareness and Training

PROTECT (PR)	**Awareness and Training (PR.AT):** The organization's personnel and partners are provided cybersecurity awareness education and are adequately trained to perform their information security-related duties and responsibilities consistent with related policies, procedures, and agreements.	**PR.AT-1:** All users are informed and trained	• **CCS CSC** 9 • **COBIT 5** APO07.03, BAI05.07 • **ISA 62443-2-1:2009** 4.3.2.4.2 • **ISO/IEC 27001:2013** A.7.2.2 • **NIST SP 800-53 Rev. 4** AT-2, PM-13
		PR.AT-2: Privileged users understand roles and responsibilities	• **CCS CSC** 9 • **COBIT 5** APO07.02, DSS06.03 • **ISA 62443-2-1:2009** 4.3.2.4.2, 4.3.2.4.3 • **ISO/IEC 27001:2013** A.6.1.1, A.7.2.2 • **NIST SP 800-53 Rev. 4** AT-3, PM-13
		PR.AT-3: Third-party stakeholders (e.g., suppliers, customers, partners) understand roles and responsibilities	• **CCS CSC** 9 • **COBIT 5** APO07.03, APO10.04, APO10.05 • **ISA 62443-2-1:2009** 4.3.2.4.2 • **ISO/IEC 27001:2013** A.6.1.1, A.7.2.2 • **NIST SP 800-53 Rev. 4** PS-7, SA-9
		PR.AT-4: Senior executives understand roles and responsibilities	• **CCS CSC** 9 • **COBIT 5** APO07.03 • **ISA 62443-2-1:2009** 4.3.2.4.2 • **ISO/IEC 27001:2013** A.6.1.1, A.7.2.2 • **NIST SP 800-53 Rev. 4** AT-3, PM-13
		PR.AT-5: Physical and information security personnel understand roles and responsibilities	• **CCS CSC** 9 • **COBIT 5** APO07.03 • **ISA 62443-2-1:2009** 4.3.2.4.2 • **ISO/IEC 27001:2013** A.6.1.1, A.7.2.2 • **NIST SP 800-53 Rev. 4** AT-3, PM-13

Table 8-8: Framework Core: Data Security

PROTECT (PR)	**Data Security (PR.DS):** Information and records (data) are managed consistent with the organization's risk strategy to protect the confidentiality, integrity, and availability of information.	**PR.DS-1:** Data-at-rest is protected	• **CCS CSC** 17 • **COBIT 5** APO01.06, BAI02.01, BAI06.01, DSS06.06 • **ISA 62443-3-3:2013** SR 3.4, SR 4.1 • **ISO/IEC 27001:2013** A.8.2.3 • **NIST SP 800-53 Rev. 4** SC-28
		PR.DS-2: Data-in-transit is protected	• **CCS CSC** 17 • **COBIT 5** APO01.06, DSS06.06 • **ISA 62443-3-3:2013** SR 3.1, SR 3.8, SR 4.1, SR 4.2 • **ISO/IEC 27001:2013** A.8.2.3, A.13.1.1, A.13.2.1, A.13.2.3, A.14.1.2, A.14.1.3 • **NIST SP 800-53 Rev. 4** SC-8
		PR.DS-3: Assets are formally managed throughout removal, transfers, and disposition	• **COBIT 5** BAI09.03 • **ISA 62443-2-1:2009** 4. 4.3.3.3.9, 4.3.4.4.1 • **ISA 62443-3-3:2013** SR 4.2 • **ISO/IEC 27001:2013** A.8.2.3, A.8.3.1, A.8.3.2, A.8.3.3, A.11.2.7 • **NIST SP 800-53 Rev. 4** CM-8, MP-6, PE-16
		PR.DS-4: Adequate capacity to ensure availability is maintained	• **COBIT 5** APO13.01 • **ISA 62443-3-3:2013** SR 7.1, SR 7.2 • **ISO/IEC 27001:2013** A.12.3.1 • **NIST SP 800-53 Rev. 4** AU-4, CP-2, SC-5
		PR.DS-5: Protections against data leaks are implemented	• **CCS CSC** 17 • **COBIT 5** APO01.06 • **ISA 62443-3-3:2013** SR 5.2 • **ISO/IEC 27001:2013** A.6.1.2, A.7.1.1, A.7.1.2, A.7.3.1, A.8.2.2, A.8.2.3, A.9.1.1, A.9.1.2, A.9.2.3, A.9.4.1, A.9.4.4, A.9.4.5, A.13.1.3, A.13.2.1, A.13.2.3, A.13.2.4, A.14.1.2, A.14.1.3 • **NIST SP 800-53 Rev. 4** AC-4, AC-5, AC-6, PE-19, PS-3, PS-6, SC-7, SC-8, SC-13, SC-31, SI-4
		PR.DS-6: Integrity checking mechanisms are used to verify software, firmware, and information integrity	• **ISA 62443-3-3:2013** SR 3.1, SR 3.3, SR 3.4, SR 3.8 • **ISO/IEC 27001:2013** A.12.2.1, A.12.5.1, A.14.1.2, A.14.1.3 • **NIST SP 800-53 Rev. 4** SI-7
		PR.DS-7: The development and testing environment(s) are separate from the production environment	• **COBIT 5** BAI07.04 • **ISO/IEC 27001:2013** A.12.1.4 • **NIST SP 800-53 Rev. 4** CM-2

Table 8-9: Framework Core: Information Protection Processes and Procedures

PROTECT (PR)	**Information Protection Processes and Procedures (PR.IP):** Security policies (that address purpose, scope, roles, responsibilities, management commitment, and coordination among organizational entities), processes, and procedures are maintained and used to manage protection of information systems and assets.	**PR.IP-1:** A baseline configuration of information technology/ industrial control systems is created and maintained	• **CCS CSC** 3, 10 • **COBIT 5** BAI10.01, BAI10.02, BAI10.03, BAI10.05 • **ISA 62443-2-1:2009** 4.3.4.3.2, 4.3.4.3.3 • **ISA 62443-3-3:2013** SR 7.6 • **ISO/IEC 27001:2013** A.12.1.2, A.12.5.1, A.12.6.2, A.14.2.2, A.14.2.3, A.14.2.4 • **NIST SP 800-53 Rev. 4** CM-2, CM-3, CM-4, CM-5, CM-6, CM-7, CM-9, SA-10
		PR.IP-2: A System Development Life Cycle to manage systems is implemented	• **COBIT 5** APO13.01 • **ISA 62443-2-1:2009** 4.3.4.3.3 • **ISO/IEC 27001:2013** A.6.1.5, A.14.1.1, A.14.2.1, A.14.2.5 • **NIST SP 800-53 Rev. 4** SA-3, SA-4, SA-8, SA-10, SA-11, SA-12, SA-15, SA-17, PL-8
		PR.IP-3: Configuration change control processes are in place	• **COBIT 5** BAI06.01, BAI01.06 • **ISA 62443-2-1:2009** 4.3.4.3.2, 4.3.4.3.3 • **ISA 62443-3-3:2013** SR 7.6 • **ISO/IEC 27001:2013** A.12.1.2, A.12.5.1, A.12.6.2, A.14.2.2, A.14.2.3, A.14.2.4 • **NIST SP 800-53 Rev. 4** CM-3, CM-4, SA-10
		PR.IP-4: Backups of information are conducted, maintained, and tested periodically	• **COBIT 5** APO13.01 • **ISA 62443-2-1:2009** 4.3.4.3.9 • **ISA 62443-3-3:2013** SR 7.3, SR 7.4 • **ISO/IEC 27001:2013** A.12.3.1, A.17.1.2A.17.1.3, A.18.1.3 • **NIST SP 800-53 Rev. 4** CP-4, CP-6, CP-9
		PR.IP-5: Policy and regulations regarding the physical operating environment for organizational assets are met	• **COBIT 5** DSS01.04, DSS05.05 • **ISA 62443-2-1:2009** 4.3.3.3.1 4.3.3.3.2, 4.3.3.3.3, 4.3.3.3.5, 4.3.3.3.6 • **ISO/IEC 27001:2013** A.11.1.4, A.11.2.1, A.11.2.2, A.11.2.3 • **NIST SP 800-53 Rev. 4** PE-10, PE-12, PE-13, PE-14, PE-15, PE-18

PROTECT (PR)		**PR.IP-6:** Data is destroyed according to policy	• **COBIT 5** BAI09.03 • **ISA 62443-2-1:2009** 4.3.4.4.4 • **ISA 62443-3-3:2013** SR 4.2 • **ISO/IEC 27001:2013** A.8.2.3, A.8.3.1, A.8.3.2, A.11.2.7 • **NIST SP 800-53 Rev. 4** MP-6
		PR.IP-7: Protection processes are continuously improved	• **COBIT 5** APO11.06, DSS04.05 • **ISA 62443-2-1:2009** 4.4.3.1, 4.4.3.2, 4.4.3.3, 4.4.3.4, 4.4.3.5, 4.4.3.6, 4.4.3.7, 4.4.3.8 • **NIST SP 800-53 Rev. 4** CA-2, CA-7, CP-2, IR-8, PL-2, PM-6
		PR.IP-8: Effectiveness of protection technologies is shared with appropriate parties	• **ISO/IEC 27001:2013** A.16.1.6 • **NIST SP 800-53 Rev. 4** AC-21, CA-7, SI-4
		PR.IP-9: Response plans (Incident Response and Business Continuity) and recovery plans (Incident Recovery and Disaster Recovery) are in place and managed	• **COBIT 5** DSS04.03 • **ISA 62443-2-1:2009** 4.3.2.5.3, 4.3.4.5.1 • **ISO/IEC 27001:2013** A.16.1.1, A.17.1.1, A.17.1.2 • **NIST SP 800-53 Rev. 4** CP-2, IR-8
		PR.IP-10: Response and recovery plans are tested	• **ISA 62443-2-1:2009** 4.3.2.5.7, 4.3.4.5.11 • **ISA 62443-3-3:2013** SR 3.3 • **ISO/IEC 27001:2013** A.17.1.3 • **NIST SP 800-53 Rev.4** CP-4, IR-3, PM-14
		PR.IP-11: Cybersecurity is included in human resources practices (e.g., deprovisioning, personnel screening)	• **COBIT 5** APO07.01, APO07.02, APO07.03, APO07.04, APO07.05 • **ISA 62443-2-1:2009** 4.3.3.2.1, 4.3.3.2.2, 4.3.3.2.3 • **ISO/IEC 27001:2013** A.7.1.1, A.7.3.1, A.8.1.4 • **NIST SP 800-53 Rev. 4** PS Family
		PR.IP-12: A vulnerability management plan is developed and implemented	• **ISO/IEC 27001:2013** A.12.6.1, A.18.2.2 • **NIST SP 800-53 Rev. 4** RA-3, RA-5, SI-2

Table 8-10: Framework Core: Maintenance

PROTECT (PR)	**Maintenance (PR.MA):** Maintenance and repairs of industrial control and information system components is performed consistent with policies and procedures.	**PR.MA-1:** Maintenance and repair of organizational assets is performed and logged in a timely manner, with approved and controlled tools	• **COBIT 5** BAI09.03 • **ISA 62443-2-1:2009** 4.3.3.3.7 • **ISO/IEC 27001:2013** A.11.1.2, A.11.2.4, A.11.2.5 • **NIST SP 800-53 Rev. 4** MA-2, MA-3, MA-5
		PR.MA-2: Remote maintenance of organizational assets is approved, logged, and performed in a manner that prevents unauthorized access	• **COBIT 5** DSS05.04 • **ISA 62443-2-1:2009** 4.3.3.6.5, 4.3.3.6.6, 4.3.3.6.7, 4.4.4.6.8 • **ISO/IEC 27001:2013** A.11.2.4, A.15.1.1, A.15.2.1 • **NIST SP 800-53 Rev. 4** MA-4

The protection section of the Framework Core concludes with Protective Technology (PR.PT; see Table 8-11). This step directs organizations to ensure the security and resilience of their systems. This step requires regular auditing to ensure that the policies established as a result of the previous steps are being followed.

8.2.3 Detect

We then begin the detection section of the Framework Core, which is first concerned with detecting Anomalies and Events (DE.AE; see Table 8-12). Whereas the Identification and Protection sections develop the security policies that are created, the following three sections all show how a firm can detect, respond to, and recover from an inevitable attack—but all that must begin with the detection of anomalies and events. Following detection, firms must then analyze any events, and determine what their potential impact might have been.

In addition to detecting anomalies and events, organizations must implement continuous monitoring in order to detect cyber threats (DE.CM; see Table 8-13). This is a critical step because it will allow firms to proactively detect early threats, and work to combat them before there is a substantial breach. Importantly, this step directs firms to monitor external service providers that may have access to the firm's internal network.

The Detection step culminates with the maintenance of Detection Processes (DE.DP; see Table 8-14). This means that firms must define roles for employees in the detection process in order to ensure accountability. Firms are also directed to regularly test and improve their detection processes.

8.2.4 Respond

The Framework Core then turns to Responses, beginning with Response Planning (RS.RP; see Table 8-15). It is critical to execute a response to a breach, or attempted

Table 8-11: Framework Core: Protective Technology

PROTECT (PR)	Protective Technology (PR.PT): Technical security solutions are managed to ensure the security and resilience of systems and assets, consistent with related policies, procedures, and agreements.	PR.PT-1: Audit/log records are determined, documented, implemented, and reviewed in accordance with policy	• **CCS CSC** 14 • **COBIT 5** APO11.04 • **ISA 62443-2-1:2009** 4.3.3.3.9, 4.3.3.5.8, 4.3.4.4.7, 4.4.2.1, 4.4.2.2, 4.4.2.4 • **ISA 62443-3-3:2013** SR 2.8, SR 2.9, SR 2.10, SR 2.11, SR 2.12 • **ISO/IEC 27001:2013** A.12.4.1, A.12.4.2, A.12.4.3, A.12.4.4, A.12.7.1 • **NIST SP 800-53 Rev. 4** AU Family
		PR.PT-2: Removable media is protected and its use restricted according to policy	• **COBIT 5** DSS05.02, APO13.01 • **ISA 62443-3-3:2013** SR 2.3 • **ISO/IEC 27001:2013** A.8.2.2, A.8.2.3, A.8.3.1, A.8.3.3, A.11.2.9 • **NIST SP 800-53 Rev. 4** MP-2, MP-4, MP-5, MP-7
		PR.PT-3: Access to systems and assets is controlled, incorporating the principle of least functionality	• **COBIT 5** DSS05.02 • **ISA 62443-2-1:2009** 4.3.3.5.1, 4.3.3.5.2, 4.3.3.5.3, 4.3.3.5.4, 4.3.3.5.5, 4.3.3.5.6, 4.3.3.5.7, 4.3.3.5.8, 4.3.3.6.1, 4.3.3.6.2, 4.3.3.6.3, 4.3.3.6.4, 4.3.3.6.5, 4.3.3.6.6, 4.3.3.6.7, 4.3.3.6.8, 4.3.3.6.9, 4.3.3.7.1, 4.3.3.7.2, 4.3.3.7.3, 4.3.3.7.4 • **ISA 62443-3-3:2013** SR 1.1, SR 1.2, SR 1.3, SR 1.4, SR 1.5, SR 1.6, SR 1.7, SR 1.8, SR 1.9, SR 1.10, SR 1.11, SR 1.12, SR 1.13, SR 2.1, SR 2.2, SR 2.3, SR 2.4, SR 2.5, SR 2.6, SR 2.7 • **ISO/IEC 27001:2013** A.9.1.2 • **NIST SP 800-53 Rev. 4** AC-3, CM-7
		PR.PT-4: Communications and control networks are protected	• **CCS CSC** 7 • **COBIT 5** DSS05.02, APO13.01 • **ISA 62443-3-3:2013** SR 3.1, SR 3.5, SR 3.8, SR 4.1, SR 4.3, SR 5.1, SR 5.2, SR 5.3, SR 7.1, SR 7.6 • **ISO/IEC 27001:2013** A.13.1.1, A.13.2.1 • **NIST SP 800-53 Rev. 4** AC-4, AC-17, AC-18, CP-8, SC-7

breach, in a timely and efficient manner. During or in the wake of a breach, firms may be chaotic places, but working from a planned response will ensure that the event is handled as efficiently and properly as possible.

Table 8-12: Framework Core: Anomalies and Events

DETECT (DE)	**Anomalies and Events (DE.AE):** Anomalous activity is detected in a timely manner and the potential impact of events is understood.	**DE.AE-1:** A baseline of network operations and expected data flows for users and systems is established and managed	• **COBIT 5** DSS03.01 • **ISA 62443-2-1:2009** 4.4.3.3 • **NIST SP 800-53 Rev. 4** AC-4, CA-3, CM-2, SI-4
		DE.AE-2: Detected events are analyzed to understand attack targets and methods	• **ISA 62443-2-1:2009** 4.3.4.5.6, 4.3.4.5.7, 4.3.4.5.8 • **ISA 62443-3-3:2013** SR 2.8, SR 2.9, SR 2.10, SR 2.11, SR 2.12, SR 3.9, SR 6.1, SR 6.2 • **ISO/IEC 27001:2013** A.16.1.1, A.16.1.4 • **NIST SP 800-53 Rev. 4** AU-6, CA-7, IR-4, SI-4
		DE.AE-3: Event data are aggregated and correlated from multiple sources and sensors	• **ISA 62443-3-3:2013** SR 6.1 • **NIST SP 800-53 Rev. 4** AU-6, CA-7, IR-4, IR-5, IR-8, SI-4
		DE.AE-4: Impact of events is determined	• **COBIT 5** APO12.06 • **NIST SP 800-53 Rev. 4** CP-2, IR-4, RA-3, SI-4
		DE.AE-5: Incident alert thresholds are established	• **COBIT 5** APO12.06 • **ISA 62443-2-1:2009** 4.2.3.10 • **NIST SP 800-53 Rev. 4** IR-4, IR-5, IR-8

We then turn to Communications (RS.CO; see Table 8-16). This is an important step because how a firm communicates its breach, and in what ways, can be of utmost importance. It is important to get governmental regulators involved early in the process to ensure the maximum likelihood of a proper response to the event.

The Framework Core then directs organizations to analyze the event (see Table 8-17) in order to ensure meaningful recovery activities. Cyberattacks in today's world are an inevitability. Being able to understand and analyze an attack can be invaluable in preventing future attacks. Forensics play a critical role in understanding the attack and preparing for future ones.

In addition to analyzing the attack, organizations must also contain and mitigate the effects of the attack (RS.MI; see Table 8-18). The scope of an attack can be incredibly wide-ranging; law firms, in the wake of an event, must ensure that they have properly contained the attack and mitigated any harm that may have resulted from it.

Table 8-13: Framework Core: Security Continuous Monitoring

DETECT (DE)	Security Continuous Monitoring (DE.CM): The information system and assets are monitored at discrete intervals to identify cybersecurity events and verify the effectiveness of protective measures.	DE.CM-1: The network is monitored to detect potential cybersecurity events	• **CCS CSC** 14, 16 • **COBIT 5** DSS05.07 • **ISA 62443-3-3:2013** SR 6.2 • **NIST SP 800-53 Rev. 4** AC-2, AU-12, CA-7, CM-3, SC-5, SC-7, SI-4
		DE.CM-2: The physical environment is monitored to detect potential cybersecurity events	• **ISA 62443-2-1:2009** 4.3.3.3.8 • **NIST SP 800-53 Rev. 4** CA-7, PE-3, PE-6, PE-20
		DE.CM-3: Personnel activity is monitored to detect potential cybersecurity events	• **ISA 62443-3-3:2013** SR 6.2 • **ISO/IEC 27001:2013** A.12.4.1 • **NIST SP 800-53 Rev. 4** AC-2, AU-12, AU-13, CA-7, CM-10, CM-11
		DE.CM-4: Malicious code is detected	• **CCS CSC** 5 • **COBIT 5** DSS05.01 • **ISA 62443-2-1:2009** 4.3.4.3.8 • **ISA 62443-3-3:2013** SR 3.2 • **ISO/IEC 27001:2013** A.12.2.1 • **NIST SP 800-53 Rev. 4** SI-3
		DE.CM-5: Unauthorized mobile code is detected	• **ISA 62443-3-3:2013** SR 2.4 • **ISO/IEC 27001:2013** A.12.5.1 • **NIST SP 800-53 Rev. 4** SC-18, SI-4. SC-44
		DE.CM-6: External service provider activity is monitored to detect potential cybersecurity events	• **COBIT 5** APO07.06 • **ISO/IEC 27001:2013** A.14.2.7, A.15.2.1 • **NIST SP 800-53 Rev. 4** CA-7, PS-7, SA-4, SA-9, SI-4
		DE.CM-7: Monitoring for unauthorized personnel, connections, devices, and software is performed	• **NIST SP 800-53 Rev. 4** AU-12, CA-7, CM-3, CM-8, PE-3, PE-6, PE-20, SI-4
		DE.CM-8: Vulnerability scans are performed	• **COBIT 5** BAI03.10 • **ISA 62443-2-1:2009** 4.2.3.1, 4.2.3.7 • **ISO/IEC 27001:2013** A.12.6.1 • **NIST SP 800-53 Rev. 4** RA-5

Table 8-14: Framework Core: Detection Processes

DETECT (DE)	Detection Processes (DE.DP): Detection processes and procedures are maintained and tested to ensure timely and adequate awareness of anomalous events.	DE.DP-1: Roles and responsibilities for detection are well defined to ensure accountability	• CCS CSC 5 • COBIT 5 DSS05.01 • ISA 62443-2-1:2009 4.4.3.1 • ISO/IEC 27001:2013 A.6.1.1 • NIST SP 800-53 Rev. 4 CA-2, CA-7, PM-14
		DE.DP-2: Detection activities comply with all applicable requirements	• ISA 62443-2-1:2009 4.4.3.2 • ISO/IEC 27001:2013 A.18.1.4 • NIST SP 800-53 Rev. 4 CA-2, CA-7, PM-14, SI-4
		DE.DP-3: Detection processes are tested	• COBIT 5 APO13.02 • ISA 62443-2-1:2009 4.4.3.2 • ISA 62443-3-3:2013 SR 3.3 • ISO/IEC 27001:2013 A.14.2.8 • NIST SP 800-53 Rev. 4 CA-2, CA-7, PE-3, PM-14, SI-3, SI-4
		DE.DP-4: Event detection information is communicated to appropriate parties	• COBIT 5 APO12.06 • ISA 62443-2-1:2009 4.3.4.5.9 • ISA 62443-3-3:2013 SR 6.1 • ISO/IEC 27001:2013 A.16.1.2 • NIST SP 800-53 Rev. 4 AU-6, CA-2, CA-7, RA-5, SI-4
		DE.DP-5: Detection processes are continuously improved	• COBIT 5 APO11.06, DSS04.05 • ISA 62443-2-1:2009 4.4.3.4 • ISO/IEC 27001:2013 A.16.1.6 • NIST SP 800-53 Rev. 4, CA-2, CA-7, PL-2, RA-5, SI-4, PM-14

Finally, the response section ends with directing organizations to improve their response plans (see Table 8-19). After an attack, a firm may learn a great deal about its own systems, as well as the types of threats it may face. This knowledge must be incorporated into future plans, as cyber threats will only become more and more common.

8.2.5 Recover

The final aspect of the Framework Core is recovering from an attack. This process begins with implementing a recovery plan (RC.RP; see Table 8-20). It is important to ensure that, in the wake of an attack, firms restore and update their systems and assets. Although a breach can be incredibly harmful to a firm, it is important to get the firm back to work and moving on from the attack.

Table 8-15: Framework Core: Response Planning

	Response Planning (RS.RP): Response processes and procedures are executed and maintained, to ensure timely response to detected cybersecurity events.	RS.RP-1: Response plan is executed during or after an event	• **COBIT 5** BAI01.10 • **CCS CSC** 18 • **ISA 62443-2-1:2009** 4.3.4.5.1 • **ISO/IEC 27001:2013** A.16.1.5 • **NIST SP 800-53 Rev. 4** CP-2, CP-10, IR-4, IR-8
RESPOND (RS)			

Table 8-16: Framework Core: Communications

		RS.CO-1: Personnel know their roles and order of operations when a response is needed	• **ISA 62443-2-1:2009** 4.3.4.5.2, 4.3.4.5.3, 4.3.4.5.4 • **ISO/IEC 27001:2013** A.6.1.1, A.16.1.1 • **NIST SP 800-53 Rev. 4** CP-2, CP-3, IR-3, IR-8
		RS.CO-2: Events are reported consistent with established criteria	• **ISA 62443-2-1:2009** 4.3.4.5.5 • **ISO/IEC 27001:2013** A.6.1.3, A.16.1.2 • **NIST SP 800-53 Rev. 4** AU-6, IR-6, IR-8
RESPOND (RS)	**Communications (RS.CO):** Response activities are coordinated with internal and external stakeholders, as appropriate, to include external support from law enforcement agencies.	RS.CO-3: Information is shared consistent with response plans	• **ISA 62443-2-1:2009** 4.3.4.5.2 • **ISO/IEC 27001:2013** A.16.1.2 • **NIST SP 800-53 Rev. 4** CA-2, CA-7, CP-2, IR-4, IR-8, PE-6, RA-5, SI-4
		RS.CO-4: Coordination with stakeholders occurs consistent with response plans	• **ISA 62443-2-1:2009** 4.3.4.5.5 • **NIST SP 800-53 Rev. 4** CP-2, IR-4, IR-8
		RS.CO-5: Voluntary information sharing occurs with external stakeholders to achieve broader cybersecurity situational awareness	• **NIST SP 800-53 Rev. 4** PM-15, SI-5

Much as firms must update their response plans after an attack, incorporating what they have learned, they should also update their recovery plans to ensure a better and more efficient recovery in the event of a future attack (see Table 8-21).

Table 8-17: Framework Core: Analysis

RESPOND (RS)	**Analysis (RS.AN):** Analysis is conducted to ensure adequate response and support recovery activities.	**RS.AN-1:** Notifications from detection systems are investigated	• **COBIT 5** DSS02.07 • **ISA 62443-2-1:2009** 4.3.4.5.6, 4.3.4.5.7, 4.3.4.5.8 • **ISA 62443-3-3:2013** SR 6.1 • **ISO/IEC 27001:2013** A.12.4.1, A.12.4.3, A.16.1.5 • **NIST SP 800-53 Rev. 4** AU-6, CA-7, IR-4, IR-5, PE-6, SI-4
		RS.AN-2: The impact of the incident is understood	• **ISA 62443-2-1:2009** 4.3.4.5.6, 4.3.4.5.7, 4.3.4.5.8 • **ISO/IEC 27001:2013** A.16.1.6 • **NIST SP 800-53 Rev. 4** CP-2, IR-4
		RS.AN-3: Forensics are performed	• **ISA 62443-3-3:2013** SR 2.8, SR 2.9, SR 2.10, SR 2.11, SR 2.12, SR 3.9, SR 6.1 • **ISO/IEC 27001:2013** A.16.1.7 • **NIST SP 800-53 Rev. 4** AU-7, IR-4
		RS.AN-4: Incidents are categorized consistent with response plans	• **ISA 62443-2-1:2009** 4.3.4.5.6 • **ISO/IEC 27001:2013** A.16.1.4 • **NIST SP 800-53 Rev. 4** CP-2, IR-4, IR-5, IR-8

Table 8-18: Framework Core: Mitigation

RESPOND (RS)	**Mitigation (RS.MI):** Activities are performed to prevent expansion of an event, mitigate its effects, and eradicate the incident.	**RS.MI-1:** Incidents are contained	• **ISA 62443-2-1:2009** 4.3.4.5.6 • **ISA 62443-3-3:2013** SR 5.1, SR 5.2, SR 5.4 • **ISO/IEC 27001:2013** A.16.1.5 • **NIST SP 800-53 Rev. 4** IR-4
		RS.MI-2: Incidents are mitigated	• **ISA 62443-2-1:2009** 4.3.4.5.6, 4.3.4.5.10 • **ISO/IEC 27001:2013** A.12.2.1, A.16.1.5 • **NIST SP 800-53 Rev. 4** IR-4
		RS.MI-3: Newly identified vulnerabilities are mitigated or documented as accepted risks	• **ISO/IEC 27001:2013** A.12.6.1 • **NIST SP 800-53 Rev. 4** CA-7, RA-3, RA-5

Table 8-19: Framework Core: Improvements

RESPOND (RS)	**Improvements (RS.IM):** Organizational response activities are improved by incorporating lessons learned from current and previous detection/response activities.	**RS.IM-1:** Response plans incorporate lessons learned	• **COBIT 5** BAI01.13 • **ISA 62443-2-1:2009** 4.3.4.5.10, 4.4.3.4 • **ISO/IEC 27001:2013** A.16.1.6 • **NIST SP 800-53 Rev. 4** CP-2, IR-4, IR-8
		RS.IM-2: Response strategies are updated	• **NIST SP 800-53 Rev. 4** CP-2, IR-4, IR-8

Table 8-20: Framework Core: Recovery Planning

RECOVER (RC)	**Recovery Planning (RC.RP):** Recovery processes and procedures are executed and maintained to ensure timely restoration of systems or assets affected by cybersecurity events.	**RC.RP-1:** Recovery plan is executed during or after an event	• **CCS CSC** 8 • **COBIT 5** DSS02.05, DSS03.04 • **ISO/IEC 27001:2013** A.16.1.5 • **NIST SP 800-53 Rev. 4** CP-10, IR-4, IR-8

Table 8-21: Framework Core: Improvements

RECOVER (RC)	**Improvements (RC.IM):** Recovery planning and processes are improved by incorporating lessons learned into future activities.	**RC.IM-1:** Recovery plans incorporate lessons learned	• **COBIT 5** BAI05.07 • **ISA 62443-2-1** 4.4.3.4 • **NIST SP 800-53 Rev. 4** CP-2, IR-4, IR-8
		RC.IM-2: Recovery strategies are updated	• **COBIT 5** BAI07.08 • **NIST SP 800-53 Rev. 4** CP-2, IR-4, IR-8

Finally, the Framework Core concludes with communications (RC.CO; see Table 8-22), which directs organizations to communicate, both internally and externally, in order to maximize reputational repair. It is important for firms to recognize that their public images must be restored, and confidence in their security must be returned to current and potential clients.

Table 8-22: Framework Core: Communications

RECOVER (RC)	Communications (RC.CO): Restoration activities are coordinated with internal and external parties, such as coordinating centers, Internet service providers, owners of attacking systems, victims, other CSIRTs, and vendors.	RC.CO-1: Public relations are managed	• COBIT 5 EDM03.02
		RC.CO-2: Reputation after an event is repaired	• COBIT 5 MEA03.02
		RC.CO-3: Recovery activities are communicated to internal stakeholders and executive and management teams	• NIST SP 800-53 Rev. 4 CP-2, IR-4

8.3   Assessing Cybersecurity Risk Management Practices Using the Framework Implementation Tiers

8.3.1   The Framework Implementation Tiers

Tiers describe the

> degree to which an organization's cybersecurity risk management practices exhibit the characteristics defined in the Framework (e.g., risk and threat aware, repeatable, and adaptive). The Tiers characterize an organization's practices over a range, from Partial (Tier 1) to Adaptive (Tier 4). These Tiers reflect a progression from informal, reactive responses to approaches that are agile and risk-informed. During the Tier selection process, an organization should consider its current risk management practices, threat environment, legal and regulatory requirements, business/mission objectives, and organizational constraints.[11]

Progression to higher tiers is encouraged when such a change would reduce cybersecurity risk and be cost effective. Successful implementation of the Framework is based upon achievement of the outcomes described in the organization's Target Profile(s) (described in Subsection 8.2.2) and not upon tier determination.

---

11 See FRAMEWORK, *supra* note 8, at p. 5.

8.3.2 The Framework Profiles: Snapshots of an Organization's Cybersecurity Practices

The Framework Profiles provide a mechanism to create "profiles" that reflect the overall state of cybersecurity risk management, including the alignment of cybersecurity activities with business requirements, risk tolerance, and resources. Profiles support business/mission requirements and aid in the communication of risk within and between organizations. An organization may create a "Current Profile" which is a snapshot of an organization's existing cybersecurity practices, as well as a "Target Profile" that reflects the desired state of its practices in the future. Organizations may compare these profiles to identify gaps and provide a roadmap for migrating to the target state.

A law firm can use the Framework as a key part of its systematic process for identifying, assessing, and managing cybersecurity risk. NIST standards do not necessarily have to replace existing processes; a law firm can use its current process and overlay it onto the Framework to determine gaps in its current cybersecurity risk approach and develop a roadmap for improvement. The Framework is useful at a high level, but NIST 800-53, ISO 27001, and other recognized cybersecurity standards provide more detailed guidance on various aspects of cybersecurity. By utilizing the Framework as a cybersecurity risk management tool, a law firm can determine activities that are most important to its business and its clients and prioritize expenditures to maximize the impact of the investment.

Risk assessments are a fundamental component of a comprehensive cybersecurity program. Law firms should consider third-party risk assessments; many large companies will insist on conducting their own risk assessments of law firm cybersecurity. For law offices, some of the relevant considerations may include the following[12]:

- What are the information technology network boundaries? If there are many offices spread across international boundaries with many devices (laptops, tablets, smartphones, devices from home), there are probably larger risks, so more robust security defenses may be necessary.[13]
- What data does the firm store and exchange? Depending on the sensitivity of the data stored at a firm, or on particular systems within a firm, different degrees of security will be necessary. It is also important to understand what client expectations are with respect to their information held by the firm.
- Who is inside the network's boundary? If there are business partners or contract attorneys with direct access to the firm's internal network, there is a greater insider threat than in a system limited to the law office members.
- What are the security controls? With bigger risks, firms will likely need more layers of more robust security controls.

---

12 NIST Special Publication (SP) 800-39, Managing Information Security Risk (Mar. 2011); NIST SP 800-37, Rev. 1, Guide for Applying the Risk Management Framework to Federal Information Systems (Feb. 2010).
13 See also IBM, supra note 6.

- Are the risks static? Of course not. As the risks escalate and shift over time, a firm's cybersecurity controls must adapt to the changing threat environment. This is why it is crucial not only to be aware that the risks are not static, but also to understand as precisely as possible *how* the risks are changing.

These factors are key examples of what goes into the risk assessments necessary for determining the effectiveness of a law office's cybersecurity defenses.[14]

---

14 David Z. Bodenheimer & Cheryl A. Falvey, *Cybersecurity Standards and Risk Assessments for Law Offices: Weighing the Security Risks and Safeguarding Against Cyber Threats*, https://www.crowell.com/files/Cybersecurity-Standards-and-Risk-Assessments-for-Law-Offices.pdf.

9

STRUCTURE YOUR FIRM TO MAKE IT HACKER-PROOF

Bill Spernow, Daniel Garrie, and Greg Kelley

Chapter 8 focused on perimeter measures that can be taken to keep hackers out of your law firm's system. Unfortunately, these are imperfect, which means that sometimes hackers can gain access to elements of your computer system. Companies are not helpless if this happens; in fact, with strong internal controls, thoughtful threat management, and competent staff, a company can effectively mitigate and eliminate the damage that might result from a hacker penetrating its system.

9.1   Internal Network Controls

Even with the best perimeter controls, there is always the possibility that a hacker gets into your environment. The next step in thwarting the hacker is to have internal controls that make it difficult for data to be exfiltrated. There are methods that can be used to protect your data in the event that someone unauthorized gains access.[1] Consider that an intruder, once inside, will likely be using a compromised user account. For example, a user in your firm might click on a malicious link that allows a hacker to take control of the user's computer. This hacker will most likely be able to traverse your network with that computer using the user's account.[2] A situation like this can be mitigated by restricting users' access to data.[3]

Restricting users' access to data limits what data a hacker can access and steal if a user's account or computer is compromised.[4] Law firms are typically comprised of attorneys, paralegals, litigation support, administrative staff, accounting, information technology (IT), and other departments. Do those in accounting need access to client files? Do attorneys, paralegals, and litigation support need access to payroll information? Do attorneys need access to client data related to matters in which they are not involved? The examples can go on and on. IT personnel, however, are typically an exception.

IT staff quite often have access to almost anywhere in the environment. They need to be able to access various areas to assist the firm in carrying out its mission. Furthermore, they often have access to administrative accounts that can give

---

1 Margaret Rouse, *Internal Control* [definition], TechTarget, http://searchcompliance.techtarget.com/definition/internal-control.

2 Christian Cawley, *How Do Trojan Horses Work?*, BrightHub, May 16, 2010, http://www.brighthub.com/computing/smb-security/articles/71376.aspx.

3 Macky Cruz, *Data Exfiltration in Targeted Attacks*, TrendMicro, Sept. 23, 2013, http://blog.trendmicro.com/trendlabs-security-intelligence/data-exfiltration-in-targeted-attacks/.

4 *See* Federal Trade Commission (FTC), *Start with Security: A Guide for Business*, https://www.ftc.gov/tips-advice/business-center/guidance/start-security-guide-business ("Not everyone on your staff needs unrestricted access to your network and the information stored on it. Put controls in place to make sure employees have access only on a 'need to know' basis . . . . If employees don't have to use personal information as part of their job, there's no need for them to have access to it.").

access to the entire environment.[5] Best practices for IT staff in dealing with network administrative duties are as follows:

1. Each IT staff member typically has two accounts. One account is for network administrative work and the other account is that person's day-to-day account. The network administrative account should be used sparingly: only when changes must be made or actions taken that require administrative rights.[6] Administrative accounts should not be used by IT staff when they are browsing the Internet, checking mail, and doing daily tasks that are the most likely entry points for hackers to compromise IT accounts. This can decrease the likelihood of an administrative account breach.[7]

2. Each IT staff member should have his or her own administrative account.[8] Sharing administrative accounts can damage accountability.[9] If a shared administrative account is compromised, it will be difficult to determine which IT person was responsible for the compromise and develop a timeline as to what data may have been stolen.[10]

Previously, we discussed intrusion detection systems (IDSs) and firewalls. However, the context of that conversation centered on a company's interaction with the Internet. Systems can be put in place to monitor files opened and accessed inside of a network.[11] What computers are accessing the company's payroll, and is that normal? Which employee accounts are accessing certain client records? Are those employees even working on those client engagements? It is important to monitor this data and create a baseline so that abnormal access can be identified.[12]

Firewalls can also be placed inside of a network to protect certain servers and their data from the rest of the company. Typically, a file server containing client files would not be used by an employee to browse the Internet. Likewise, that server would not be used to access someone's email and open attachments. Limiting those activities on a file server helps protect that server from being compromised. The other way that the server can be compromised is when other workstations in the environment are compromised; those workstations can then be used to attack the file server. Putting a firewall between your file servers and

---

5 Warwick Ashford, *One in Four IT Security Staff Abuse Admin Rights, Survey Shows*, Computer Weekly, Dec. 5, 2011, http://www.computerweekly.com/news/2240111956/One-in-four-IT-security-staff-abuse-admin-rights-survey-shows.

6 *What Is a Network Administrator Account?*, Microsoft, https://technet.microsoft.com/en-us/library/network-admin-account-1.aspx.

7 For a discussion on what might occur if an administrative account is compromised, *see* Jesper Johansson, *Why You Should Disable the Administrator Account*, Microsoft:Technet, Jan.-Feb. 2006, https://technet.microsoft.com/en-us/magazine/2006.01.securitywatch.aspx.

8 David J. Johnson, *The Use and Administration of Shared Accounts*, SANS, 2003, https://www.sans.org/reading-room/whitepapers/basics/administration-shared-accounts-1271.

9 *Id.* ("There is also minimal accountability for shared accounts as users do what they want/need with the accounts but the account really isn't their account.")

10 *Id.*

11 Margaret Rouse, *Security Information Management (SIM)* [definition], TechTarget, http://searchsecurity.techtarget.com/definition/security-information-management-SIM.

12 *Risk Management: Implementation of Baseline Controls*, TechTarget, http://searchsecurity.techtarget.com/tutorial/Risk-management-Implementation-of-baseline-controls.

the workstations on your network can limit traffic between those devices.[13] Limiting the traffic limits the types and number of attacks that can take place on a server, which would assist in protecting the server and its contents.[14]

9.2 # Threat Management vs. Risk Management

Protecting an organization's data starts with understanding a company's assets, the threats to those assets, the vulnerabilities those assets have, and the eventual risk to the environment.[15] A company's assets include not only the data maintained, but also the devices holding, transmitting, and protecting that data. *Vulnerabilities* are the weaknesses of those assets, and can be inherent in the technology or due to an interaction with those assets.[16] The *threats* are the people (hackers) and tools (malware, social engineering) that attempt to gain access to the assets, usually by exploiting a vulnerability.[17] Finally, the *risk* is the likelihood of exposure of assets and the damage that is done when an asset is exposed.[18]

Practicing threat management is an important step in protecting a company's assets and keeping hackers from getting at your sensitive information. It takes an understanding of what threats are out there from both a human and a technology perspective. Identifying threats when they become known is the first, and possibly the most important, step in protecting your environment. By managing threats a company can mitigate risks.

Threat management allows an organization to quickly respond to evolving threats to its environment. This involves intelligence gathering that allows an organization to spot threats early, before they become a problem. Usually threat management involves implementation of multiple systems that are dynamically updated based on new threats. Those systems include:

1. Anti-virus. Anti-virus (AV) applications detect, quarantine, and respond to viruses based on file signatures or behavior patterns. Therefore, AV apps must already have experience with a virus in order to detect it. AV solutions are provided by software vendors who have the advantage of a customer base across multiple geographic regions and industries. As a result, when

---

13 For an example of a firewall that operates within a network to segment servers and workstations, *see, e.g., Internal Segmentation Firewall (ISFW)*, Fortinet, http://www.fortinet.com/solutions/internal-network-segmentation-firewall.html.
14 *Id.*
15 *See, e.g.,* Symantec, Assets, Threats and Vulnerabilities: Discovery and Analysis, https://www.symantec.com/content/en/us/enterprise/media/security_response/whitepapers/Risk_Management.pdf.
16 *Vulnerability*, Techopedia, https://www.techopedia.com/definition/13484/vulnerability.
17 *Threat*, Techopedia, https://www.techopedia.com/definition/25263/threat.
18 *Risk Analysis*, Techopedia, https://www.techopedia.com/definition/16522/risk-analysis.

one organization detects a new virus, the AV provider can quickly update the rest of its installation base.[19]

2. Anti-spam. While spam was historically more of a nuisance than anything else, spam has evolved into a vehicle for social engineering attempts. Threat management utilizes anti-spam software to block potentially malicious emails that may contain malicious attachments or links to malicious websites. Anti-spam systems can block email servers that are known sources for spam emails through what are known as realtime blackhole lists (RBLs).[20]

3. Content filtering. Content filtering monitors and blocks websites from being viewed. One of the main uses of content filtering is an HR tool to prevent employees from viewing websites that may be inappropriate for a work environment (pornography, gambling, hate sites) or offensive to others. Often these types of websites, which are not mainstream, are delivery vehicles for malware.[21]

4. Centralized patch management. Patch management systems make sure computers in an environment have their updates applied in a timely fashion. Patch management systems can also notify IT when a patch is critical and requires immediate attention.[22]

5. Data loss prevention (DLP). DLP systems monitor activity on a network, including workstations and servers, in order to detect when sensitive information is accessed or moved in an unauthorized fashion. DLP systems can change to respond to new methods of data exfiltration, such as the proliferation of private cloud storage sites (Dropbox, Box.net, etc.).[23]

6. Training. Often the most overlooked method of threat management is employee training. Training employees to spot malicious emails or social engineering attempts can be an effective means of stopping those attacks. When new types of threats emerge, communication with employees as to those new threats can help stop the threats in their tracks. Furthermore, consistent reminders of the types of threats out there will keep the subject at the front of each employee's mind. A skeptical staff that inquires about emails before acting on them, though this sometimes may seem like a nuisance, is much better than a successful attack.[24]

The strength of threat management systems is the pooling of resources across multiple industries and geographic locations.[25] A threat detected in the banking industry, for instance, can result in the implementation of protection and

---

19 Margaret Rouse, *Antivirus Software* [definition], TECHTARGET, http://searchsecurity.techtarget.com/definition/antivirus-software.

20 *Anti-Spam*, TECHOPEDIA, https://www.techopedia.com/definition/1629/anti-spam; *RBL—Realtime Blackhole List*, WEBOPEDIA, http://www.webopedia.com/TERM/R/RBL.html.

21 Margaret Rouse, *Content Filtering (Information Filtering)* [definition], TECHTARGET, http://searchsecurity.techtarget.com/definition/content-filtering.

22 Margaret Rouse, *Patch Management* [definition], TECHTARGET, http://searchenterprisedesktop.techtarget.com/definition/patch-management.

23 *Data Loss Prevention (DLP)* [definition], WHATIS.COM, http://whatis.techtarget.com/definition/data-loss-prevention-DLP.

24 *See, e.g.,* Margaret Rouse, *Security Awareness Training* [definition], TECHTARGET, http://searchsecurity.techtarget.com/definition/security-awareness-training.

25 Jacob Williams, *Practical Threat Management and Incident Response for the Small- to Medium-Sized Enterprises*, SANS, June 2014, https://www.sans.org/reading-room/whitepapers/analyst/practical-threat-management-incident-response-small-medium-sized-enterprises-35257.

prevention techniques by companies in the retail industry. A threat detected at the beginning of the work day in Japan can stimulate a patch or update to be released before the work day begins in the United States. Going back to the statistics in the Verizon data breach report, proper threat management can prevent many breaches by providing a process for updating systems before an attack occurs.[26]

Threats come in a variety of forms. They can be internal or external. They may be human or electronic in nature. A threat can come over email, from a website, or from someone on the Internet sitting in front of a computer.[27]

Often the biggest threat to an organization is internal.[28] Employees are given access to data because they need it to do their work. Frequently employees are given unfettered access to data for fear that limiting or controlling those persons' access may impede their work. Firms rarely monitor what data employees access and what they do with that data. Some employees, motivated by greed or disappointment in their job, might abuse their access to company data. Careless or untrained employees can also pose a threat.[29] These individuals may transfer sensitive data to an unencrypted USB drive. Or maybe they email sensitive data to an unsecure personal account so that the data can be accessed from home. Understanding the employee as a threat is critical to developing policies and processes to safeguard your data.[30] It may start with compartmentalizing company data so that it is easier to provide access to just those pieces of data that an employee needs, rather than allowing each employee access to all company data.[31] It may extend to limitations on or elimination of the use of USB devices.[32] For larger organizations with bigger budgets, understanding the internal threat may lead to the implementation of data loss prevention technologies that identify, monitor, and scan information in your environment and alert the security team to violations of rules regarding that information.[33]

Another threat comes from the interaction of your employees with the outside world: social engineering. Social engineering is not something new that developed with computers. Humans trusting other humans and falling victim to lies and misdirection can be seen in the old story of the Trojan horse. In fact, our use of the word "Trojan" in describing certain types of malware has its roots in the story of the Trojan horse. Today, social engineering is typically used in email and telephone communications. Often, the goal in social engineering is to get the target to act on

---

26 *2015 Data Breach Investigations Report*, VERIZON ENTERPRISE SOLUTIONS, https://msisac.cisecurity.org/whitepaper/documents/1.pdf.

27 For a more in-depth discussion of the types of cyber threats that a firm may face, *see* Chapter 3.

28 Warwick Ashford, *Internal Threat Among Biggest Cyber Security Challenges, Says Former FBI Investigator*, COMPUTER WEEKLY, June 29, 2015, http://www.computerweekly.com/news/4500248908/Internal-threat-among-biggest-cyber-security-challenges-says-former-FBI-investigator.

29 Neal O'Farrell, *Employees: Your Best Defense, or Your Greatest Vulnerability*, TECHTARGET, http://searchsecurity.techtarget.com/tip/Employees-Your-best-defense-or-your-greatest-vulnerability.

30 *Id.*

31 *Security Mistakes That Leave You Vulnerable to Compromise #7: Failure to Compartmentalize Your Network*, NETCRAFTSMEN, Sept. 25, 2011, http://www.netcraftsmen.com/security-mistakes-that-leave-you-vulnerable-to-compromise-7-failure-to-compartmentalize-your-network/.

32 Andy Greenberg, *Why the Security of USB Is Fundamentally Broken*, WIRED, July 31, 2014, http://www.wired.com/2014/07/usb-security/.

33 *Data Loss Prevention (DLP)*, WHATIS.COM, http://whatis.techtarget.com/definition/data-loss-prevention-DLP.

an email. The email may have an attachment that, when opened, starts the process of surreptitiously encrypting all data, rendering the data inaccessible and the company hostage. There may be a link in an email with the goal of getting employees to download malicious software or provide credentials in order to "verify" their account. These are but a few of the many forms social engineering can take.

9.3 Staff—Finding the Right People and Services

Companies relying on computers and digital information need a staff to manage that data.[34] Smaller organizations will tend to outsource their IT services, whereas larger organizations will have a mix of employed staff and outsourced services.[35] Unfortunately, in small organizations, the person who runs IT is often either the young employee who knows more about computers than others in the company or is the office administrator. With today's cybersecurity threats and increased emphasis on protecting data, there are not many worse actions a company can take than not having the proper staff.[36]

The old adage "you don't know what you don't know" applies to information technology and cybersecurity in a profound way. In the early days of IT, I recall not having tight enough controls on my firewall. An outside vendor came in to do some additional work, part of which involved scanning our network perimeter. I recall being embarrassed to find out that they were able to read our entire active directory and iterate through all of the user accounts and other objects. Fast-forward to years later: I recall speaking with a client who had a computer that was the subject of an investigation. A former employee had allegedly stolen information during the last few days of employment. The client explained that they considered the most important piece of information to be who had opened what files and when. The client then described what was done with the computer. Upon termination of the employee, the client turned on the computer and opened up nearly every important file on the computer. So, who was the last person to open up these important files and when? Why, the client itself!

A misconception about computers and IT professionals is that the someone who "knows the most" about computers in an organization can handle almost anything. In fact, the computer industry is filled with specializations, in the same

---

34 *Every Company Needs to Have a Security Program*, APPLIEDTRUST (2008), https://www.appliedtrust.com/resources/security/every-company-needs-to-have-a-security-program.

35 *See, e.g.*, Arif Mohamed, *IT Outsourcing for Small Businesses (SMEs)—Essential Guide*, COMPUTER WEEKLY, July 2009, http://www.computerweekly.com/feature/IT-outsourcing-for-small-businesses-SMEs-Essential-Guide.

36 Luke Forsyth, *Poor Data Security Can Cause Lasting Damage to Your Enterprise*, THE GUARDIAN, Dec. 13, 2012, http://www.theguardian.com/media-network/media-network-blog/2012/dec/13/internet-data-security-enterprise.

way that the medical and legal industries have their specialties.[37] Typically one would not hire an attorney who specializes in tax law to give advice on labor and employment issues. One would also not seek out a cardiologist to repair a knee that had gone sideways in a skiing accident. With information technology, there are just as many specialties, including:

- **Programmers.** Individuals specializing in programming have intimate knowledge of one or more programming languages (in reality, the programming specialty can be further broken down by knowledge of different programming languages). These individuals understand the methods and processes undertaken to model a product, design the interface with inputs and outputs, and program the application in the most efficient way.[38]

- **Desktop support.** Desktop support personnel understand standard computer setup as well as the programs being run in the organization. Their knowledge and experience helps them determine the best ways to support and fix computers, as well as how to research problems in a timely manner.[39]

- **Database administrator.** Larger organizations relying on applications that interface with Oracle, SQL Server, or other database applications need individuals who specialize in databases. These individuals can model an environment and convert that environment into a series of tables, fields, and queries to store information about that environment. Database administrators understand how to maximize the efficiency of a database so that it can store and serve up large amounts of data in an acceptable time frame.[40]

- **Network administrator.** These individuals have responsibilities that may include managing the switches, routers, and hubs that are the physical backbone of a company's network. They may also have responsibilities with respect to adding, removing, and otherwise managing user accounts. Network administrators may also deal with a company's email system, although that too can be a specialty in and of itself.[41]

- **Information security.** Information security specialists have the responsibility to ensure that a company's digital information is protected. Their realm of influence includes security policies (such as setting password policies that are implemented by others), firewall configuration, and monitoring of a company's network for signs of intrusion. Depending on the size of the team and its makeup, information security specialists may be involved not only in the prevention of attacks, but also in investigation if an attack occurs.[42]

---

37 Chris Levin, *8 Kinds of IT Professionals: Which One Does Your Company Need?*, ANSWERQUEST, Aug. 4, 2015, http://answer-quest.net/8-kinds-of-it-professionals-which-one-does-your-company-need/.
38 *Id.*
39 *Id.*
40 *Id.*
41 *Id.*
42 *Id.*

The preceding descriptions are just a sampling of the numerous specialties within the information technology field. In fact, they may be too generalized for some people's tastes. The point is to show that it takes the right people with the right skills to handle the various aspects of information technology, especially information security.[43]

Not everyone can hire multiple IT staff members, but it is important, when hiring people for your IT positions, that they be of the proper mindset when it comes to security. Policies, systems, applications, and the like all should be designed with security in mind from the beginning.[44] Many companies choose to share data with their clients in a portal.[45] When designing the portal, the first question to be asked should be what type of information will be shared; and second, how will that information be protected.[46] It is the responsibility of the IT security department to come up with those questions.

The right IT security professionals will understand that from the beginning they are underequipped.[47] IT security is a lot like playing offense for a football team. Think about the last game you watched. Do you remember the 50 plays in which the offensive tackle successfully blocked the defensive lineman, or do you remember the one time the defensive lineman got through and sacked the quarterback? Managing IT security is very similar. To be successful, you have to protect the environment against any and all attacks. The hacker only has to get through once to be successful.[48] The right IT security professional understands this concept, and will use the resources at hand to practice threat management as discussed in the previous section.

The IT security professional also understands that he or she is a team of one; or, in very large organizations, a team of about a dozen.[49] These professionals also know that their opponent is composed of teams of hundreds, thousands, or more.[50] The hacker world works tirelessly to exploit the latest vulnerabilities and find new vulnerabilities.[51] Hackers also share a good deal of information.[52] When one considers state-sponsored hacking in this mix, there is the realization that not only do

---

43 David Mortman, *Best Practices for Choosing an Information Security Team New Hire*, TechTarget, http://searchsecurity. techtarget.com/answer/Best-practices-for-choosing-an-information-security-team-new-hire.

44 *See, e.g., Information Security Policy—A Development Guide for Large and Small Companies*, SANS, 2007, https://www.sans.org/ reading-room/whitepapers/policyissues/information-security-policy-development-guide-large-small-companies-1331.

45 For an example of an organization that provides secure client portals, *see* Joanna Slusarz, *How to Securely Share Documents with Clients*, Laserfiche, https://www.laserfiche.com/ecmblog/how-to-securely-share-documents-with-clients/.

46 Steve Barnes, *Three Basics of Secure Client Portal Design*, CoreTech Revolution, June 28, 2012, http://www.coretechrevolution.com/latest-news/139-three-basics-of-secure-client-portal-design.

47 Gil Press, *6 Observations About Cybersecurity Based on Two New Surveys*, Forbes:Tech, Aug. 12, 2015, http://www.forbes.com/sites/gilpress/2015/08/12/6-observations-about-cybersecurity-based-on-two-new-surveys/#7df04c3d552c.

48 Chris Triolo, *Hackers Only Need to Get It Right Once, We Need to Get It Right Every Time*, SCMagazine, July 24, 2015, http://www.scmagazine.com/hackers-only-need-to-get-it-right-once-we-need-to-get-it-right-every-time/article/362462/.

49 Tom Scholtz & Rob McMillan, *Tips and Guidelines for Sizing Your Information Security Organization*, Gartner, Aug. 19, 2015, https://www.gartner.com/doc/2718319/tips-guidelines-sizing-information-security.

50 Triolo, *supra* note 48.

51 *Id.*

52 Tom Groenfeldt, *Hackers Collaborate, Now White Hats Can Share Cyber Crime Info*, Forbes:Tech, Nov. 4, 2013, http://www. forbes.com/sites/tomgroenfeldt/2013/11/04/hackers-collaborate-now-white-hats-can-share-cyber-crime-info/#421a5d3d17a1 ("The bad guys use social media to communicate and share information but the good guys don't do that.").

the hackers have more people and more time, but they also have more money and computing resources.

Good IT security professionals spend time doing research and staying up to date with the latest in security and hacking trends.[53] Whether it is articles, blogs, conferences, or formal training, many avenues for continuous learning are available for people with different learning methods and budgets.[54] It is critical that security be supported and taken seriously from the top of the organization down.[55]

What if you do not have those resources internally? Many firms outsource their IT security to an outside vendor.[56] Typically, the firms that outsource are smaller firms that do not have a budget for multiple IT disciplines. In that case, look for an IT vendor that not only can respond to an IT security incident, but also puts a lot of its resources into the prevention of IT security incidents. If your firm's entire IT department is outsourced, do not assume that the outsourcing company is considering IT security. Review with the outsourced IT department to understand from their perspective what services they are providing. The benefit of an outsourced IT department is that the rest of the firm should not have to think about IT and IT security; however, quarterly or yearly updates on services provided can prevent miscommunications that lead to security breaches.[57]

9.4   Summary

Every organization with a computer network is potentially threatened. While some organizations are specifically targeted for hacking, most organizations are compromised because they took no, or very minimal, steps to prevent being hacked.[58] It is not uncommon for an organization's perimeter defenses to be breached, but strong internal controls, as well as competent staff, can be instrumental in mitigating or avoiding harm when a breach does occur. Law firms must

---

53 Ondrej Krehel, *Getting Your Information Security Team Right*, CSO, Oct. 14, 2015, http://www.csoonline.com/article/2991282/infosec-staffing/getting-your-information-security-team-right.html.

54 For a list of some of the places where information security professionals can get this information, *see Top 100+ Cyber Security Blogs & Infosec Resources*, DDOS PROTECTION SERVICES, 2016, http://ddosattackprotection.org/blog/cyber-security-blogs/.

55 APPLIEDTRUST, *supra* note 34.

56 For a list of vendors, *see* VENDORS, INFORMATION SECURITY BUZZ, http://www.informationsecuritybuzz.com/directory/vendors/.

57 For a broader discussion on best practices when outsourcing information security, *see* Warwick Ashford, *Best Practice in Outsourcing Security*, COMPUTER WEEKLY, July 2012, http://www.computerweekly.com/feature/Best-practice-in-outsourcing-security.

58 John Pullen, *How to Protect Your Small Business Against a Cyber Attack*, ENTREPRENEUR, Feb. 27, 2013, https://www.entrepreneur.com/article/225468 ("According to a Verizon study of data breaches in 2011, more than 80 percent of victims were targets of opportunity—which means they did not protect their Wi-Fi systems with passwords and otherwise had poor security, if any at all.").

implement internal controls to protect their data in the event that a system is compromised. Practicing threat management rather than risk management is a way for an IT environment to be flexible and change its protection schemes when different types of attacks come to light. Threat management also allows for notification to users when new attacks take place. Finally, having the proper staff, whether internal or outsourced, helps with putting in place the processes discussed in this chapter. Proper security requires a lot of work and attention, but every law firm should implement some, if not all, of these security measures in order to protect its sensitive data. The consequences of not doing so are exponentially more damaging, expensive, and time-consuming.

Framework for Improving Critical Infrastructure Cybersecurity

Version 1.0

National Institute of Standards and Technology

February 12, 2014

Framework for Improving Critical Infrastructure Cybersecurity

Executive Summary

The national and economic security of the United States depends on the reliable functioning of critical infrastructure. Cybersecurity threats exploit the increased complexity and connectivity of critical infrastructure systems, placing the Nation's security, economy, and public safety and health at risk. Similar to financial and reputational risk, cybersecurity risk affects a company's bottom line. It can drive up costs and impact revenue. It can harm an organization's ability to innovate and to gain and maintain customers.

To better address these risks, the President issued Executive Order 13636, "Improving Critical Infrastructure Cybersecurity," on February 12, 2013, which established that "[i]t is the Policy of the United States to enhance the security and resilience of the Nation's critical infrastructure and to maintain a cyber environment that encourages efficiency, innovation, and economic prosperity while promoting safety, security, business confidentiality, privacy, and civil liberties." In enacting this policy, the Executive Order calls for the development of a voluntary risk-based Cybersecurity Framework—a set of industry standards and best practices to help organizations manage cybersecurity risks. The resulting Framework, created through collaboration between government and the private sector, uses a common language to address and manage cybersecurity risk in a cost-effective way based on business needs without placing additional regulatory requirements on businesses.

The Framework focuses on using business drivers to guide cybersecurity activities and considering cybersecurity risks as part of the organization's risk management processes. The Framework consists of three parts: the Framework Core, the Framework Profile, and the Framework Implementation Tiers. The Framework Core is a set of cybersecurity activities, outcomes, and informative references that are common across critical infrastructure sectors, providing the detailed guidance for developing individual organizational Profiles. Through use of the Profiles, the Framework will help the organization align its cybersecurity activities with its business requirements, risk tolerances, and resources. The Tiers provide a mechanism for organizations to view and understand the characteristics of their approach to managing cybersecurity risk.

The Executive Order also requires that the Framework include a methodology to protect individual privacy and civil liberties when critical infrastructure organizations conduct cybersecurity activities. While processes and existing needs will differ, the Framework can assist organizations in incorporating privacy and civil liberties as part of a comprehensive cybersecurity program.

The Framework enables organizations—regardless of size, degree of cybersecurity risk, or cybersecurity sophistication—to apply the principles and best practices of risk management to improving the security and resilience of critical infrastructure. The Framework provides organization and structure to today's multiple approaches to cybersecurity by assembling standards, guidelines, and practices that are working effectively in industry today. Moreover, because it references globally recognized standards for cybersecurity, the Framework can also be used by organizations located outside the United States and can serve as a model for international cooperation on strengthening critical infrastructure cybersecurity.

The Framework is not a one-size-fits-all approach to managing cybersecurity risk for critical infrastructure. Organizations will continue to have unique risks—different threats, different vulnerabilities, different risk tolerances—and how they implement the practices in the Framework will vary. Organizations can determine activities that are important to critical service delivery and can prioritize investments to maximize the impact of each dollar spent. Ultimately, the Framework is aimed at reducing and better managing cybersecurity risks.

The Framework is a living document and will continue to be updated and improved as industry provides feedback on implementation. As the Framework is put into practice, lessons learned will be integrated into future versions. This will ensure it is meeting the needs of critical infrastructure owners and operators in a dynamic and challenging environment of new threats, risks, and solutions.

Use of this voluntary Framework is the next step to improve the cybersecurity of our Nation's critical infrastructure—providing guidance for individual organizations, while increasing the cybersecurity posture of the Nation's critical infrastructure as a whole.

1.0   Framework Introduction

The national and economic security of the United States depends on the reliable functioning of critical infrastructure. To strengthen the resilience of this infrastructure, President Obama issued Executive Order 13636 (EO), "Improving Critical Infrastructure Cybersecurity," on February 12, 2013.[1] This Executive Order calls for the development of a voluntary Cybersecurity Framework ("Framework") that provides a "prioritized, flexible, repeatable, performance-based, and cost-effective approach" to manage cybersecurity risk for those processes, information, and systems directly involved in the delivery of critical infrastructure services.

---

1 Executive Order no. 13636, Improving Critical Infrastructure Cybersecurity, DCPD-201300091, February 12, 2013. http://www.gpo.gov/fdsys/pkg/FR-2013-02-19/pdf/2013-03915.pdf

The Framework, developed in collaboration with industry, provides guidance to an organization on managing cybersecurity risk.

Critical infrastructure is defined in the EO as "systems and assets, whether physical or virtual, so vital to the United States that the incapacity or destruction of such systems and assets would have a debilitating impact on security, national economic security, national public health or safety, or any combination of those matters." Due to the increasing pressures from external and internal threats, organizations responsible for critical infrastructure need to have a consistent and iterative approach to identifying, assessing, and managing cybersecurity risk. This approach is necessary regardless of an organization's size, threat exposure, or cybersecurity sophistication today.

The critical infrastructure community includes public and private owners and operators, and other entities with a role in securing the Nation's infrastructure. Members of each critical infrastructure sector perform functions that are supported by information technology (IT) and industrial control systems (ICS).[2] This reliance on technology, communication, and the interconnectivity of IT and ICS has changed and expanded the potential vulnerabilities and increased potential risk to operations. For example, as ICS and the data produced in ICS operations are increasingly used to deliver critical services and support business decisions, the potential impacts of a cybersecurity incident on an organization's business, assets, health and safety of individuals, and the environment should be considered. To manage cybersecurity risks, a clear understanding of the organization's business drivers and security considerations specific to its use of IT and ICS is required. Because each organization's risk is unique, along with its use of IT and ICS, the tools and methods used to achieve the outcomes described by the Framework will vary.

Recognizing the role that the protection of privacy and civil liberties plays in creating greater public trust, the Executive Order requires that the Framework include a methodology to protect individual privacy and civil liberties when critical infrastructure organizations conduct cybersecurity activities. Many organizations already have processes for addressing privacy and civil liberties. The methodology is designed to complement such processes and provide guidance to facilitate privacy risk management consistent with an organization's approach to cybersecurity risk management. Integrating privacy and cybersecurity can benefit organizations by increasing customer confidence, enabling more standardized sharing of information, and simplifying operations across legal regimes.

To ensure extensibility and enable technical innovation, the Framework is technology neutral. The Framework relies on a variety of existing standards, guidelines, and practices to enable critical infrastructure providers to achieve resilience. By relying on those global standards, guidelines, and practices developed, managed, and updated by industry, the tools and methods available to achieve the Framework outcomes will scale across borders, acknowledge the global nature of cybersecurity risks, and evolve with technological advances and business requirements. The use of

---

2 The DHS Critical Infrastructure program provides a listing of the sectors and their associated critical functions and value chains. http://www.dhs.gov/critical-infrastructure-sectors

existing and emerging standards will enable economies of scale and drive the development of effective products, services, and practices that meet identified market needs. Market competition also promotes faster diffusion of these technologies and practices and realization of many benefits by the stakeholders in these sectors.

Building from those standards, guidelines, and practices, the Framework provides a common taxonomy and mechanism for organizations to:

1. Describe their current cybersecurity posture;
2. Describe their target state for cybersecurity;
3. Identify and prioritize opportunities for improvement within the context of a continuous and repeatable process;
4. Assess progress toward the target state;
5. Communicate among internal and external stakeholders about cybersecurity risk.

The Framework complements, and does not replace, an organization's risk management process and cybersecurity program. The organization can use its current processes and leverage the Framework to identify opportunities to strengthen and communicate its management of cybersecurity risk while aligning with industry practices. Alternatively, an organization without an existing cybersecurity program can use the Framework as a reference to establish one.

Just as the Framework is not industry-specific, the common taxonomy of standards, guidelines, and practices that it provides also is not country-specific. Organizations outside the United States may also use the Framework to strengthen their own cybersecurity efforts, and the Framework can contribute to developing a common language for international cooperation on critical infrastructure cybersecurity.

1.1   Overview of the Framework

The Framework is a risk-based approach to managing cybersecurity risk, and is composed of three parts: the Framework Core, the Framework Implementation Tiers, and the Framework Profiles. Each Framework component reinforces the connection between business drivers and cybersecurity activities. These components are explained below.

- The *Framework Core* is a set of cybersecurity activities, desired outcomes, and applicable references that are common across critical infrastructure sectors. The Core presents industry standards, guidelines, and practices in a manner that allows for communication of cybersecurity activities and outcomes across the organization from the executive level to the implementation/operations level. The Framework Core consists of five concurrent and continuous Functions—Identify, Protect, Detect, Respond, Recover. When considered together, these Functions provide a high-level, strategic view of the lifecycle of an organization's management of cybersecurity risk. The Framework Core then identifies underlying key Categories and Subcategories for each Function, and matches them with example Informative References such as existing standards, guidelines, and practices for each Subcategory.

- *Framework Implementation Tiers* ("Tiers") provide context on how an organization views cybersecurity risk and the processes in place to manage that risk. Tiers describe the degree to which an organization's cybersecurity risk management practices exhibit the characteristics defined in the Framework (e.g., risk and threat aware, repeatable, and adaptive). The Tiers characterize an organization's practices over a range, from Partial (Tier 1) to Adaptive (Tier 4). These Tiers reflect a progression from informal, reactive responses to approaches that are agile and risk-informed. During the Tier selection process, an organization should consider its current risk management practices, threat environment, legal and regulatory requirements, business/mission objectives, and organizational constraints.

- A *Framework Profile* ("Profile") represents the outcomes based on business needs that an organization has selected from the Framework Categories and Subcategories. The Profile can be characterized as the alignment of standards, guidelines, and practices to the Framework Core in a particular implementation scenario. Profiles can be used to identify opportunities for improving cybersecurity posture by comparing a "Current" Profile (the "as is" state) with a "Target" Profile (the "to be" state). To develop a Profile, an organization can review all of the Categories and Subcategories and, based on business drivers and a risk assessment, determine which are most important; they can add Categories and Subcategories as needed to address the organization's risks. The Current Profile can then be used to support prioritization and measurement of progress toward the Target Profile, while factoring in other business needs including cost-effectiveness and innovation. Profiles can be used to conduct self-assessments and communicate within an organization or between organizations.

1.2 Risk Management and the Cybersecurity Framework

Risk management is the ongoing process of identifying, assessing, and responding to risk. To manage risk, organizations should understand the likelihood that an event will occur and the resulting impact. With this information, organizations can determine the acceptable level of risk for delivery of services and can express this as their risk tolerance.

With an understanding of risk tolerance, organizations can prioritize cybersecurity activities, enabling organizations to make informed decisions about cybersecurity expenditures. Implementation of risk management programs offers organizations the ability to quantify and communicate adjustments to their cybersecurity programs. Organizations may choose to handle risk in different ways, including mitigating the risk, transferring the risk, avoiding the risk, or accepting the risk, depending on the potential impact to the delivery of critical services.

The Framework uses risk management processes to enable organizations to inform and prioritize decisions regarding cybersecurity. It supports recurring risk assessments and validation of business drivers to help organizations select target states for cybersecurity activities that reflect desired outcomes. Thus, the Framework gives organizations the ability to dynamically select and direct improvement in cybersecurity risk management for the IT and ICS environments.

The Framework is adaptive to provide a flexible and risk-based implementation that can be used with a broad array of cybersecurity risk management processes. Examples of cybersecurity risk management processes include International Organization for Standardization (ISO) 31000:2009[3], ISO/IEC 27005:2011[4], National Institute of Standards and Technology (NIST) Special Publication (SP) 800-39[5], and the *Electricity Subsector Cybersecurity Risk Management Process* (RMP) guideline[6].

1.3   Document Overview

The remainder of this document contains the following sections and appendices:

- Section 2 describes the Framework components: the Framework Core, the Tiers, and the Profiles.
- Section 3 presents examples of how the Framework can be used.
- Appendix A presents the Framework Core in a tabular format: the Functions, Categories, Subcategories, and Informative References.
- Appendix B contains a glossary of selected terms.
- Appendix C lists acronyms used in this document.

---

3 International Organization for Standardization, *Risk management—Principles and guidelines*, ISO 31000:2009, 2009. http://www.iso.org/iso/home/standards/iso31000.htm

4 International Organization for Standardization/International Electrotechnical Commission, *Information technology—Security techniques—Information security risk management*, ISO/IEC 27005:2011, 2011. http://www.iso.org/iso/catalogue_detail?csnumber=56742

5 Joint Task Force Transformation Initiative, *Managing Information Security Risk: Organization, Mission, and Information System View*, NIST Special Publication 800-39, March 2011. http://csrc.nist.gov/publications/nistpubs/800-39/SP800-39-final.pdf

6 U.S. Department of Energy, *Electricity Subsector Cybersecurity Risk Management Process*, DOE/OE-0003, May 2012. http://energy.gov/sites/prod/files/Cybersecurity%20Risk%20Management%20Process%20Guideline%20-%20Final%20-%20May%202012.pdf

2.0   Framework Basics

The Framework provides a common language for understanding, managing, and expressing cybersecurity risk both internally and externally. It can be used to help identify and prioritize actions for reducing cybersecurity risk, and it is a tool for aligning policy, business, and technological approaches to managing that risk. It can be used to manage cybersecurity risk across entire organizations or it can be focused on the delivery of critical services within an organization. Different types of entities—including sector coordinating structures, associations, and organizations—can use the Framework for different purposes, including the creation of common Profiles.

2.1   Framework Core

The *Framework Core* provides a set of activities to achieve specific cybersecurity outcomes, and references examples of guidance to achieve those outcomes. The Core is not a checklist of actions to perform. It presents key cybersecurity outcomes identified by industry as helpful in managing cybersecurity risk. The Core comprises four elements: Functions, Categories, Subcategories, and Informative References, depicted in **Figure 1**:

Functions	Categories	Subcategories	Informative References
IDENTIFY			
PROTECT			
DETECT			
RESPOND			
RECOVER			

Figure 1: Framework Core Structure

The Framework Core elements work together as follows:

- **Functions** organize basic cybersecurity activities at their highest level. These Functions are Identify, Protect, Detect, Respond, and Recover. They aid an organization in expressing its management of cybersecurity risk by organizing information, enabling risk management decisions, addressing threats, and improving by learning from previous activities. The Functions also align with existing methodologies for incident management and help show the impact of investments in cybersecurity. For example, investments in planning and exercises support timely response and recovery actions, resulting in reduced impact to the delivery of services.

- **Categories** are the subdivisions of a Function into groups of cybersecurity outcomes closely tied to programmatic needs and particular activities. Examples of Categories include "Asset Management," "Access Control," and "Detection Processes."

- **Subcategories** further divide a Category into specific outcomes of technical and/or management activities. They provide a set of results that, while not exhaustive, help support achievement of the outcomes in each Category. Examples of Subcategories include "External information systems are catalogued," "Data-at-rest is protected," and "Notifications from detection systems are investigated."

- **Informative References** are specific sections of standards, guidelines, and practices common among critical infrastructure sectors that illustrate a method to achieve the outcomes associated with each Subcategory. The Informative References presented in the Framework Core are illustrative and not exhaustive. They are based upon cross-sector guidance most frequently referenced during the Framework development process.[7]

The five Framework Core Functions are defined below. These Functions are not intended to form a serial path, or lead to a static desired end state. Rather, the Functions can be performed concurrently and continuously to form an operational culture that addresses the dynamic cybersecurity risk. See Appendix A for the complete Framework Core listing.

- **Identify**—Develop the organizational understanding to manage cybersecurity risk to systems, assets, data, and capabilities.
  The activities in the Identify Function are foundational for effective use of the Framework. Understanding the business context, the resources that support critical functions, and the related cybersecurity risks enables an organization to focus and prioritize its efforts, consistent with its risk

---

7 NIST developed a Compendium of informative references gathered from the Request for Information (RFI) input, Cybersecurity Framework workshops, and stakeholder engagement during the Framework development process. The Compendium includes standards, guidelines, and practices to assist with implementation. The Compendium is not intended to be an exhaustive list, but rather a starting point based on initial stakeholder input. The Compendium and other supporting material can be found at http://www.nist.gov/cyberframework/.

management strategy and business needs. Examples of outcome Categories within this Function include: Asset Management; Business Environment; Governance; Risk Assessment; and Risk Management Strategy.

- **Protect**—Develop and implement the appropriate safeguards to ensure delivery of critical infrastructure services.

  The Protect Function supports the ability to limit or contain the impact of a potential cybersecurity event. Examples of outcome Categories within this Function include: Access Control; Awareness and Training; Data Security; Information Protection Processes and Procedures; Maintenance; and Protective Technology.

- **Detect**—Develop and implement the appropriate activities to identify the occurrence of a cybersecurity event.

  The Detect Function enables timely discovery of cybersecurity events. Examples of outcome Categories within this Function include: Anomalies and Events; Security Continuous Monitoring; and Detection Processes.

- **Respond**—Develop and implement the appropriate activities to take action regarding a detected cybersecurity event.

  The Respond Function supports the ability to contain the impact of a potential cybersecurity event. Examples of outcome Categories within this Function include: Response Planning; Communications; Analysis; Mitigation; and Improvements.

- **Recover**—Develop and implement the appropriate activities to maintain plans for resilience and to restore any capabilities or services that were impaired due to a cybersecurity event.

  The Recover Function supports timely recovery to normal operations to reduce the impact from a cybersecurity event. Examples of outcome Categories within this Function include: Recovery Planning; Improvements; and Communications.

2.2 Framework Implementation Tiers

The Framework Implementation Tiers ("Tiers") provide context on how an organization views cybersecurity risk and the processes in place to manage that risk. The Tiers range from Partial (Tier 1) to Adaptive (Tier 4) and describe an increasing degree of rigor and sophistication in cybersecurity risk management practices and the extent to which cybersecurity risk management is informed by business needs and is integrated into an organization's overall risk management practices. Risk management considerations include many aspects of cybersecurity, including the degree to which privacy and civil liberties considerations are integrated into an organization's management of cybersecurity risk and potential risk responses.

The Tier selection process considers an organization's current risk management practices, threat environment, legal and regulatory requirements, business/mission objectives, and organizational constraints. Organizations should determine the desired Tier, ensuring that the selected level meets the organizational goals, is feasible to implement, and reduces cybersecurity risk to critical assets and resources to levels acceptable to the organization. Organizations should consider leveraging external guidance obtained from Federal government departments and agencies, Information Sharing and Analysis Centers (ISACs), existing maturity models, or other sources to assist in determining their desired tier.

While organizations identified as Tier 1 (Partial) are encouraged to consider moving toward Tier 2 or greater, Tiers do not represent maturity levels. Progression to higher Tiers is encouraged when such a change would reduce cybersecurity risk and be cost effective. Successful implementation of the Framework is based upon achievement of the outcomes described in the organization's Target Profile(s) and not upon Tier determination.

The Tier definitions are as follows:

Tier 1: Partial

- *Risk Management Process*—Organizational cybersecurity risk management practices are not formalized, and risk is managed in an *ad hoc* and sometimes reactive manner. Prioritization of cybersecurity activities may not be directly informed by organizational risk objectives, the threat environment, or business/mission requirements.

- *Integrated Risk Management Program*—There is limited awareness of cybersecurity risk at the organizational level and an organization-wide approach to managing cybersecurity risk has not been established. The organization implements cybersecurity risk management on an irregular, case-by-case basis due to varied experience or information gained from outside sources. The organization may not have processes that enable cybersecurity information to be shared within the organization.

- *External Participation*—An organization may not have the processes in place to participate in coordination or collaboration with other entities.

Tier 2: Risk Informed

- *Risk Management Process*—Risk management practices are approved by management but may not be established as organizational-wide policy. Prioritization of cybersecurity activities is directly informed by organizational risk objectives, the threat environment, or business/mission requirements.

- *Integrated Risk Management Program*—There is an awareness of cybersecurity risk at the organizational level but an organization-wide approach to managing cybersecurity risk has not been established. Risk-informed, management-approved processes and procedures are defined and implemented, and staff has adequate resources to perform their cybersecurity duties. Cybersecurity information is shared within the organization on an informal basis.

- *External Participation*—The organization knows its role in the larger ecosystem, but has not formalized its capabilities to interact and share information externally.

Tier 3: Repeatable

- *Risk Management Process*—The organization's risk management practices are formally approved and expressed as policy. Organizational cybersecurity practices are regularly updated based on the application of risk management processes to changes in business/mission requirements and a changing threat and technology landscape.
- *Integrated Risk Management Program*—There is an organization-wide approach to manage cybersecurity risk. Risk-informed policies, processes, and procedures are defined, implemented as intended, and reviewed. Consistent methods are in place to respond effectively to changes in risk. Personnel possess the knowledge and skills to perform their appointed roles and responsibilities.
- *External Participation*—The organization understands its dependencies and partners and receives information from these partners that enables collaboration and risk-based management decisions within the organization in response to events.

Tier 4: Adaptive

- *Risk Management Process*—The organization adapts its cybersecurity practices based on lessons learned and predictive indicators derived from previous and current cybersecurity activities. Through a process of continuous improvement incorporating advanced cybersecurity technologies and practices, the organization actively adapts to a changing cybersecurity landscape and responds to evolving and sophisticated threats in a timely manner.
- *Integrated Risk Management Program*—There is an organization-wide approach to managing cybersecurity risk that uses risk-informed policies, processes, and procedures to address potential cybersecurity events. Cybersecurity risk management is part of the organizational culture and evolves from an awareness of previous activities, information shared by other sources, and continuous awareness of activities on their systems and networks.
- *External Participation*—The organization manages risk and actively shares information with partners to ensure that accurate, current information is being distributed and consumed to improve cybersecurity before a cybersecurity event occurs.

2.3   Framework Profile

The Framework Profile ("Profile") is the alignment of the Functions, Categories, and Subcategories with the business requirements, risk tolerance, and resources of the organization. A Profile enables organizations to establish a roadmap for reducing cybersecurity risk that is well aligned with organizational and sector goals, considers legal/regulatory requirements and industry best practices, and reflects risk management priorities. Given the complexity of many organizations, they may choose to have multiple profiles, aligned with particular components and recognizing their individual needs.

Framework Profiles can be used to describe the current state or the desired target state of specific cybersecurity activities. The Current Profile indicates the cybersecurity outcomes that are currently being achieved. The Target Profile indicates the outcomes needed to achieve the desired cybersecurity risk management goals. Profiles support business/mission requirements and aid in the communication of risk within and between organizations. This Framework document does not prescribe Profile templates, allowing for flexibility in implementation.

Comparison of Profiles (e.g., the Current Profile and Target Profile) may reveal gaps to be addressed to meet cybersecurity risk management objectives. An action plan to address these gaps can contribute to the roadmap described above. Prioritization of gap mitigation is driven by the organization's business needs and risk management processes. This risk-based approach enables an organization to gauge resource estimates (e.g., staffing, funding) to achieve cybersecurity goals in a cost-effective, prioritized manner.

2.4   Coordination of Framework Implementation

Figure 2 describes a common flow of information and decisions at the following levels within an organization:

- Executive
- Business/Process
- Implementation/Operations

The executive level communicates the mission priorities, available resources, and overall risk tolerance to the business/process level. The business/process level uses the information as inputs into the risk management process, and then collaborates with the implementation/operations level to communicate business needs and create a Profile. The implementation/operations level communicates the Profile implementation progress to the business/process level. The business/process level uses this information to perform an impact assessment. Business/process level management reports the outcomes of that impact assessment to the executive level to inform the organization's overall risk management process and to the implementation/operations level for awareness of business impact.

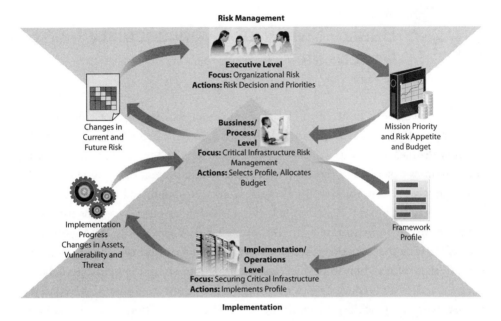

Risk Management

Executive Level
Focus: Organizational Risk
Actions: Risk Decision and Priorities

Changes in
Current and
Future Risk

**Bussiness/
Process/
Level**
Focus: Critical Infrastructure Risk
Management
Actions: Selects Profile, Allocates
Budget

Mission Priority
and Risk Appetite
and Budget

Implementation
Progress
Changes in Assets,
Vulnerability and
Threat

Framework
Profile

**Implementation/
Operations
Level**
Focus: Securing Critical Infrastructure
Actions: Implements Profile

Implementation

Figure 2: Notional Information and Decision Flows within an Organization

3.0   How to Use the Framework

An organization can use the Framework as a key part of its systematic process for identifying, assessing, and managing cybersecurity risk. The Framework is not designed to replace existing processes; an organization can use its current process and overlay it onto the Framework to determine gaps in its current cybersecurity risk approach and develop a roadmap to improvement. Utilizing the Framework as a cybersecurity risk management tool, an organization can determine activities that are most important to critical service delivery and prioritize expenditures to maximize the impact of the investment.

The Framework is designed to complement existing business and cybersecurity operations. It can serve as the foundation for a new cybersecurity program or a mechanism for improving an existing program. The Framework provides a means of expressing cybersecurity requirements to business partners and customers and can help identify gaps in an organization's cybersecurity practices. It also provides a general set of considerations and processes for considering privacy and civil liberties implications in the context of a cybersecurity program.

The following sections present different ways in which organizations can use the Framework.

3.1 Basic Review of Cybersecurity Practices

The Framework can be used to compare an organization's current cybersecurity activities with those outlined in the Framework Core. Through the creation of a Current Profile, organizations can examine the extent to which they are achieving the outcomes described in the Core Categories and Subcategories, aligned with the five high-level Functions: Identify, Protect, Detect, Respond, and Recover. An organization may find that it is already achieving the desired outcomes, thus managing cybersecurity commensurate with the known risk. Conversely, an organization may determine that it has opportunities to (or needs to) improve. The organization can use that information to develop an action plan to strengthen existing cybersecurity practices and reduce cybersecurity risk. An organization may also find that it is overinvesting to achieve certain outcomes. The organization can use this information to reprioritize resources to strengthen other cybersecurity practices.

While they do not replace a risk management process, these five high-level Functions will provide a concise way for senior executives and others to distill the fundamental concepts of cybersecurity risk so that they can assess how identified risks are managed, and how their organization stacks up at a high level against existing cybersecurity standards, guidelines, and practices. The Framework can also help an organization answer fundamental questions, including "How are we doing?" Then they can move in a more informed way to strengthen their cybersecurity practices where and when deemed necessary.

3.2 Establishing or Improving a Cybersecurity Program

The following steps illustrate how an organization could use the Framework to create a new cybersecurity program or improve an existing program. These steps should be repeated as necessary to continuously improve cybersecurity.

Step 1: Prioritize and Scope. The organization identifies its business/mission objectives and high-level organizational priorities. With this information, the organization makes strategic decisions regarding cybersecurity implementations and determines the scope of systems and assets that support the selected business line or process. The Framework can be adapted to support the different business lines or processes within an organization, which may have different business needs and associated risk tolerance.

Step 2: Orient. Once the scope of the cybersecurity program has been determined for the business line or process, the organization identifies related systems and assets, regulatory requirements, and overall risk approach. The organization then identifies threats to, and vulnerabilities of, those systems and assets.

Step 3: Create a Current Profile. The organization develops a Current Profile by indicating which Category and Subcategory outcomes from the Framework Core are currently being achieved.

Step 4: Conduct a Risk Assessment. This assessment could be guided by the organization's overall risk management process or previous risk assessment activities. The organization analyzes the operational environment in order to discern the likelihood of a cybersecurity event and the impact that the event could have on the organization. It is important that organizations seek to incorporate emerging risks and threat and vulnerability data to facilitate a robust understanding of the likelihood and impact of cybersecurity events.

Step 5: Create a Target Profile. The organization creates a Target Profile that focuses on the assessment of the Framework Categories and Subcategories describing the organization's desired cybersecurity outcomes. Organizations also may develop their own additional Categories and Subcategories to account for unique organizational risks. The organization may also consider influences and requirements of external stakeholders such as sector entities, customers, and business partners when creating a Target Profile.

Step 6: Determine, Analyze, and Prioritize Gaps. The organization compares the Current Profile and the Target Profile to determine gaps. Next it creates a prioritized action plan to address those gaps that draws upon mission drivers, a cost/benefit analysis, and understanding of risk to achieve the outcomes in the Target Profile. The organization then determines resources necessary to address the gaps. Using Profiles in this manner enables the organization to make informed decisions about cybersecurity activities, supports risk management, and enables the organization to perform cost-effective, targeted improvements.

Step 7: Implement Action Plan. The organization determines which actions to take in regards to the gaps, if any, identified in the previous step. It then monitors its current cybersecurity practices against the Target Profile. For further guidance, the Framework identifies example Informative References regarding the Categories and Subcategories, but organizations should determine which standards, guidelines, and practices, including those that are sector specific, work best for their needs.

An organization may repeat the steps as needed to continuously assess and improve its cybersecurity. For instance, organizations may find that more frequent repetition of the orient step improves the quality of risk assessments. Furthermore, organizations may monitor progress through iterative updates to the Current Profile, subsequently comparing the Current Profile to the Target Profile. Organizations may also utilize this process to align their cybersecurity program with their desired Framework Implementation Tier.

3.3 Communicating Cybersecurity Requirements with Stakeholders

The Framework provides a common language to communicate requirements among interdependent stakeholders responsible for the delivery of essential critical infrastructure services. Examples include:

- An organization may utilize a Target Profile to express cybersecurity risk management requirements to an external service provider (e.g., a cloud provider to which it is exporting data).
- An organization may express its cybersecurity state through a Current Profile to report results or to compare with acquisition requirements.
- A critical infrastructure owner/operator, having identified an external partner on whom that infrastructure depends, may use a Target Profile to convey required Categories and Subcategories.
- A critical infrastructure sector may establish a Target Profile that can be used among its constituents as an initial baseline Profile to build their tailored Target Profiles.

3.4 Identifying Opportunities for New or Revised Informative References

The Framework can be used to identify opportunities for new or revised standards, guidelines, or practices where additional Informative References would help organizations address emerging needs. An organization implementing a given Subcategory, or developing a new Subcategory, might discover that there are few Informative References, if any, for a related activity. To address that need, the organization might collaborate with technology leaders and/or standards bodies to draft, develop, and coordinate standards, guidelines, or practices.

3.5 Methodology to Protect Privacy and Civil Liberties

This section describes a methodology as required by the Executive Order to address individual privacy and civil liberties implications that may result from cybersecurity operations. This methodology is intended to be a general set of considerations and processes since privacy and civil liberties implications may differ by sector or over time and organizations may address these considerations and processes with a range of technical implementations. Nonetheless, not all activities in a cybersecurity program may give rise to these considerations. Consistent with Section 3.4, technical privacy standards, guidelines, and additional best practices may need to be developed to support improved technical implementations.

Privacy and civil liberties implications may arise when personal information is used, collected, processed, maintained, or disclosed in connection with an organization's cybersecurity activities. Some examples of activities that bear privacy or civil liberties considerations may include: cybersecurity activities that result in the over-collection or over-retention of personal information; disclosure or use of personal information unrelated to cybersecurity activities; cybersecurity mitigation activities that result in denial of service or other similar potentially adverse impacts, including activities such as some types of incident detection or monitoring that may impact freedom of expression or association.

The government and agents of the government have a direct responsibility to protect civil liberties arising from cybersecurity activities. As referenced in the methodology below, government or agents of the government that own or operate critical infrastructure should have a process in place to support compliance of cybersecurity activities with applicable privacy laws, regulations, and Constitutional requirements.

To address privacy implications, organizations may consider how, in circumstances where such measures are appropriate, their cybersecurity program might incorporate privacy principles such as: data minimization in the collection, disclosure, and retention of personal information material related to the cybersecurity incident; use limitations outside of cybersecurity activities on any information collected specifically for cybersecurity activities; transparency for certain cybersecurity activities; individual consent and redress for adverse impacts arising from use of personal information in cybersecurity activities; data quality, integrity, and security; and accountability and auditing.

As organizations assess the Framework Core in Appendix A, the following processes and activities may be considered as a means to address the above-referenced privacy and civil liberties implications:

Governance of cybersecurity risk

- An organization's assessment of cybersecurity risk and potential risk responses considers the privacy implications of its cybersecurity program
- Individuals with cybersecurity-related privacy responsibilities report to appropriate management and are appropriately trained
- Process is in place to support compliance of cybersecurity activities with applicable privacy laws, regulations, and Constitutional requirements
- Process is in place to assess implementation of the foregoing organizational measures and controls

Approaches to identifying and authorizing individuals to access organizational assets and systems

- Steps are taken to identify and address the privacy implications of access control measures to the extent that they involve collection, disclosure, or use of personal information

Awareness and training measures

- Applicable information from organizational privacy policies is included in cybersecurity workforce training and awareness activities
- Service providers that provide cybersecurity-related services for the organization are informed about the organization's applicable privacy policies

Anomalous activity detection and system and assets monitoring

- Process is in place to conduct a privacy review of an organization's anomalous activity detection and cybersecurity monitoring

Response activities, including information sharing or other mitigation efforts

- Process is in place to assess and address whether, when, how, and the extent to which personal information is shared outside the organization as part of cybersecurity information sharing activities
- Process is in place to conduct a privacy review of an organization's cybersecurity mitigation efforts

Appendix A: Framework Core

This appendix presents the Framework Core: a listing of Functions, Categories, Subcategories, and Informative References that describe specific cybersecurity activities that are common across all critical infrastructure sectors. The chosen presentation format for the Framework Core does not suggest a specific implementation order or imply a degree of importance of the Categories, Subcategories, and Informative References. The Framework Core presented in this appendix represents a common set of activities for managing cybersecurity risk. While the Framework is not exhaustive, it is extensible, allowing organizations, sectors, and other entities to use Subcategories and Informative References that are cost-effective and efficient and that enable them to manage their cybersecurity risk. Activities can be selected from the Framework Core during the Profile creation process and additional Categories, Subcategories, and Informative References may be added to the Profile. An organization's risk management processes, legal/regulatory requirements, business/mission objectives, and organizational constraints guide the selection of these activities during Profile creation. Personal information is considered a component of data or assets referenced in the Categories when assessing security risks and protections.

While the intended outcomes identified in the Functions, Categories, and Subcategories are the same for IT and ICS, the operational environments and considerations for IT and ICS differ. ICS have a direct effect on the physical world, including potential risks to the health and safety of individuals, and impact on the environment. Additionally, ICS have unique performance and reliability requirements compared with IT, and the goals of safety and efficiency must be considered when implementing cybersecurity measures.

For ease of use, each component of the Framework Core is given a unique identifier. Functions and Categories each have a unique alphabetic identifier, as shown in Table 1. Subcategories within each Category are referenced numerically; the unique identifier for each Subcategory is included in Table 2.

Additional supporting material relating to the Framework can be found on the NIST website at http://www.nist.gov/cyberframework/.

Table 1: Function and Category Unique Identifiers

Function Unique Identifier	Function	Category Unique Identifier	Category
ID	Identify	ID.AM	Asset Management
		ID.BE	Business Environment
		ID.GV	Governance
		ID.RA	Risk Assessment
		ID.RM	Risk Management Strategy
PR	Protect	PR.AC	Access Control
		PR.AT	Awareness and Training
		PR.DS	Data Security
		PR.IP	Information Protection Processes and Procedures
		PR.MA	Maintenance
		PR.PT	Protective Technology
DE	Detect	DE.AE	Anomalies and Events
		DE.CM	Security Continuous Monitoring
		DE.DP	Detection Processes
RS	Respond	RS.RP	Response Planning
		RS.CO	Communications
		RS.AN	Analysis
		RS.MI	Mitigation
		RS.IM	Improvements
RC	Recover	RC.RP	Recovery Planning
		RC.IM	Improvements
		RC.CO	Communications

Table 2: Framework Core

Function	Category	Subcategory	Informative References
IDENTIFY (ID)	**Asset Management (ID.AM):** The data, personnel, devices, systems, and facilities that enable the organization to achieve business purposes are identified and managed consistent with their relative importance to business objectives and the organization's risk strategy.	**ID.AM-1:** Physical devices and systems within the organization are inventoried	• **CCS CSC** 1 • **COBIT 5** BAI09.01, BAI09.02 • **ISA 62443-2-1:2009** 4.2.3.4 • **ISA 62443-3-3:2013** SR 7.8 • **ISO/IEC 27001:2013** A.8.1.1, A.8.1.2 • **NIST SP 800-53 Rev. 4** CM-8
		ID.AM-2: Software platforms and applications within the organization are inventoried	• **CCS CSC** 2 • **COBIT 5** BAI09.01, BAI09.02, BAI09.05 • **ISA 62443-2-1:2009** 4.2.3.4 • **ISA 62443-3-3:2013** SR 7.8 • **ISO/IEC 27001:2013** A.8.1.1, A.8.1.2 • **NIST SP 800-53 Rev. 4** CM-8
		ID.AM-3: Organizational communication and data flows are mapped	• **CCS CSC** 1 • **COBIT 5** DSS05.02 • **ISA 62443-2-1:2009** 4.2.3.4 • **ISO/IEC 27001:2013** A.13.2.1 • **NIST SP 800-53 Rev. 4** AC-4, CA-3, CA-9, PL-8
		ID.AM-4: External information systems are catalogued	• **COBIT 5** APO02.02 • **ISO/IEC 27001:2013** A.11.2.6 • **NIST SP 800-53 Rev. 4** AC-20, SA-9
		ID.AM-5: Resources (e.g., hardware, devices, data, and software) are prioritized based on their classification, criticality, and business value	• **COBIT 5** APO03.03, APO03.04, BAI09.02 • **ISA 62443-2-1:2009** 4.2.3.6 • **ISO/IEC 27001:2013** A.8.2.1 • **NIST SP 800-53 Rev. 4** CP-2, RA-2, SA-14
		ID.AM-6: Cybersecurity roles and responsibilities for the entire workforce and third-party stakeholders (e.g., suppliers, customers, partners) are established	• **COBIT 5** APO01.02, DSS06.03 • **ISA 62443-2-1:2009** 4.3.2.3.3 • **ISO/IEC 27001:2013** A.6.1.1 • **NIST SP 800-53 Rev. 4** CP-2, PS-7, PM-11

(continued)

Table 2: Framework Core *(continued)*

Function	Category	Subcategory	Informative References
IDENTIFY (ID)	**Business Environment (ID.BE):** The organization's mission, objectives, stakeholders, and activities are understood and prioritized; this information is used to inform cybersecurity roles, responsibilities, and risk management decisions.	**ID.BE-1:** The organization's role in the supply chain is identified and communicated	• **COBIT 5** APO08.04, APO08.05, APO10.03, APO10.04, APO10.05 • **ISO/IEC 27001:2013** A.15.1.3, A.15.2.1, A.15.2.2 • **NIST SP 800-53 Rev. 4** CP-2, SA-12
		ID.BE-2: The organization's place in critical infrastructure and its industry sector are identified and communicated	• **COBIT 5** APO02.06, APO03.01 • **NIST SP 800-53 Rev. 4** PM-8
		ID.BE-3: Priorities for organizational mission, objectives, and activities are established and communicated	• **COBIT 5** APO02.01, APO02.06, APO03.01 • **ISA 62443-2-1:2009** 4.2.2.1, 4.2.3.6 • **NIST SP 800-53 Rev. 4** PM-11, SA-14
		ID.BE-4: Dependencies and critical functions for delivery of critical services are established	• **ISO/IEC 27001:2013** A.11.2.2, A.11.2.3, A.12.1.3 • **NIST SP 800-53 Rev. 4** CP-8, PE-9, PE-11, PM-8, SA-14
		ID.BE-5: Resilience requirements to support delivery of critical services are established	• **COBIT 5** DSS04.02 • **ISO/IEC 27001:2013** A.11.1.4, A.17.1.1, A.17.1.2, A.17.2.1 • **NIST SP 800-53 Rev. 4** CP-2, CP-11, SA-14
	Governance (ID.GV): The policies, procedures, and processes to manage and monitor the organization's regulatory, legal, risk, environmental, and operational requirements are understood and inform the management of cybersecurity risk.	**ID.GV-1:** Organizational information security policy is established	• **COBIT 5** APO01.03, EDM01.01, EDM01.02 • **ISA 62443-2-1:2009** 4.3.2.6 • **ISO/IEC 27001:2013** A.5.1.1 • **NIST SP 800-53 Rev. 4-1** controls from all families

Function	Category	Subcategory	Informative References
IDENTIFY (ID		**ID.GV-2:** Information security roles and responsibilities are coordinated and aligned with internal roles and external partners	• **COBIT 5** APO13.12 • **ISA 62443-2-1:2009** 4.3.2.3.3 • **ISO/IEC 27001:2013** A.6.1.1, A.7.2.1 • **NIST SP 800-53 Rev. 4** PM-1, PS-7
		ID.GV-3: Legal and regulatory requirements regarding cybersecurity, including privacy and civil liberties obligations, are understood and managed	• **COBIT 5** MEA03.01, MEA03.04 • **ISA 62443-2-1:2009** 4.4.3.7 • **ISO/IEC 27001:2013** A.18.1 • **NIST SP 800-53 Rev. 4-1** controls from all families (except PM-1)
		ID.GV-4: Governance and risk management processes address cybersecurity risks	• **COBIT 5** DSS04.02 • **ISA 62443-2-1:2009** 4.2.3.1, 4.2.3.3, 4.2.3.8, 4.2.3.9, 4.2.3.11, 4.3.2.4.3, 4.3.2.6.3 • **NIST SP 800-53 Rev. 4** PM-9, PM-11
	Risk Assessment (ID.RA): The organization understands the cybersecurity risk to organizational operations (including mission, functions, image, or reputation), organizational assets, and individuals.	**ID.RA-1:** Asset vulnerabilities are identified and documented	• **CCS CSC** 4 • **COBIT 5** APO12.01, APO12.02, APO12.03, APO12.04 • **ISA 62443-2-1:2009** 4.2.3, 4.2.3.7, 4.2.3.9, 4.2.3.12 • **ISO/IEC 27001:2013** A.12.6.1, A.18.2.3 • **NIST SP 800-53 Rev. 4** CA-2, CA-7, CA-8, RA-3, RA-5, SA-5, SA-11, SI-2, SI-4, SI-5
		ID.RA-2: Threat and vulnerability information is received from information-sharing forums and sources	• **ISA 62443-2-1:2009** 4.2.3, 4.2.3.9, 4.2.3.12 • **ISO/IEC 27001:2013** A.6.1.4 • **NIST SP 800-53 Rev. 4** PM-15, PM-16, SI-5

(continued)

Table 2: Framework Core *(continued)*

Function	Category	Subcategory	Informative References
IDENTIFY (ID)		**ID.RA-3**: Threats, both internal and external, are identified and documented	• **COBIT 5** APO12.01, APO12.02, APO12.03, APO12.04 • **ISA 62443-2-1:2009** 4.2.3, 4.2.3.9, 4.2.3.12 • **NIST SP 800-53 Rev. 4** RA-3, SI-5, PM-12, PM-16
		ID.RA-4: Potential business impacts and likelihoods are identified	• **COBIT 5** DSS04.02 • **ISA 62443-2-1:2009** 4.2.3, 4.2.3.9, 4.2.3.12 • **NIST SP 800-53 Rev. 4** RA-2, RA-3, PM-9, PM-11, SA-14
		ID.RA-5: Threats, vulnerabilities, likelihoods, and impacts are used to determine risk	• **COBIT 5** APO12.02 • **ISO/IEC 27001:2013** A.12.6.1 • **NIST SP 800-53 Rev. 4** RA-2, RA-3, PM-16
		ID.RA-6: Risk responses are identified and prioritized	• **COBIT 5** APO12.05, APO13.02 • **NIST SP 800-53 Rev. 4** PM-4, PM-9
	Risk Management Strategy (ID.RM): The organization's priorities, constraints, risk tolerances, and assumptions are established and used to support operational risk decisions.	**ID.RM-1**: Risk management processes are established, managed, and agreed to by organizational stakeholders	• **COBIT 5** APO12.04, APO12.05, APO13.02, BAI02.03, BAI04.02 • **ISA 62443-2-1:2009** 4.3.4.2 • **NIST SP 800-53 Rev. 4** PM-9
		ID.RM-2: Organizational risk tolerance is determined and clearly expressed	• **COBIT 5** APO12.06 • **ISA 62443-2-1:2009** 4.3.2.6.5 • **NIST SP 800-53 Rev. 4** PM-9
		ID.RM-3: The organization's determination of risk tolerance is informed by its role in critical infrastructure and sector-specific risk analysis	• **NIST SP 800-53 Rev. 4** PM-8, PM-9, PM-11, SA-14

Function	Category	Subcategory	Informative References
PROTECT (PR)	**Access Control (PR.AC):** Access to assets and associated facilities is limited to authorized users, processes, or devices, and to authorized activities and transactions.	**PR.AC-1:** Identities and credentials are managed for authorized devices and users	• **CCS CSC** 16 • **COBIT 5** DSS05.04, DSS06.03 • **ISA 62443-2-1:2009** 4.3.3.5.1 • **ISA 62443-3-3:2013** SR 1.1, SR 1.2, SR 1.3, SR 1.4, SR 1.5, SR 1.7, SR 1.8, SR 1.9 • **ISO/IEC 27001:2013** A.9.2.1, A.9.2.2, A.9.2.4, A.9.3.1, A.9.4.2, A.9.4.3 • **NIST SP 800-53 Rev. 4** AC-2, IA Family
		PR.AC-2: Physical access to assets is managed and protected	• **COBIT 5** DSS01.04, DSS05.05 • **ISA 62443-2-1:2009** 4.3.3.3.2, 4.3.3.3.8 • **ISO/IEC 27001:2013** A.11.1.1, A.11.1.2, A.11.1.4, A.11.1.6, A.11.2.3 • **NIST SP 800-53 Rev. 4** PE-2, PE-3, PE-4, PE-5, PE-6, PE-9
		PR.AC-3: Remote access is managed	• **COBIT 5** APO13.01, DSS01.04, DSS05.03 • **ISA 62443-2-1:2009** 4.3.3.6.6 • **ISA 62443-3-3:2013** SR 1.13, SR 2.6 • **ISO/IEC 27001:2013** A.6.2.2, A.13.1.1, A.13.2.1 • **NIST SP 800-53 Rev. 4** AC-17, AC-19, AC-20
		PR.AC-4: Access permissions are managed, incorporating the principles of least privilege and separation of duties	• **CCS CSC** 12, 15 • **ISA 62443-2-1:2009** 4.3.3.7.3 • **ISA 62443-3-3:2013** SR 2.1 • **ISO/IEC 27001:2013** A.6.1.2, A.9.1.2, A.9.2.3, A.9.4.1, A.9.4.4 • **NIST SP 800-53 Rev. 4** AC-2, AC-3, AC-5, AC-6, AC-16
		PR.AC-5: Network integrity is protected, incorporating network segregation where appropriate	• **ISA 62443-2-1:2009** 4.3.3.4 • **ISA 62443-3-3:2013** SR 3.1, SR 3.8 • **ISO/IEC 27001:2013** A.13.1.1, A.13.1.3, A.13.2.1 • **NIST SP 800-53 Rev. 4** AC-4, SC-7

(continued)

Table 2: Framework Core *(continued)*

Function	Category	Subcategory	Informative References
PROTECT (PR)	**Awareness and Training (PR.AT):** The organization's personnel and partners are provided cybersecurity awareness education and are adequately trained to perform their information security-related duties and responsibilities consistent with related policies, procedures, and agreements.	**PR.AT-1:** All users are informed and trained	• **CCS CSC** 9 • **COBIT 5** APO07.03, BAI05.07 • **ISA 62443-2-1:2009** 4.3.2.4.2 • **ISO/IEC 27001:2013** A.7.2.2 • **NIST SP 800-53 Rev. 4** AT-2, PM-13
		PR.AT-2: Privileged users understand roles & responsibilities	• **CCS CSC** 9 • **COBIT 5** APO07.02, DSS06.03 • **ISA 62443-2-1:2009** 4.3.2.4.2, 4.3.2.4.3 • **ISO/IEC 27001:2013** A.6.1.1, A.7.2.2 • **NIST SP 800-53 Rev. 4** AT-3, PM-13
		PR.AT-3: Third-party stakeholders (e.g., suppliers, customers, partners) understand roles & responsibilities	• **CCS CSC** 9 • **COBIT 5** APO07.03, APO10.04, APO10.05 • **ISA 62443-2-1:2009** 4.3.2.4.2 • **ISO/IEC 27001:2013** A.6.1.1, A.7.2.2 • **NIST SP 800-53 Rev. 4** PS-7, SA-9
		PR.AT-4: Senior executives understand roles & responsibilities	• **CCS CSC** 9 • **COBIT 5** APO07.03 • **ISA 62443-2-1:2009** 4.3.2.4.2 • **ISO/IEC 27001:2013** A.6.1.1, A.7.2.2 • **NIST SP 800-53 Rev. 4** AT-3, PM-13
		PR.AT-5: Physical and information security personnel understand roles & responsibilities	• **CCS CSC** 9 • **COBIT 5** APO07.03 • **ISA 62443-2-1:2009** 4.3.2.4.2 • **ISO/IEC 27001:2013** A.6.1.1, A.7.2.2 • **NIST SP 800-53 Rev. 4** AT-3, PM-13

Function	Category	Subcategory	Informative References
PROTECT (PR)	**Data Security (PR.DS):** Information and records (data) are managed consistent with the organization's risk strategy to protect the confidentiality, integrity, and availability of information.	**PR.DS-1:** Data-at-rest is protected	• **CCS CSC** 17 • **COBIT 5** APO01.06, BAI02.01, BAI06.01, DSS06.06 • **ISA 62443-3-3:2013** SR 3.4, SR 4.1 • **ISO/IEC 27001:2013** A.8.2.3 • **NIST SP 800-53 Rev. 4** SC-28
		PR.DS-2: Data-in-transit is protected	• **CCS CSC** 17 • **COBIT 5** APO01.06, DSS06.06 • **ISA 62443-3-3:2013** SR 3.1, SR 3.8, SR 4.1, SR 4.2 • **ISO/IEC 27001:2013** A.8.2.3, A.13.1.1, A.13.2.1, A.13.2.3, A.14.1.2, A.14.1.3 • **NIST SP 800-53 Rev. 4** SC-8
		PR.DS-3: Assets are formally managed throughout removal, transfers, and disposition	• **COBIT 5** BAI09.03 • **ISA 62443-2-1:2009** 4. 4.3.3.3.9, 4.3.4.4.1 • **ISA 62443-3-3:2013** SR 4.2 • **ISO/IEC 27001:2013** A.8.2.3, A.8.3.1, A.8.3.2, A.8.3.3, A.11.2.7 • **NIST SP 800-53 Rev. 4** CM-8, MP-6, PE-16
		PR.DS-4: Adequate capacity to ensure availability is maintained	• **COBIT 5** APO13.01 • **ISA 62443-3-3:2013** SR 7.1, SR 7.2 • **ISO/IEC 27001:2013** A.12.3.1 • **NIST SP 800-53 Rev. 4** AU-4, CP-2, SC-5
		PR.DS-5: Protections against data leaks are implemented	• **CCS CSC** 17 • **COBIT 5** APO01.06 • **ISA 62443-3-3:2013** SR 5.2 • **ISO/IEC 27001:2013** A.6.1.2, A.7.1.1, A.7.1.2, A.7.3.1, A.8.2.2, A.8.2.3, A.9.1.1, A.9.1.2, A.9.2.3, A.9.4.1, A.9.4.4, A.9.4.5, A.13.1.3, A.13.2.1, A.13.2.3, A.13.2.4, A.14.1.2, A.14.1.3 • **NIST SP 800-53 Rev. 4** AC-4, AC-5, AC-6, PE-19, PS-3, PS-6, SC-7, SC-8, SC-13, SC-31, SI-4
		PR.DS-6: Integrity checking mechanisms are used to verify software, firmware, and information integrity	• **ISA 62443-3-3:2013** SR 3.1, SR 3.3, SR 3.4, SR 3.8 • **ISO/IEC 27001:2013** A.12.2.1, A.12.5.1, A.14.1.2, A.14.1.3 • **NIST SP 800-53 Rev. 4** SI-7
		PR.DS-7: The development and testing environment(s) are separate from the production environment	• **COBIT 5** BAI07.04 • **ISO/IEC 27001:2013** A.12.1.4 • **NIST SP 800-53 Rev. 4** CM-2

(continued)

Table 2: Framework Core *(continued)*

Function	Category	Subcategory	Informative References
PROTECT (PR)	**Information Protection Processes and Procedures (PR.IP):** Security policies (that address purpose, scope, roles, responsibilities, management commitment, and coordination among organizational entities), processes, and procedures are maintained and used to manage protection of information systems and assets.	**PR.IP-1:** A baseline configuration of information technology/ industrial control systems is created and maintained	• **CCS CSC** 3, 10 • **COBIT 5** BAI10.01, BAI10.02, BAI10.03, BAI10.05 • **ISA 62443-2-1:2009** 4.3.4.3.2, 4.3.4.3.3 • **ISA 62443-3-3:2013** SR 7.6 • **ISO/IEC 27001:2013** A.12.1.2, A.12.5.1, A.12.6.2, A.14.2.2, A.14.2.3, A.14.2.4 • **NIST SP 800-53 Rev. 4** CM-2, CM-3, CM-4, CM-5, CM-6, CM-7, CM-9, SA-10
		PR.IP-2: A System Development Life Cycle to manage systems is implemented	• **COBIT 5** APO13.01 • **ISA 62443-2-1:2009** 4.3.4.3.3 • **ISO/IEC 27001:2013** A.6.1.5, A.14.1.1, A.14.2.1, A.14.2.5 • **NIST SP 800-53 Rev. 4** SA-3, SA-4, SA-8, SA-10, SA-11, SA-12, SA-15, SA-17, PL-8
		PR.IP-3: Configuration change control processes are in place	• **COBIT 5** BAI06.01, BAI01.06 • **ISA 62443-2-1:2009** 4.3.4.3.2, 4.3.4.3.3 • **ISA 62443-3-3:2013** SR 7.6 • **ISO/IEC 27001:2013** A.12.1.2, A.12.5.1, A.12.6.2, A.14.2.2, A.14.2.3, A.14.2.4 • **NIST SP 800-53 Rev. 4** CM-3, CM-4, SA-10
		PR.IP-4: Backups of information are conducted, maintained, and tested periodically	• **COBIT 5** APO13.01 • **ISA 62443-2-1:2009** 4.3.4.3.9 • **ISA 62443-3-3:2013** SR 7.3, SR 7.4 • **ISO/IEC 27001:2013** A.12.3.1, A.17.1.2A.17.1.3, A.18.1.3 • **NIST SP 800-53 Rev. 4** CP-4, CP-6, CP-9
		PR.IP-5: Policy and regulations regarding the physical operating environment for organizational assets are met	• **COBIT 5** DSS01.04, DSS05.05 • **ISA 62443-2-1:2009** 4.3.3.3.1 4.3.3.3.2, 4.3.3.3.3, 4.3.3.3.5, 4.3.3.3.6 • **ISO/IEC 27001:2013** A.11.1.4, A.11.2.1, A.11.2.2, A.11.2.3 • **NIST SP 800-53 Rev. 4** PE-10, PE-12, PE-13, PE-14, PE-15, PE-18

Function	Category	Subcategory	Informative References
PROTECT (PR)		**PR.IP-6:** Data is destroyed according to policy	• **COBIT 5** BAI09.03 • **ISA 62443-2-1:2009** 4.3.4.4.4 • **ISA 62443-3-3:2013** SR 4.2 • **ISO/IEC 27001:2013** A.8.2.3, A.8.3.1, A.8.3.2, A.11.2.7 • **NIST SP 800-53 Rev. 4** MP-6
		PR.IP-7: Protection processes are continuously improved	• **COBIT 5** APO11.06, DSS04.05 • **ISA 62443-2-1:2009** 4.4.3.1, 4.4.3.2, 4.4.3.3, 4.4.3.4, 4.4.3.5, 4.4.3.6, 4.4.3.7, 4.4.3.8 • **NIST SP 800-53 Rev. 4** CA-2, CA-7, CP-2, IR-8, PL-2, PM-6
		PR.IP-8: Effectiveness of protection technologies is shared with appropriate parties	• **ISO/IEC 27001:2013** A.16.1.6 • **NIST SP 800-53 Rev. 4** AC-21, CA-7, SI-4
		PR.IP-9: Response plans (Incident Response and Business Continuity) and recovery plans (Incident Recovery and Disaster Recovery) are in place and managed	• **COBIT 5** DSS04.03 • **ISA 62443-2-1:2009** 4.3.2.5.3, 4.3.4.5.1 • **ISO/IEC 27001:2013** A.16.1.1, A.17.1.1, A.17.1.2 • **NIST SP 800-53 Rev. 4** CP-2, IR-8
		PR.IP-10: Response and recovery plans are tested	• **ISA 62443-2-1:2009** 4.3.2.5.7, 4.3.4.5.11 • **ISA 62443-3-3:2013** SR 3.3 • **ISO/IEC 27001:2013** A.17.1.3 • **NIST SP 800-53 Rev.4** CP-4, IR-3, PM-14
		PR.IP-11: Cybersecurity is included in human resources practices (e.g., deprovisioning, personnel screening)	• **COBIT 5** APO07.01, APO07.02, APO07.03, APO07.04, APO07.05 • **ISA 62443-2-1:2009** 4.3.3.2.1, 4.3.3.2.2, 4.3.3.2.3 • **ISO/IEC 27001:2013** A.7.1.1, A.7.3.1, A.8.1.4 • **NIST SP 800-53 Rev. 4** PS Family
		PR.IP-12: A vulnerability management plan is developed and implemented	• **ISO/IEC 27001:2013** A.12.6.1, A.18.2.2 • **NIST SP 800-53 Rev. 4** RA-3, RA-5, SI-2

(continued)

Table 2: Framework Core *(continued)*

Function	Category	Subcategory	Informative References
PROTECT (PR)	**Maintenance (PR.MA):** Maintenance and repairs of industrial control and information system components is performed consistent with policies and procedures.	**PR.MA-1:** Maintenance and repair of organizational assets is performed and logged in a timely manner, with approved and controlled tools	• **COBIT 5** BAI09.03 • **ISA 62443-2-1:2009** 4.3.3.3.7 • **ISO/IEC 27001:2013** A.11.1.2, A.11.2.4, A.11.2.5 • **NIST SP 800-53 Rev. 4** MA-2, MA-3, MA-5
		PR.MA-2: Remote maintenance of organizational assets is approved, logged, and performed in a manner that prevents unauthorized access	• **COBIT 5** DSS05.04 • **ISA 62443-2-1:2009** 4.3.3.6.5, 4.3.3.6.6, 4.3.3.6.7, 4.4.4.6.8 • **ISO/IEC 27001:2013** A.11.2.4, A.15.1.1, A.15.2.1 • **NIST SP 800-53 Rev. 4** MA-4
	Protective Technology (PR.PT): Technical security solutions are managed to ensure the security and resilience of systems and assets, consistent with related policies, procedures, and agreements.	**PR.PT-1:** Audit/log records are determined, documented, implemented, and reviewed in accordance with policy	• **CCS CSC** 14 • **COBIT 5** APO11.04 • **ISA 62443-2-1:2009** 4.3.3.3.9, 4.3.3.5.8, 4.3.4.4.7, 4.4.2.1, 4.4.2.2, 4.4.2.4 • **ISA 62443-3-3:2013** SR 2.8, SR 2.9, SR 2.10, SR 2.11, SR 2.12 • **ISO/IEC 27001:2013** A.12.4.1, A.12.4.2, A.12.4.3, A.12.4.4, A.12.7.1 • **NIST SP 800-53 Rev. 4** AU Family
		PR.PT-2: Removable media is protected and its use restricted according to policy	• **COBIT 5** DSS05.02, APO13.01 • **ISA 62443-3-3:2013** SR 2.3 • **ISO/IEC 27001:2013** A.8.2.2, A.8.2.3, A.8.3.1, A.8.3.3, A.11.2.9 • **NIST SP 800-53 Rev. 4** MP-2, MP-4, MP-5, MP-7
		PR.PT-3: Access to systems and assets is controlled, incorporating the principle of least functionality	• **COBIT 5** DSS05.02 • **ISA 62443-2-1:2009** 4.3.3.5.1, 4.3.3.5.2, 4.3.3.5.3, 4.3.3.5.4, 4.3.3.5.5, 4.3.3.5.6, 4.3.3.5.7, 4.3.3.5.8, 4.3.3.6.1, 4.3.3.6.2, 4.3.3.6.3, 4.3.3.6.4, 4.3.3.6.5, 4.3.3.6.6, 4.3.3.6.7, 4.3.3.6.8, 4.3.3.6.9, 4.3.3.7.1, 4.3.3.7.2, 4.3.3.7.3, 4.3.3.7.4 • **ISA 62443-3-3:2013** SR 1.1, SR 1.2, SR 1.3, SR 1.4, SR 1.5, SR 1.6, SR 1.7, SR 1.8, SR 1.9, SR 1.10, SR 1.11, SR 1.12, SR 1.13, SR 2.1, SR 2.2, SR 2.3, SR 2.4, SR 2.5, SR 2.6, SR 2.7 • **ISO/IEC 27001:2013** A.9.1.2 • **NIST SP 800-53 Rev. 4** AC-3, CM-7

Function	Category	Subcategory	Informative References
PROTECT (PR)		**PR.PT-4:** Communications and control networks are protected	• **CCS CSC** 7 • **COBIT 5** DSS05.02, APO13.01 • **ISA 62443-3-3:2013** SR 3.1, SR 3.5, SR 3.8, SR 4.1, SR 4.3, SR 5.1, SR 5.2, SR 5.3, SR 7.1, SR 7.6 • **ISO/IEC 27001:2013** A.13.1.1, A.13.2.1 • **NIST SP 800-53 Rev. 4** AC-4, AC-17, AC-18, CP-8, SC-7
DETECT (DE)	**Anomalies and Events (DE.AE):** Anomalous activity is detected in a timely manner and the potential impact of events is understood.	**DE.AE-1:** A baseline of network operations and expected data flows for users and systems is established and managed	• **COBIT 5** DSS03.01 • **ISA 62443-2-1:2009** 4.4.3.3 • **NIST SP 800-53 Rev. 4** AC-4, CA-3, CM-2, SI-4
		DE.AE-2: Detected events are analyzed to understand attack targets and methods	• **ISA 62443-2-1:2009** 4.3.4.5.6, 4.3.4.5.7, 4.3.4.5.8 • **ISA 62443-3-3:2013** SR 2.8, SR 2.9, SR 2.10, SR 2.11, SR 2.12, SR 3.9, SR 6.1, SR 6.2 • **ISO/IEC 27001:2013** A.16.1.1, A.16.1.4 • **NIST SP 800-53 Rev. 4** AU-6, CA-7, IR-4, SI-4
		DE.AE-3: Event data are aggregated and correlated from multiple sources and sensors	• **ISA 62443-3-3:2013** SR 6.1 • **NIST SP 800-53 Rev. 4** AU-6, CA-7, IR-4, IR-5, IR-8, SI-4
		DE.AE-4: Impact of events is determined	• **COBIT 5** APO12.06 • **NIST SP 800-53 Rev. 4** CP-2, IR-4, RA-3, SI-4
		DE.AE-5: Incident alert thresholds are established	• **COBIT 5** APO12.06 • **ISA 62443-2-1:2009** 4.2.3.10 • **NIST SP 800-53 Rev. 4** IR-4, IR-5, IR-8

(continued)

Table 2: Framework Core *(continued)*

Function	Category	Subcategory	Informative References
DETECT (DE)	**Security Continuous Monitoring (DE.CM):** The information system and assets are monitored at discrete intervals to identify cybersecurity events and verify the effectiveness of protective measures.	**DE.CM-1:** The network is monitored to detect potential cybersecurity events	• **CCS CSC** 14, 16 • **COBIT 5** DSS05.07 • **ISA 62443-3-3:2013** SR 6.2 • **NIST SP 800-53 Rev. 4** AC-2, AU-12, CA-7, CM-3, SC-5, SC-7, SI-4
		DE.CM-2: The physical environment is monitored to detect potential cybersecurity events	• **ISA 62443-2-1:2009** 4.3.3.3.8 • **NIST SP 800-53 Rev. 4** CA-7, PE-3, PE-6, PE-20
		DE.CM-3: Personnel activity is monitored to detect potential cybersecurity events	• **ISA 62443-3-3:2013** SR 6.2 • **ISO/IEC 27001:2013** A.12.4.1 • **NIST SP 800-53 Rev. 4** AC-2, AU-12, AU-13, CA-7, CM-10, CM-11
		DE.CM-4: Malicious code is detected	• **CCS CSC** 5 • **COBIT 5** DSS05.01 • **ISA 62443-2-1:2009** 4.3.4.3.8 • **ISA 62443-3-3:2013** SR 3.2 • **ISO/IEC 27001:2013** A.12.2.1 • **NIST SP 800-53 Rev. 4** SI-3
		DE.CM-5: Unauthorized mobile code is detected	• **ISA 62443-3-3:2013** SR 2.4 • **ISO/IEC 27001:2013** A.12.5.1 • **NIST SP 800-53 Rev. 4** SC-18, SI-4. SC-44
		DE.CM-6: External service provider activity is monitored to detect potential cybersecurity events	• **COBIT 5** APO07.06 • **ISO/IEC 27001:2013** A.14.2.7, A.15.2.1 • **NIST SP 800-53 Rev. 4** CA-7, PS-7, SA-4, SA-9, SI-4
		DE.CM-7: Monitoring for unauthorized personnel, connections, devices, and software is performed	• **NIST SP 800-53 Rev. 4** AU-12, CA-7, CM-3, CM-8, PE-3, PE-6, PE-20, SI-4
		DE.CM-8: Vulnerability scans are performed	• **COBIT 5** BAI03.10 • **ISA 62443-2-1:2009** 4.2.3.1, 4.2.3.7 • **ISO/IEC 27001:2013** A.12.6.1 • **NIST SP 800-53 Rev. 4** RA-5

Function	Category	Subcategory	Informative References
DETECT (DE)	**Detection Processes (DE.DP):** Detection processes and procedures are maintained and tested to ensure timely and adequate awareness of anomalous events.	**DE.DP-1:** Roles and responsibilities for detection are well defined to ensure accountability	• **CCS CSC** 5 • **COBIT 5** DSS05.01 • **ISA 62443-2-1:2009** 4.4.3.1 • **ISO/IEC 27001:2013** A.6.1.1 • **NIST SP 800-53 Rev. 4** CA-2, CA-7, PM-14
		DE.DP-2: Detection activities comply with all applicable requirements	• **ISA 62443-2-1:2009** 4.4.3.2 • **ISO/IEC 27001:2013** A.18.1.4 • **NIST SP 800-53 Rev. 4** CA-2, CA-7, PM-14, SI-4
		DE.DP-3: Detection processes are tested	• **COBIT 5** APO13.02 • **ISA 62443-2-1:2009** 4.4.3.2 • **ISA 62443-3-3:2013** SR 3.3 • **ISO/IEC 27001:2013** A.14.2.8 • **NIST SP 800-53 Rev. 4** CA-2, CA-7, PE-3, PM-14, SI-3, SI-4
		DE.DP-4: Event detection information is communicated to appropriate parties	• **COBIT 5** APO12.06 • **ISA 62443-2-1:2009** 4.3.4.5.9 • **ISA 62443-3-3:2013** SR 6.1 • **ISO/IEC 27001:2013** A.16.1.2 • **NIST SP 800-53 Rev. 4** AU-6, CA-2, CA-7, RA-5, SI-4
		DE.DP-5: Detection processes are continuously improved	• **COBIT 5** APO11.06, DSS04.05 • **ISA 62443-2-1:2009** 4.4.3.4 • **ISO/IEC 27001:2013** A.16.1.6 • **NIST SP 800-53 Rev. 4**, CA-2, CA-7, PL-2, RA-5, SI-4, PM-14
RESPOND (RS)	**Response Planning (RS.RP):** Response processes and procedures are executed and maintained, to ensure timely response to detected cybersecurity events.	**RS.RP-1:** Response plan is executed during or after an event	• **COBIT 5** BAI01.10 • **CCS CSC** 18 • **ISA 62443-2-1:2009** 4.3.4.5.1 • **ISO/IEC 27001:2013** A.16.1.5 • **NIST SP 800-53 Rev. 4** CP-2, CP-10, IR-4, IR-8
	Communications (RS.CO): Response activities are coordinated with internal and external stakeholders, as appropriate, to include external support from law enforcement agencies.	**RS.CO-1:** Personnel know their roles and order of operations when a response is needed	• **ISA 62443-2-1:2009** 4.3.4.5.2, 4.3.4.5.3, 4.3.4.5.4 • **ISO/IEC 27001:2013** A.6.1.1, A.16.1.1 • **NIST SP 800-53 Rev. 4** CP-2, CP-3, IR-3, IR-8

(continued)

Table 2: Framework Core *(continued)*

Function	Category	Subcategory	Informative References
RESPOND (RS)		**RS.CO-2:** Events are reported consistent with established criteria	• **ISA 62443-2-1:2009** 4.3.4.5.5 • **ISO/IEC 27001:2013** A.6.1.3, A.16.1.2 • **NIST SP 800-53 Rev. 4** AU-6, IR-6, IR-8
		RS.CO-3: Information is shared consistent with response plans	• **ISA 62443-2-1:2009** 4.3.4.5.2 • **ISO/IEC 27001:2013** A.16.1.2 • **NIST SP 800-53 Rev. 4** CA-2, CA-7, CP-2, IR-4, IR-8, PE-6, RA-5, SI-4
		RS.CO-4: Coordination with stakeholders occurs consistent with response plans	• **ISA 62443-2-1:2009** 4.3.4.5.5 • **NIST SP 800-53 Rev. 4** CP-2, IR-4, IR-8
		RS.CO-5: Voluntary information sharing occurs with external stakeholders to achieve broader cybersecurity situational awareness	• **NIST SP 800-53 Rev. 4** PM-15, SI-5
	Analysis (RS.AN): Analysis is conducted to ensure adequate response and support recovery activities.	**RS.AN-1:** Notifications from detection systems are investigated	• **COBIT 5** DSS02.07 • **ISA 62443-2-1:2009** 4.3.4.5.6, 4.3.4.5.7, 4.3.4.5.8 • **ISA 62443-3-3:2013** SR 6.1 • **ISO/IEC 27001:2013** A.12.4.1, A.12.4.3, A.16.1.5 • **NIST SP 800-53 Rev. 4** AU-6, CA-7, IR-4, IR-5, PE-6, SI-4
		RS.AN-2: The impact of the incident is understood	• **ISA 62443-2-1:2009** 4.3.4.5.6, 4.3.4.5.7, 4.3.4.5.8 • **ISO/IEC 27001:2013** A.16.1.6 • **NIST SP 800-53 Rev. 4** CP-2, IR-4
		RS.AN-3: Forensics are performed	• **ISA 62443-3-3:2013** SR 2.8, SR 2.9, SR 2.10, SR 2.11, SR 2.12, SR 3.9, SR 6.1 • **ISO/IEC 27001:2013** A.16.1.7 • **NIST SP 800-53 Rev. 4** AU-7, IR-4
		RS.AN-4: Incidents are categorized consistent with response plans	• **ISA 62443-2-1:2009** 4.3.4.5.6 • **ISO/IEC 27001:2013** A.16.1.4 • **NIST SP 800-53 Rev. 4** CP-2, IR-4, IR-5, IR-8

Function	Category	Subcategory	Informative References
RESPOND (RS)	**Mitigation (RS.MI):** Activities are performed to prevent expansion of an event, mitigate its effects, and eradicate the incident.	**RS.MI-1:** Incidents are contained	• **ISA 62443-2-1:2009** 4.3.4.5.6 • **ISA 62443-3-3:2013** SR 5.1, SR 5.2, SR 5.4 • **ISO/IEC 27001:2013** A.16.1.5 • **NIST SP 800-53 Rev. 4** IR-4
		RS.MI-2: Incidents are mitigated	• **ISA 62443-2-1:2009** 4.3.4.5.6, 4.3.4.5.10 • **ISO/IEC 27001:2013** A.12.2.1, A.16.1.5 • **NIST SP 800-53 Rev. 4** IR-4
		RS.MI-3: Newly identified vulnerabilities are mitigated or documented as accepted risks	• **ISO/IEC 27001:2013** A.12.6.1 • **NIST SP 800-53 Rev. 4** CA-7, RA-3, RA-5
	Improvements (RS.IM): Organizational response activities are improved by incorporating lessons learned from current and previous detection/response activities.	**RS.IM-1:** Response plans incorporate lessons learned	• **COBIT 5** BAI01.13 • **ISA 62443-2-1:2009** 4.3.4.5.10, 4.4.3.4 • **ISO/IEC 27001:2013** A.16.1.6 • **NIST SP 800-53 Rev. 4** CP-2, IR-4, IR-8
		RS.IM-2: Response strategies are updated	• **NIST SP 800-53 Rev. 4** CP-2, IR-4, IR-8
RECOVER (RC)	**Recovery Planning (RC.RP):** Recovery processes and procedures are executed and maintained to ensure timely restoration of systems or assets affected by cybersecurity events.	**RC.RP-1:** Recovery plan is executed during or after an event	• **CCS CSC** 8 • **COBIT 5** DSS02.05, DSS03.04 • **ISO/IEC 27001:2013** A.16.1.5 • **NIST SP 800-53 Rev. 4** CP-10, IR-4, IR-8
	Improvements (RC.IM): Recovery planning and processes are improved by incorporating lessons learned into future activities.	**RC.IM-1:** Recovery plans incorporate lessons learned	• **COBIT 5** BAI05.07 • **ISA 62443-2-1** 4.4.3.4 • **NIST SP 800-53 Rev. 4** CP-2, IR-4, IR-8
		RC.IM-2: Recovery strategies are updated	• **COBIT 5** BAI07.08 • **NIST SP 800-53 Rev. 4** CP-2, IR-4, IR-8

(continued)

Table 2: Framework Core *(continued)*

Function	Category	Subcategory	Informative References
RECOVER (RC)	**Communications (RC.CO):** Restoration activities are coordinated with internal and external parties, such as coordinating centers, Internet service providers, owners of attacking systems, victims, other CSIRTs, and vendors.	**RC.CO-1:** Public relations are managed	• **COBIT 5** EDM03.02
		RC.CO-2: Reputation after an event is repaired	• **COBIT 5** MEA03.02
		RC.CO-3: Recovery activities are communicated to internal stakeholders and executive and management teams	• **NIST SP 800-53 Rev. 4** CP-2, IR-4

Information regarding Informative References described in Appendix A may be found at the following locations:

- Control Objectives for Information and Related Technology (COBIT): http://www.isaca.org/COBIT/Pages/default.aspx
- Council on CyberSecurity (CCS) Top 20 Critical Security Controls (CSC): http://www.counciloncybersecurity.org
- ANSI/ISA-62443-2-1 (99.02.01)-2009, *Security for Industrial Automation and Control Systems: Establishing an Industrial Automation and Control Systems Security Program*: http://www.isa.org/Template.cfm?Section=Standards-8&Template=/Ecommerce/ProductDisplay.cfm&ProductID=10243
- ANSI/ISA-62443-3-3 (99.03.03)-2013, *Security for Industrial Automation and Control Systems: System Security Requirements and Security Levels*: http://www.isa.org/Template.cfm?Section=Standards2&template=/Ecommerce/ProductDisplay.cfm&ProductID=13420
- ISO/IEC 27001, *Information technology—Security techniques—Information security management systems—Requirements*: http://www.iso.org/iso/home/store/catalogue_ics/catalogue_detail_ics.htm?csnumber=54534
- NIST SP 800-53 Rev. 4: NIST Special Publication 800-53 Revision 4, *Security and Privacy Controls for Federal Information Systems and Organizations*, April 2013 (including updates as of January 15, 2014). http://dx.doi.org/10.6028/NIST.SP.800-53r4.

Mappings between the Framework Core Subcategories and the specified sections in the Informative References represent a general correspondence and are not intended to definitively determine whether the specified sections in the Informative References provide the desired Subcategory outcome.

Appendix B: Glossary

This appendix defines selected terms used in the publication.

Category
The subdivision of a Function into groups of cybersecurity outcomes, closely tied to programmatic needs and particular activities. Examples of Categories include "Asset Management," "Access Control," and "Detection Processes."

Critical Infrastructure
Systems and assets, whether physical or virtual, so vital to the United States that the incapacity or destruction of such systems and assets would have a debilitating impact on cybersecurity, national economic security, national public health or safety, or any combination of those matters.

Cybersecurity
The process of protecting information by preventing, detecting, and responding to attacks.

Cybersecurity Event
A cybersecurity change that may have an impact on organizational operations (including mission, capabilities, or reputation).

Detect (function)
Develop and implement the appropriate activities to identify the occurrence of a cybersecurity event.

Framework
A risk-based approach to reducing cybersecurity risk composed of three parts: the Framework Core, the Framework Profile, and the Framework Implementation Tiers. Also known as the "Cybersecurity Framework."

Framework Core
A set of cybersecurity activities and references that are common across critical infrastructure sectors and are organized around particular outcomes. The Framework Core comprises four types of elements: Functions, Categories, Subcategories, and Informative References.

Framework Implementation Tier
A lens through which to view the characteristics of an organization's approach to risk—how an organization views cybersecurity risk and the processes in place to manage that risk.

Framework Profile
A representation of the outcomes that a particular system or organization has selected from the Framework Categories and Subcategories.

Function
One of the main components of the Framework. Functions provide the highest level of structure for organizing basic cybersecurity activities into Categories and Subcategories. The five functions are Identify, Protect, Detect, Respond, and Recover.

Identify (function)
Develop the organizational understanding to manage cybersecurity risk to systems, assets, data, and capabilities.

Informative Reference
A specific section of standards, guidelines, and practices common among critical infrastructure sectors that illustrates a method to achieve the outcomes associated with each Subcategory.

Mobile Code	A program (e.g., script, macro, or other portable instruction) that can be shipped unchanged to a heterogeneous collection of platforms and executed with identical semantics.
Protect (function)	Develop and implement the appropriate safeguards to ensure delivery of critical infrastructure services.
Privileged User	A user that is authorized (and, therefore, trusted) to perform security-relevant functions that ordinary users are not authorized to perform.
Recover (function)	Develop and implement the appropriate activities to maintain plans for resilience and to restore any capabilities or services that were impaired due to a cybersecurity event.
Respond (function)	Develop and implement the appropriate activities to take action regarding a detected cybersecurity event.
Risk	A measure of the extent to which an entity is threatened by a potential circumstance or event, and typically a function of: (i) the adverse impacts that would arise if the circumstance or event occurs; and (ii) the likelihood of occurrence.
Risk Management	The process of identifying, assessing, and responding to risk.
Subcategory	The subdivision of a Category into specific outcomes of technical and/or management activities. Examples of Subcategories include "External information systems are catalogued," "Data-at-rest is protected," and "Notifications from detection systems are investigated."

Appendix C: Acronyms

This appendix defines selected acronyms used in the publication.

CCS	Council on CyberSecurity
COBIT	Control Objectives for Information and Related Technology
DCS	Distributed Control System
DHS	Department of Homeland Security
EO	Executive Order
ICS	Industrial Control Systems
IEC	International Electrotechnical Commission
IR	Interagency Report
ISA	International Society of Automation
ISAC	Information Sharing and Analysis Center
ISO	International Organization for Standardization
IT	Information Technology
NIST	National Institute of Standards and Technology
RFI	Request for Information
RMP	Risk Management Process
SCADA	Supervisory Control and Data Acquisition
SP	Special Publication

Vendor Security Alliance (VSA) Definitions

Definitions Relating to Vendor Security from the Vendor Security Alliance 2016 Questionnaire

Term	Description
Bug Bounty Program:	Any method by which members of the public can submit to company information regarding security vulnerabilities, software to fix an issue, or any other deviation of the company's software that does not fit its intended purpose.
Critical Security Vulnerability:	A vulnerability is a state in a computing system (or set of systems) that either: 1) allows an attacker to execute commands as another user, or 2) allows an attacker to access data that is contrary to the specified access restrictions for that data, or 3) allows an attacker to pose as another entity, or 4) allows an attacker to conduct a denial of service.
Data Classification Policy (or Matrix):	A policy or matrix classifying data by risk and applying appropriate controls to safeguard the data.
Data Encryption Standard:	A document describing the security method (including Algorithms) used to encrypt information, e.g., AES-256.
Data Flow Diagram:	A diagram showing how data flow through the infrastructure and applications, from ingestion onwards.
Individual Contractors:	Any nonemployee that works under the direct control of the employer.
Multifactor Authentication (MFA):	A security system that requires more than one method of authentication from independent categories of credentials to verify the user's identity for a login or other transaction.
Partner:	Any person or business entity with an agreement to share work with the company.
Penetration Test Approved Methodology:	A penetration test that follows one of the frameworks listed here: https://www.owasp.org/index.php/Penetration_testing_methodologies.
Penetration Test:	The practice of testing a computer system, network, or web application to find vulnerabilities that an attacker could exploit. Every vulnerability discovered is disclosed to the customer.

* The authors would like to thank Dr. Ken Baylor for providing the VSA Glossary of Terms for use in this book.

Term	Description
Personally Identifiable Information (PII):	Any information that can be individually attributed to identify an individual. This information includes, but is not limited to, drivers license numbers, social security numbers (or their equivalent), health and financial records.
Personnel:	Includes employees and contractors under the direct control of management.
Privacy Incident:	A privacy incident results from the loss of control, compromise, unauthorized disclosure, unauthorized acquisition, unauthorized access, or any similar term referring to situations where persons other than authorized users, and for an other than authorized purpose, have access or potential access to PII in usable form, whether physical or electronic. The term encompasses both suspected and confirmed incidents involving PII that raise a reasonable risk of harm.
Protected Data:	Includes PII, sensitive data, HIPAA, financial data and other data defined as sensitive data.
Rule-Based Access Control:	A methodology to assign and manage appropriate level of access control to all computer systems in an organization or enterprise based on job functions and responsibilities.
Security Incident:	An incident is any event that threatens the security, confidentiality, integrity, or availability of information assets (electronic or paper), information systems, and/or the networks that deliver the information. An incident can involve: 1) violation of an explicit or implied security policy 2) attempts to gain unauthorized access 3) unwanted denial of resources 4) unauthorized use 5) changes without the owner's knowledge, instruction, or consent
Sensitive Data:	Any information a reasonable person would consider private, or not choose to share with the public.
Vendor Audit:	A process in which a vendor's security controls are validated by an approved method. The deliverable is access to the audited report(s) of the vendor service, which involves either triggering a new audit or gaining access to a current audit report for the vendor.
Web Application Firewall (WAF):	An appliance, server plugin, or filter that applies a set of rules to an HTTP conversation. Generally, these rules cover common attacks such as cross-site scripting (XSS) and SQL injection. By customizing the rules to your application, many attacks can be identified and blocked. The effort to perform this customization can be significant and needs to be maintained as the application is modified.

EU-Specific Terms from Directive 95/46/EC (Current Data Protection Regime in the EU)

Term	Description
Personal Data:	any information relating to an identified or identifiable natural person ("data subject"); an identifiable natural person is one who can be identified, directly or indirectly, in particular by reference to an identifier such as a name, an identification number, location data, an online identifier or to one or more factors specific to the physical, physiological, genetic, mental, economic, cultural, or social identity of that natural person.
Controller:	the natural or legal person, public authority, agency or other body which, alone or jointly with others, determines the purposes and means of the processing of personal data.
Processor:	a natural or legal person, public authority, agency, or other body which processes personal data on behalf of the controller.
Consent of the Data Subject:	any freely given, specific, informed, and unambiguous indication of the data subject's wishes by which he or she, by a statement or by a clear affirmative action, signifies agreement to the processing of personal data relating to him or her.
Personal Data Breach:	a breach of security leading to the accidental or unlawful destruction, loss, alteration, unauthorized disclosure of, or access to, personal data transmitted, stored, or otherwise processed.
Processing:	any operation or set of operations which is performed on personal data or on sets of personal data, whether or not by automated means, such as collection, recording, organization, structuring, storage, adaptation or alteration, retrieval, consultation, use, disclosure by transmission, dissemination or otherwise making available, alignment or combination, restriction, erasure, or destruction.
Recipient:	a natural or legal person, public authority, agency, or another body, to which the personal data are disclosed, whether a third party, or not.
Third Party:	a natural or legal person, public authority, agency, or body other than the data subject, controller, processor, and persons who, under the direct authority of the controller or processor, are authorized to process personal data.

* https://www.vendorsecurityalliance.org/questions/definitions

Index